"In the hour of its greatest achievement, the state is driven onto unexpected paths by the bounds of the system." Sudden, unexpected shifts in the trend of relative power underlie both the transformation of the international system and the massive warfare historically associated with it. In *Systems in crisis: new imperatives of high politics at century's end*, Professor Doran develops a theory of the power cycle that reveals the structural bounds on statecraft and the trauma of adjusting to these shifting tides of history.

In a bold and wide-ranging analysis, Doran considers the rise and fall in relative power of the major states from 1815 to the present. Demonstrating the conflicting messages in absolute and relative power change, and the unique international political perspective of statecraft that emerges, he comes to very different conclusions from Paul Kennedy's *The rise and fall of the great powers*. The dynamic conception of relative power invokes a paradigm shift in international political thought. Power cycle theory offers new insights into the causes of major war, explaining why confrontation led to one world war in 1914 and appeasement to another in 1939.

Systems change can, however, be peaceful. The priority of statecraft today is to find peaceful solutions to the shifting trends in relative power and role involving the U.S.A., the Soviet Union, China, Japan, and Europe. Doran proposes a managed solution to peaceful change, presenting a guide to avoiding the pitfalls that might make war more likely. Thus power cycle theory is a foundation upon which to build a cumulative conception of world politics.

Systems in crisis: new imperatives of high politics at century's end presents a broad and original analysis of one of the most important questions in world politics today. Charles Doran addresses problems of economics and history as well as of international relations, and this book will be essential reading for students and specialists in these fields as well as for policy analysts.

SYSTEMS IN CRISIS

CAMBRIDGE STUDIES IN INTERNATIONAL RELATIONS

SYSTEMS IN CRISIS

New imperatives of high politics at century's end

CHARLES F. DORAN

Professor of International Relations
The Johns Hopkins University
Paul H. Nitze School of Advanced International Studies
Washington, D. C.

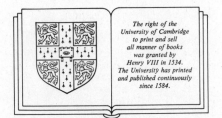

The right of the University of Cambridge to print and sell all manner of books was granted by Henry VIII in 1534. The University has printed and published continuously since 1584.

CAMBRIDGE UNIVERSITY PRESS

Cambridge

New York   Port Chester   Melbourne   Sydney

Published by the Press Syndicate of the University of Cambridge
The Pitt Building, Trumpington Street, Cambridge CB2 1RP
40 West 20th Street, New York, NY 10011, USA
10 Stamford Road, Oakleigh, Melbourne 3166, Australia

First published 1991

Printed in Great Britain at the University Press, Cambridge

British Library cataloguing in publication data

Doran, Charles F. (Charles Francis), *1943 –*
Systems in crisis : new imperatives of high politics at
century's end. – (Cambridge studies in international
relations : 16)
1. Foreign relations
I. Title
327

Library of Congress cataloguing in publication data

Doran, Charles F.
Systems in crisis : new imperatives of high politics at century's
end / Charles F. Doran.
     p.   cm. – (Cambridge studies in international relations : 16)
Includes bibliographical references and index.
ISBN 0 521 40185 2 (hardback)
1. Peaceful change (International relations) 2. World
politics – 1945- I. Title. II. Series.
JX1952.D665 1991
327'.09'04 – dc20   90–2557   CIP

ISBN 0 521 40185 2 hardback

"Spes Anchora Vitae"

CONTENTS

PREFACE

Uncertainty is the watchword of contemporary world politics. In the last decade of the century as in the first, the international system confronts transformation. During bipolarity and the Cold War, the markers for strategic policy were clear, containment worked, and Soviet expansion turned inward upon itself, feeding reform. But what are the guides for policy now? What is the threat? Is the Soviet Union acquiescing in decline with diminished foreign policy ambitions? Or is the Kremlin merely throwing out ballast in preparation for a new surge of growth in power and influence? Is Japan perhaps growing too fast, threatening its own, as well as the system's, ability to adjust when its ebullience suddenly bumps against the limits to relative power growth? How are China's awkward surges to be explained and to be assimilated? How far and how fast will Europe coalesce under the strains of structural adjustment occurring inside and outside West and East? Might the Cold War return? Clearly, the uncertainties of systems transformation are not the ordinary kind, but monumental structural uncertainties that reach deep into the core of cherished ideological preferences and domestic policy.

With systems change comes new hope but also new fear. The eagerness of some to accommodate domestic economic change and long-suppressed freedom is met with increased rigidities and opposition to social change by others. As bipolarity yields in the coming decades to some as yet undetermined new international system, world order and the other imperatives of high politics will increasingly have to face this uncertainty and its psychological and behavioral underpinnings. The inescapable reality of systems transformation is that statesmen must navigate these unexplored waters. But if statesmen are to succeed where those of previous systems transformations have fared so poorly, a new chart is needed. Power cycle analysis is a map that may help cross difficult passages.

What causes systems transformation and the massive war historically associated with it? That is the question which drives this study.

The study does not pretend to examine all war, but only a subset of major war, including the massive confrontations that have periodically fractured the international system. Such war is thankfully a rare event, and, according to power cycle analysis, it is tied to an equally rare occurrence in the history of a major power and of the system. These wars are associated with existential moments in the international political development of the state known as "critical points" where foreign policy expectations suddenly are proven wrong. When several leading states undergo critical change at about the same time, everything in foreign policy terms seems to have changed. Long-standing contradictions in the system are exposed, and equilibrium among states may be on the verge of snapping as a backlog of adjustments between interests and power suddenly demand resolution. It is a system in crisis.

History records these existential moments when governments discover that their foreign policy expectations are no longer valid. The policy maker does not come to know these changes by some sophisticated set of charts and tables or calculation of growth rates. The strategist may not even be aware of the overall power cycle dynamic. Such calculations and awareness are not assumed, and their absence only verifies the shock of discovery for the unsuspecting government and society. But, at some point in the nation's history, the policy maker finds that past assumptions about long-term security and status no longer make sense. Power cycle analysis puts into meaningful international political terms how these troubling discontinuities of foreign policy perception occur, and how and why governments have reacted to them in ways that all too often have been violent.

The analysis fuses three substantive and analytic foci of international relations scholarship: analysis of normative options and choices in foreign policy behavior; analysis of major war and its causes; analysis of the system's structure and relative power. Underlying the first two foci was the conviction that only by understanding the causes of major war can idealists and realists alike hope to channel their "intense revulsion against war" (Howard 1984, p. 21) into effective policies to prevent it. Underlying the third focus was the equally strong conviction that the concept of relative power is central to the understanding of statecraft, that the structure of the international system uniquely affects the opportunity, constraints, and behavior of the statesman. There was the sense that, just as the more encompassing perspective of macroeconomics revolutionized understanding of the economy, so might systemic structural (relative power) analysis provide a clearer "Copernican" perspective on the causes of major war, the trauma of systems transformation, and the path to world order (Hoffmann 1960, Waltz 1979).

Power cycle theory emerged from historical sociological analysis of the first three epochs of systems transformation and the postwar efforts to establish world order (Doran 1971). Why did statesmen fail to preserve the peace? What strategies did they employ, what political obstacles did they face? What was it about the rise and decline of great powers that repeatedly proved so traumatic? Once conceptualized, the "idealized power cycle" disclosed conflicting messages and surprises in relative growth itself. It became apparent that the state power cycle involves much more than mere rise and decline, and that the heart of what the statesman considers important in world politics is ensconced in the uniqueness of the relative power dynamic. In power cycle analysis, the concern of the statesman that the "tides of history have changed" takes on very specific meaning, a meaning absent from the balance-of-power assessment of state behavior.

Economics stresses the importance of change in the absolute levels of power. At the heart of international politics are changes in relative power. The power cycle encompasses state and system in a single dynamic of relative power change within that system. When conceived in terms of such a single historical dynamic, the perspective of changing relative power opens up a whole new structural interpretation. A light bulb comes on, illuminating the discommodious complexity of world politics. In the hour of its greatest achievement, the state is driven onto unexpected paths by the bounds of the system.

That complexity is not only structural. It must also encompass the essential behavioral component of statecraft. Hence "power cycle" is an abbreviation of "cycle of power and role" and its operationalization as the "cycle of relative capability." The power cycle is, in essence, the state's development as a major international political actor involving a variety of leadership roles. It depends on both actualized capabilities and the latent capabilities which are necessary to sustain its long-term growth in power and role. The cycle traces a state's changing performance and size relative to other leading states over long time periods, and hence, in the broadest (simplest) sense, its rise and decline as a great power. While it does offer historians a clear depiction of the "shifting balance of world forces" (Mowat 1968), of the trends of history (Dehio 1962, Kennedy 1988), the power cycle is an even more potent analytical device. It is a key to the uniquely international political mind-set of the contemporaneous statesman.

The power cycle records, at each moment in time, the state's clearly defined past and the likely trajectory of its yet-to-be-determined future. It records the political development of the state as an evolving phenomenon, revealing at each step how contemporaneous statesmen perceive the state, its past history, and its projected future. The power cycle thus is a concept that encompasses the requirements of the statesman and the analyst of international political behavior, and thereby R. G. Collingwood's requirement that the historian "re-enact the past in his own mind" (1956, p. 282).

Hence, while the analysis is based solely on the facts of history as they unfold, its approach is that of historical sociology which analyzes history holistically (Hoffmann 1960). Historical sociology studies international political behavior from a variety of sociological perspectives, and it requires methods, concepts, and analyses that go beyond the descriptions and explanations of the events that evolved. It invites (rather than eschews) speculation about the likely effects of alternative responses which decision makers did indeed consider, and about the morality or justice of various alternatives which decision makers did (and do) explicitly evaluate. In turn, the resulting analytical constructs and speculations attempt to provide new understanding and clarity to historical description.

Power cycle theory thus provides a uniquely international political perspective for the understanding of statecraft, in past history and in contemporary policy. It demonstrates that relative power, and hence the international political issues confronting statesmen, cannot be fully understood outside the context of the full relative power dynamic. Removed from the singular preoccupation with the flat chessboard of military strategy, with the perceptions and concerns of statesmen correctly focused, the origins of the First World War look quite different. So does the possibility for a resolution to the so-called "dilemma of peaceful change."

Derived from international political assessment, and quite intuitive once explained, the logic of the political dynamic at critical points, including the likelihood for instability there, is supported by the rigor of mathematical logic. Critical points are mathematically unique points of abrupt change in the dynamic, the very opposite of gradual change. Uniquely at the critical points, the state experiences a sudden, unanticipated, and ineluctable *inversion* in the trend of foreign policy expectation. During critical periods, when the tides of history suddenly change, adjustment is both necessary and more difficult.

Notwithstanding the inherent structural instability at critical points, why have governments so often failed to adjust? Why is the occurrence of a critical point so potentially unsettling and traumatic?

First, with very high uncertainty about systemic structure, the familiar policy anchors are either gone or in question. It is uncertain whether a state remains in the central system, how many major players will count in the future, who alliance partners are and how steadfast, whether security arrangements are less certain or open to reinterpretation, and whether foreign policy role is in jeopardy. All of these are high stakes matters manifested in radically altered foreign policy expectations. Such uncertainty is not a secure basis for new foreign policy initiative.

Second, gaps between interests and power long in the making are squeezed to the surface of awareness by the stress of state interaction in the critical interval. Governments probe and struggle for advantage when opportunities previously restricted suddenly appear within grasp, or just beyond reach. What rationalization or subterfuge has earlier foreclosed now seems ripe for taking. But the atmosphere has been poisoned by the resulting tension. Governments are defensive and are not prone to bargain as rationally as during normal times. Overreaction and anxiety occur, and decision making may take on a crisis quality. Inversions of force expectation are of a much higher probability, for state policy initiatives and systemic responses are likely to be less controlled.

Third, even if policy makers are able to overcome uncertainty and act in as controlled a manner as at other times in the state's history, they still must translate policy choice into action. To do so they must convince reluctant policy elites to yield long-held foreign policy interests or to assume new interests they are hesitant to support. Policy makers may have to call for increases in military spending or for expeditious cutbacks, policy choices determined by the requirements of external equilibrium. Because of their abstruse nature, when set against practical matters of territorial concessions or financial expenditure, the dictates of external equilibrium are difficult to explain to publics, and difficult to sell to the bureaucracy or the political party. Inertia is as common to the implementation of policy as it is to the making of decisions.

But can governments learn from history? Can they learn to adjust to the determinants of structural change? Of course they can. That is the imperative for which this book has been written. A clue to adjustment lies within the power cycle dynamic.

"Policy makers can, if they will, use history more discriminatingly." Ernest May's (1973) prescription for the more discriminate use of history has an uncanny resemblance to the clue within power cycle theory: "Instead of merely projecting a trend, [analysts] can dissect the forces that produced it and ask whether or not those forces will persist with the same vectors" (p. xii). The perceptive historian or political scientist, like the perceptive commodity trader or perceptive politician at election time, knows that critical points do exist when *everything changes*, when forces suddenly do *not* "persist with the same vectors." In international politics, a complete *inversion* in the prior trend of *relative* power occurs at a critical point, inverting the very assumptions upon which the state has long become accustomed to viewing its future. Power cycle theory warns statesmen that existing trends in relative power will someday change, even as trends in absolute power continue unchanged. When relative power trends do change, there will be a need and a demand for adjustments.

Just as the politician, commodity broker, or coach learns to capture the "existential moment" of change and turn it to advantage, so the statesman must learn to adapt to the dynamic of the power cycle and to adjust foreign relations accordingly. But the analyst should not assume that such adjustment will be easy. Confusions regarding the appropriate adjustment increase multifold during the trauma and massive uncertainty of a critical period. When to accommodate and when to oppose – the dilemma of peaceful change – has too often resulted in the wrong choice.

At the height of crisis in the 1930s, the dilemma of peaceful change was the focus of practicing diplomats and their foreign policy advisors, of international lawyers and legal scholars, who watched it fail in policies of "appeasement of aggressors" (Wright 1942, p. 1075). Stimulated by events in Japan and Germany early in the decade, widely discussed at conferences and in books by the policy elite in New York, London, and Paris, the dilemma was not a theoretical contrivance but a real-world diplomatic conundrum. Norms and legal regimes were even then at the heart of the search for solutions. Yet the debate was overtaken by events, because the underlying structural problem was never solved concerning how to reconcile changing power with legitimate interest. What kinds of international political demands are legitimate and what is a just response? This book proposes a possible solution to that dilemma based on the power cycle dynamic, a solution that puts the burden on decision makers to eliminate power-role fissures *prior to* the crisis of critical change.

International relations as a field has attempted to explain foreign policy outcomes through an integration of strategy with the dictates of the systems structure, and with norms later to be encompassed in the notion of international regimes. As the paradigm shift to an international political perspective evolved, a number of enigmas required sorting out: (1) the complex relationship between absolute and relative power change; (2) how to distinguish state and systemic level analysis without distorting either; (3) how to proceed from a static conception of structure to a truly dynamic interpretation, and (4) how to dissociate economic processes and concerns from that which is uniquely international political in the structural dynamic and in the behavioral responses of statesmen. Power cycle theory addresses each enigma directly.

But there was also a tendency in structural analyses either to reject balance-of-power thinking as invalid, or to accept it unquestioningly. Only belatedly has the vertical international relations perspective been integrated more fully with a modified horizontal balance perspective. Likewise, the idea of foreign policy role had to be reunited with the parallel notion of national capability. Within power cycle theory, management of systems change is viewed as a restoration of conceptions of morality and legitimacy on a par with the structural foundation of international political order.

In the midst of far-reaching structural change, what set of policies will contribute to global security and political stability? Viewed from the systemic perspective, the challenge for policy in a transforming world looks at once clearer and more complex.

ACKNOWLEDGMENTS

The bibliography only partially acknowledges the long list of intellectual debt. Particular gratitude goes to Rodolfo Mosca, my old mentor in European diplomatic history, who first opened my eyes to the concert and to the Continental perspective on the balance of power. Some who read part or all of this manuscript or prior related manuscripts, posed questions, or called ideas to my attention in important correspondence and conversation, include the following: Josef Becker, Davis Bobrow, Max Corden, Richard Giusti, Isiah Frank, Takashi Inogouchi, Brian Job, Yasuhiro Kodama, Robert Kuderle, Jack Levy, George Liska, Gregory Marchildon, Susan McInnis, Timothy McKeown, Kenneth Mayer, Peter Mayer-Tasch, Manus Midlarsky, Joseph Nye, Catherine Perry, Richard Rosecrance, Bruce Russett, J. David Singer, Randolph Siverson, Richard Smoke, William Thompson, Robert Thrall, Robert W. Tucker, John Vasquez, William Zartman. Many very able students kept the flame alive: Walter Brill, Daniel Chiu, Dale Copeland, David Dessler, Eduardo Marcucci, Wes Parsons, James Voorhees, Terry Ward, Young Yoon. Richard Holtzapple helped me through the last editorial tasks. Tyson Liotta created the graphics. Steve Smith and his reviewers were demanding and thorough and are responsible for much of the clarity in this exposition. Michael Holdsworth and Gill Thomas sharpened its focus with important suggestions. Sheila McEnery provided skilful editorial guidance. Any mistakes of interpretation and content are solely of my own making.

Most important was my extraordinary family, for whom this manuscript was yet another burden to shoulder up the long "down escalator" of chlordane poisoning that much delayed the book's appearance. Along the way, Charles, Jr., developed the algorithm for the best-fit asymmetric logistic in 1986–87. Brent manned the computer thereafter. Kirk showed he could carry his own pack. Connemara lightened the load. What made it all worth while was my *raison d'être*, my wife Barbara, to whom I dedicate this book.

INTRODUCTION: NEW PERSPECTIVES ON THE CAUSES AND MANAGEMENT OF SYSTEMS CRISIS

A fundamental concern of international relations is maintenance of world order while providing security for the nation–state. Instability has many causes, and the massive wars accompanying systems transformation are not simply explained. Structural explanations establish a broad historical framework around which other sources of explanation may be integrated.

SYSTEMS STRUCTURE AS KEY TO AN INTERNATIONAL POLITICAL VIEW OF FOREIGN POLICY

By systemic stability and instability we mean how much peace versus massive conflict characterizes the system at a particular time. System stability does not refer to the degree to which the internal components of the system (its structure) are stable in the sense of unchanging. The system is constantly changing, and transformation occurs not as a discontinuity but as an "evolutionary novelty" emerging from the continuum of long-term changes in systemic structure, systemic changes which reflect the dynamics of the various state power cycles within that system (Doran 1971, pp. 1–11, 46–58). Systemic stability is equivalent to the absence of major war, to territorial security combined with peace, or peace based upon the acceptance of a legitimate international political order.

In the late nineteenth century, analysts spoke of the problem of peaceful change to connote the perils of nationalism and imperialism, and challenges to the status quo created by newly rising states. With the obvious failure of the balance of power prior to the First World War, and the struggle to overcome that failure at Versailles, this problem acquired a meaning that was highly structural in concept and useage. A wrong solution to the problem in appeasing Hitler shifted the focus of analysis after 1945 to the reasons why it failed, to the reasons why changes in the structure of the system have repeatedly ended in world war.

1

But if structure is what gives each international system its special character and substance, what are the essential components of structure? At a minimum, structure involves the number of actors within the central or great power system, their relative power, their systemic roles, the extent of polarization (ideological as well as structural), the nature and extent of alliance association, and the nature of the norms and codes of governing behavior constituting the prevailing international regime. These considerations form the basis of judgment whether a particular type of system is likely to be more or less conducive to stability, or whether the origins of political stablility lie with the nature of the change in systemic structure.

Contributions to this systemic structural perspective have come from many directions and contrasting approaches to analysis, but something like consensus now exists regarding the principal concepts of system, structure, and distribution of power. As Morton Kaplan (1961) warned, any attempt to describe the differences between types of theoretical international systems in terms other than structure "would founder under the weight of the parameters which individualize these systems" (pp. 8–9). Richard Rosecrance (1963) showed that systems are stable at maturity and that the problem is getting from one stable system to another. "System structure" was defined as "the distribution and hierarchy of power" by Stanley Hoffmann (1968a, p. 17), or equivalently as "the distribution of capabilities across the units" by Kenneth Waltz (1979, p. 69), who emphasized that "to be politically pertinent, power has to be defined in terms of the distribution of capabilities" (p. 192). The notion of system structure is tied to that of power, and power (in whatever issue area) involves a relative relationship. The distribution and hierarchy of capability reflect the relative power of each member of the system, operationalized as "percentage share of systemic power" by J. David Singer and his associates (1972). Hence, the distribution of capability, systemic shares, and relative power are used interchangeably to express what is meant by systems structure.

Waltz recognized that the definition of systems structure as distribution of capabilities is necessary "to bring off the Copernican revolution" of systems level understanding (p. 69). "The structure of a system changes with changes in the distribution of capabilities across the system's units. And changes in structure change expectations about how the units of the system will behave and about the outcomes their interactions will produce" (p. 97). After extensive debate centered on this "structural realist" view, Robert Keohane (1989) concluded: "systemic theory is important because we must understand the context of action before we can understand the action itself

... structural theory [relative power, or the concept of systemic shares] is important because it provides an irreplaceable *component* for a thorough analysis of action, by states or non-state actors, in world politics" (p. 61). Note for example Stephen Krasner's (1985) contrast between a structural interpretation of North–South relations and the economistic focus on the behavior of utility-maximizing individuals (p. 306). The concepts of system and structure capture much that is important in the behavior of states and accordingly form the basis for the emergent paradigm shift even if a theory of international relations must go beyond structural realism.

Why must theory go beyond realism, classical and structural? While a number of reasons could be adduced, we here focus on the reason identified by Keohane: existing theories of international relations "do not offer a theory of peaceful change" (p. 65). Keohane was responding at once to the crucial insight into international relations, and the fundamental limitations of the hegemonic stability paradigm, which appeared in Robert Gilpin's (1981) study of "war and change in world politics." Asserting that "the fundamental problem of international relations in the contemporary world is the problem of peaceful adjustment to the consequences of the uneven growth of power among states, just as it was in the past" (p. 230), Gilpin examined the unsuccessful efforts of analysts to overcome this dilemma of peaceful change before and after the Second World War. Keohane concluded that the resolution to the dilemma lies in regimes and international institutions, and thus that system and structure are involved in the problem but not in its solution.

But, according to power cycle analysis, system and structure are indeed involved in the solution to peaceful change. Without a foundation in terms of state power and foreign policy role, other perhaps more elaborate solutions are likely to collapse because they will have been eroded from beneath by the absence of an adequate structural base.

While part of a wider tradition of systemic and structural theories, the power cycle perspective may however be obscured by certain assumptions that do not apply to it. Its conception of the system is totally dynamic and stresses the nonlinearities of state power change that suddenly alter the view of the future. And while its focus on vertical change also emerged within the power transition and hegemonic stability research traditions, this common perspective has masked the true commonalities and divergences between these three distinct theories, leading to confusions about both the causes of war and the path to world order.

3

THE THEORY AS INITIALLY FORMULATED

Power cycle theory saw its first articulation in *The Politics of Assimilation: Hegemony and Its Aftermath* (1971). Why had the balance of power repeatedly failed to preserve order? Why were certain times in history so traumatic for states individually and collectively? Those questions guided examination of the first three world wars of the modern state system, and the postwar efforts to establish a new world order at the Peace of Westphalia (1648), the Treaty of Utrecht (1713), and the Congress of Vienna (1815). This summary relates only the theoretical aspects of that study.

The book argued that such structural crisis can be understood only by examining how a state becomes a hegemonic threat. What factors or conditions enable a state to rise above others in the system and aspire to hegemony? Efforts to understand the dynamic of French capability over three centuries (seventeenth through nineteenth), reinforced by "thought experiments," yielded an answer that was elegant in its simplicity: *A state's relative capability in a system will increase when its rate of absolute growth is greater than the absolute growth rate for that system as a whole (the systemic norm)*. A table (p. 47) summarized the steps needed to determine whether a state was converging or diverging from the systemic norm, and hence the direction of its relative power trajectory.

What then enables a state to grow faster than the systemic norm? If a state does begin to diverge from the systemic norm, what is the nature of its growth or decline in relative power, and how does that dynamic influence the behaviors of states throughout the system? Further "thought experiments" yielded a second principle of relative power change: *a state's relative capability growth will accelerate for a time and then (at a point of inflection) begin a process of deceleration*. As the state rises in level of relative capability (due to its greater absolute growth rate), it acquires progressively larger systemic shares *until* it reaches a level at which its absolute growth rate increasingly dominates the systemic norm and hence becomes increasingly "less greater" than that norm. Subsequent to that level, the state acquires ever smaller systemic shares although absolute growth rates have not changed throughout the system. Viewed alternatively, the finiteness of systemic shares means that a rising state eventually will have increasing difficulty in acquiring additional shares.

The analysis demonstrated that long-term changes in relative power for each state in the system and changing systemic structure are two aspects of a single dynamic. Moreover, these changes in a state's relative power over time reflect its rise and decline as a major power within the system, its cycle of power and role capability. Once the process of state rise and decline is recognized as a process amenable to systematic analysis, the dynamic can be fully explicated and the impact of changing systems structure on the behaviors of statemen directly assessed. The occurrence of *critical times in the state's international political development*, times when it abruptly experiences a new perception of future security and foreign policy role, then seems as naturally and firmly deductive as it was inductively derived from the study of history.

The power cycle was seen as an evolution of what Klaus Knoor (1956) called war potential. Relative war potential, or relative national capability, was shown to index the "curve" of the power cycle, as developed conceptually in chapter 4, historically for the three hegemonies in chapters 9, 12, and 19, and graphically as a generalized power cycle in chapter 21. Chapter 5 emphasized the thesis that "intra-actor organic [relative capability] changes are vital to the potential rise of hegemonies, to their eventual emergence as a major systemic threat, and to the success or failure of their reintegration into the system" (p. 60). The last chapter summarized the thesis in a series of generalizations about the state cycle of political development, its implications for hegemony and major war, and the associated implications for order maintenance.

First, it presented the *theory of the state power cycle*, namely, the generalized dynamic of relative power. Curves of the absolute growth rate for the hegemon and for the system were drawn together with a curve which "roughly depicts the war potential of a hegemon relative to the average war-potential change of the major powers in the system" (p. 194), the state power cycle: "The war potential of a state *relative* to that of other major individual states or to the average war-potential variation of all major states appears to follow largely a cyclical development" (p. 192). Chapter 3 reproduces that figure, disaggregating the absolute and relative dynamics to enhance explanation (Figure 3.1).

Remember that Figure 3.1 depicts the *rates of growth* in absolute capability. As explained above, the absolute growth rates for the state and for the system will determine whether the state's relative power trajectory is rising or declining. The particular rates of growth depicted were chosen to emphasize the very important fact that even when each state in the system is undergoing increasing rates of absolute growth, a state can rise, peak, and then enter decline in relative power. Although the power cycle appears simple, even intuitive, its dynamics are actually quite complex and sometimes are counterintuitive.

Second, the three historical cases suggested a relation between *specific points* on the power cycle and the *likelihood for hegemony*, "although the respective curves have never been drawn. Such analyses deny that the relationship is the simple one normally asserted by the balance-of-power theorists who automatically equate hegemonic activity with excessive maximized power" (p. 192). Louis XIV's paramountcy seemed to have occurred "perhaps considerably in advance of France's peak potential" where the state "is stimulated to grasp quickly the supremacy it has so long anticipated and been denied." Napoleon's "drive for supremacy must have occurred early on the downward slope of France's relative latent war-potential curve" where the government tries "to achieve a role which the state assuredly will not again be in a position to contemplate seriously." In each case, the state feels frustrated about its systemic role, and "the dynamics of war-potential change may aggravate the psychology ('irrational' as this may be from the analyst's perspective) of the errant actor" at two particular points (p. 193). Labeled on the figure, these two points – the first inflection point (F) and the zenith (Z) – were identified as the points of highest expansionist motivation for a potential hegemon because, at those points, the state suddenly must confront a switch from ever increasing to ever declining rate (F) or level (Z) of relative power.

> The two points of highest expansionist motivation may be singularly frustrating for the state, for, while its latent war potential may be increasing at very high absolute rates, the *acceleration of its relative war potential* will be falling off and may continue to fall off at everincreasing rates ... Given a sufficient time lag for the realization to strike policy makers, the first expansionist outburst probably occurs after the state perceives a shift from *acceleration* to *deceleration* in its relative war potential. Both of these types of change ought to hold immense shock value for a government highly intent upon a major world, or systemic, role. (p. 193).

Third, a very surprising fact was added in a footnote (p. 192, n. 3): on key economic indicators, Germany's relative power appeared to peak early in the century. This empirical observation was especially striking because Germany's absolute gains were ever increasing on those indicators, and because its continued rising trajectory in relative as well as absolute terms was the prevalent historical interpretation. Germany's second expansionist attempt appeared to fall after the second inflection point (L) of sudden *improved* rate of relative power change. This fact was discussed as further evidence for *instability at that critical point as well*. And it was proposed that the Franco-Prussian War and Bismarck's wars of unification may have been a response to Germany's first inflection point. Thus, although the purpose of the book was to examine the conditions underlying massive systemic wars, the trauma of critical change in future power and role projection was proposed as *a potential cause of other major wars* as well. Suggestions for how to operationalize the theory were made at various points (pp. 47–51, 59–61, 192, 210), but that was a task for the future.

The purpose there was rather to emphasize the implications of the study for how to reintegrate the defeated hegemon harmoniously into the system in a way which would *prevent further hegemonic attempts* by that or other states:

> In the absolute theoretical sense, assimilation [order-maintenance, its third phase] is never complete, for in this sense it cannot stop in less than a motionless system in which interests and power have been equilibrated among all the major states in an unchanging international political universe. The universe of international political discourse is dynamic, however, and assimilation is a historical process, not an absolute one. In this sense assimilation ends when an entirely new systemic context supersedes the former context. (p. 194)

This fourth generalization was emphasized throughout: order-maintenance is an on-going process which must be "based on observations of long-term changes in relative [capability]" (p. 1). Therein lie the *clues to peaceful change*.

The long-term changes which the designers of the peace treaties must "deal with" in order to preserve the peace must not be limited to "the long-range factors ... *as they present themselves for extrapolation at the time* of the peace negotiations." The designers of assimilation "must ever consider the possibility that *new forces* [new states, and/or an inversion of the prior extrapolation which abruptly occurs at a critical point on the relative power curve] may emerge in the future to *transform systemic conditions*. With respect to the latter responsibility, [they] must take care not to create an *artificial inequality of systemic roles* which could encourage unstable developments" (p. 31, emphasis added). The key to successful peaceful change requires awareness that future change in the system will involve new conditions that *could not be predicted at the time of the peace treaties by linear projections*, and that those new conditions will create uncertainties and anxieties when they do suddenly occur. Peaceful change also requires that *a sense of justice be consciously applied*: to sustain the territorial integrity of states and to assure that a disequilibrium between power and systemic roles is not allowed to disrupt the peace during those critical intervals.

Finally, peaceful change requires recognition that the "dynamics of international politics" is not restricted to either cyclical conceptions of history or the Marxian negation of opposites, each of which supports the notion that peaceful change is not possible. The book postulated general "mechanisms of change in the international system" that could "effect evolutionary developments" and others that could "lead to cyclical repetition." Principles of complementarity (productive reinforcement by supplying a lack, exploiting reciprocal strengths, minimizing corresponding weaknesses, or specialization) and of competitiveness (elimination of contradictions, inefficiencies, and superfluities) explain the emergent cycles of relative power and facilitate the evolution of a world order that is both secure and more just (pp. 2–11).

The present book takes up where the earlier book left off. It has the same purpose, to argue a more viable basis for systemic equilibrium and order maintenance than the balance of power. But it has been enriched by the work of many scholars in the intervening two decades of theoretical and empirical analysis devoted to a host of related questions.

EXTENSIONS AND OPERATIONALIZATION

Many theoretical and empirical questions had to be answered before the generalized power cycle and its implications for systemic stability could be tested. Can power be effectively indexed, and can the notion of power be interpreted consistently by respondents? Background questions had to be resolved regarding causation, indexation, the dynamic interaction between interests and power, and modeling of a nonlinear dynamical process. J. David Singer's path-breaking Correlates of War Project guided development of our "yardstick" for a state's political evolution as a major power.

The rank disequilibrium literature influenced how the notion of general equilibrium has been schematically represented and further articulated. The mechanics of disequilibrium (how the *causes* of war yield the *decision* for war) required study of decision making in normal circumstances versus critical periods of abrupt massive structural uncertainty and perceived threat, a question explored in a widely diverse literature encompassing economic forecasting, arms race modeling, and social psychology as well.

Long before the index was conceptualized, attempts were made to find an efficient way to determine the times of critical change, when the trend of relative power undergoes inversion. The approach suggested in Doran (1971) was used: analyzing *rates of growth* in absolute capability for a state versus the system readily identifies its period of rise, peak, and decline relative to that system. Accordingly, graphs of relative scores depict that pattern, including the occurrence of inflection points. Analysis of the *rates of change* of the relative power data easily identifies the times of inflection.

This exercise, applied to a number of indicators and test systems, demonstrated that the underlying factors of growth are broad-based and strongly reinforce the trend of the power cycle. It also verified that the nonlinear dynamic of the power cycle, its inflection and turning points, is inherent in relative change in a limited system, that the concepts "relative," "system," and the "cycle of relative power" are inextricably united. Search of the literature on nonlinear dynamics indicated that understanding of such processes was still quite nascent. Meanwhile, the system dynamics modeling approach of Jay Forrester (1968, 1971) despite its shortcomings *vis-à-vis* global equilibrium, was used successfully to model the dynamics of Germany's rise and decline and its associated instability (Doran 1974b). But it was not a general test.

This modeling exercise led to the literature on predator-prey models in ecology, and to analyses of growth processes of animal and human populations. The belief that the correct mathematical model for the dynamic of the power cycle was logistic growth emerged from that study. Logistic growth involves nonlinear growth in the context of limited resources, and relative power involves the distribution of the 100 percentage shares of systemic power among the states in the major power subsystem. The critical points in the relative power dynamic can also be calculated by means of the logistic, substantiating those identified via analysis of successive rates of growth in absolute power and rates of change in relative power. Further search led to the so-called Verhulst or Pearl curve for modeling asymmetric logistic growth (Pearl 1925). Hence, it was not until 1978 that research had been completed on the nature of the yardstick, the required data collected, the mathematical model operationalized, and the test of power cycle theory finally undertaken.

Carried out with the important assistance of a student, the empirical test (Doran and Parsons 1980) established the reality of the power cycle for nine major states in the system. It also confirmed a causal relation between abrupt nonlinear change in power and role projection at critical points on the cycle, and the initiation of major war (not just the weaker claims of incidence and association).

9

Concerns raised about the statistical procedure for calculating critical points via the generalized asymmetric logistic prompted reliability tests of the critical points via a variety of approaches. This exercise demonstrated once again that the critical points are present in the data and are not an artifact of the analytic imagination or method. While undertaking this effort, a mathematician examined that broader statistical issue, involving estimation of the asymptotes, in the context of dynamical systems analysis. The very uniqueness of the inflection point of logistic growth suggested an efficient algorithm to resolve that problem. In addition, this technique enabled us to verify a number of assumptions of the theory regarding the "abruptness" of change at a critical point, and regarding perception and direction of causation (chapter 4).

The question regarding the mechanics of disequilibrium during critical intervals received new understanding from an unexpected source, the nation–state response during the two "oil crises" of the 1970s. Normal market behavior was inverted, and prices escalated. The phenomenon of inverted expectations and its effect on price, likewise witnessed during crises such as a depression, provided a clear analogy to the nation-state response to threatened future power and role during critical periods of the power cycle, already conceptualized via the supply/demand paradigm (see chapters 1 and 7). This explanation for why and how the decision for war is likely to occur in critical intervals was first presented in the context of the transformation of systems (Doran 1980a)

CONCEPTUAL CONFUSIONS SURROUNDING ALTERNATIVE EXPLANATORY MODELS

Some confusions arise because of the label "power cycle theory." The label refers to the *two-part* theory regarding (1) the dynamic of state rise and decline itself (the power cycle), and (2) the implications of that dynamic for major war. I had not given a name to this theory, referring variously (depending upon the aspect of the cycle being emphasized) to the "*generalized* cycle of relative power" or the "cycle of relative power *and role*" or the "cycle of *political development of the state*" and, as a separate issue, to the implications of that cycle for major war. At a conference shortly after the empirical demonstration of the generalized cycle, the term "power cycle theory" was coined by colleagues comparing this concept of the state relative power dynamic with the "power transition" and "long cycle" notions. When I adopted this usage, I always emphasized that power cycle

10

theory had these two parts, so that scholars could accept the first half of the theory (the theory of the cycle of power and role) without necessarily accepting the second half (the theory of how that cycle relates to major war). In my view, the notions of power transition and a declining hegemon can (must) be interpreted within the context of such a power cycle dynamic (whether or not proponents of those theories agree with the indicators utilized in the ultimate empirical test of the power cycle). The power cycle is an analytic paradigm within which many explanations for war may find understanding.

This is not to claim that the authors of power transition theory or of hegemonic stability theory would accept the notion of a state power cycle, much less the particular dynamic hypothesized in power cycle theory and its implications for world order. Some scholars have questioned the logistic nature of relative power, the existence of inflection points, the existence of a state power cycle itself, and Germany's peak prior to 1914 (chapter 3 responds to those questions directly). And certainly the words "rising" and "declining" have clear meaning outside a conception of the power cycle. But many scholars comparing these three models do interpret Kenneth Organski's and Jacek Kugler's (1980) power transition notion and Robert Gilpin's (1981) "cycles of hegemonic decline" as though they involve such a state power cycle (Levy 1987; Thompson 1983).

Regardless of their respective conceptions of rise and decline, hegemonic stability, power transition, and power cycle theories involve three very different explanations of major war and require-ments for world order. In transition theory, a rising challenger contests a dominant state for position at the top of the international hierarchy, initiating war to change the status quo. In hegemonic stability theory, a hegemon facing imminent decline initiates preven-tive war in an effort to prevent its subordination by a challenger and eventual decline. The crisis of a critical point is in no way equivalent to either a power transition or hegemonic decline as has sometimes been asserted.

Furthermore, Gilpin's (1981, p. 161) observation that the hegemon possibly traced the "S-shaped [logistic] curve for the [*absolute*] growth of an economy" postulated by Simon Kuznets (1930) and examined by Harvey Leibenstein (1978) must not be confused with the logistic of relative power growth. The logistic of absolute growth does not underlie and does not explain the logistic relative power dynamic, much less its political consequences. Gilpin also referred to the publications on power cycle theory for an "understanding of the dynamics of international relations," from which one might infer either that he did or did not believe they are equivalent (p. 95). But analysts must assess and acknowledge the *unique* causes and nature of the *logistic* growth and decline in *relative* power which underlies and is required for conceptualizing the dynamic of the power cycle and its implications. The analyst's intuitive sense about the rise and decline of states, like the layman's intuitive sense of gravity that requires much fuller elaboration, can and must proceed to deeper understanding of the power cycle dynamic.

In his brilliant assessment of the underpinnings of neomercantilism, Gilpin (1987) also ties the logistic nature of absolute rise and decline of leading sectors of the economy – the "product cycle" of Kuznets (1930) and Vernon (1966) – to international political conflict. "Political conflict ensues between declining and rising sectors over the control of economic policy. This political tension is especially acute when the expanding sector is located in one nation and the declining sector is located in another ... interstate conflicts arise as individual states seek either to promote their expanding industries or to protect their declining ones" (p. 99). While this argument is not incorrect, it is incomplete and misfocused. It takes attention away from his other important argument about the international political causes of world wars, an argument that is consistent with power cycle theory: the disjuncture between the existing governance of the system and the new distribution of relative power (Gilpin 1981, pp. 186–87).

The preoccupation with absolute growth of different product sectors thus confuses the absolute and relative curves in a way that obscures the international political dynamic. Of course, the logistic pattern of absolute growth for a product in a limited market is *analogous with* the logistic pattern of a state's changing share of the system's 100 percentage shares, and it does impact on the relative power trajectories. But the logistic nature of relative power change is *different from*, and *is not directly nor necessarily tied to*, the logistic nature of absolute growth and hence must explicitly be distinguished from it, in concept and in historical interpretation.

Consider one simple but historically important situation: even as a state is experiencing very rapid absolute growth on a given indicator (product sector) so that its absolute trajectory is nowhere near the upper end of the logistic, the state may have peaked and even entered decline in its relative trajectory on that same indicator. This was precisely the situation which occurred for Germany (even in the European subsystem) in the decade prior to 1914 on a number of key economic indicators (chapter 3). And it was the reason for choosing the absolute growth rate curves depicted in the first publication of the theory. Hence, although "rapid shifts in comparative advantage give rise to intense economic conflict between rising and declining economies" (Gilpin 1987, pp. 112, 56), focus on the logistic effect of absolute growth can distort the issue of where on the logistic of relative power each economy really is. Namely, while declining rate of absolute industrial growth may account in part for Britain's decline in relative power at the end of the century, it cannot account for Germany's logistic peak in relative power well before the First World War.

A restriction to the product cycle argument precludes going beyond the perspective of the "political economy of international relations," tied to the declining hegemon thesis with its important *economic* implications, so as to explore the truly *international political* implications. Recall the second principle of relative power change. As a major state moves up and down the systemic hierarchy, the logistic nature of relative capability results from the varying degree to which the state's absolute growth rate itself affects the systemic norm. Expressed non-dynamically, the logistic nature of relative capability is due to the fixed number of systemic shares. This logistic nature of relative power growth is intrinsic to the bounds established by the system, and insofar, is uniquely international political.

This confusion about the absolute and relative dynamics is not limited to the political economy perspective. It is widespread in the literature, and is at the heart of interpretive confusion surrounding the First World War and conceptual difficulty in addressing the dilemma of peaceful change.

We do not dispute the primary assumption of the international political economy literature. Gilpin (1975, p. 38) quotes R. B. Hawtrey (1930, p. 120) as representative: "Every conflict is one of power and power depends upon resources." Economic resources are the material basis of power, Klaus Knoor's war potential, our indicators of national capability. Without questioning the economic as well as the political concerns of a declining state, or the political as well as economic ambitions of a rising state, we ask whether uneven growth is in itself what is so troubling politically. Unequal growth rates are nearly universal and scarcely manageable; changes in the operation of political economy are endemic; changes in the hierarchy of wealth and power are inevitable. Perhaps it is only a certain kind of change in the relative power of states that is more difficult for state and system to absorb politically. A focus on state foreign policy behavior yields a view on the causes of world war, and how to prevent it, which is not incompatible with that of international political economy. But unless the unique logistic nature of relative power growth is fully incorporated into the analysis, serious conceptual and interpretive confusion will obscure understanding of both economic and political causation.

Additional confusion arises because of three other conceptions of "cycle" which are quite distinct from the power cycle and are part of other traditions of scholarship. First, building upon the Kondratieff notion of a "long cycle" of technological change and its implications for peace and war, a large literature has emerged (Garvy 1943; Rostow 1975; Modelski 1978; Thompson and Zuk 1982; Goldstein 1988). The *"long cycle"* is a systemic-level cycle representing successive domination of the global system by the leading maritime trading state (perhaps Gilpin intends such a *systemic* cycle rather than the state cycle of power cycle theory). Second, are the *cycles of conflict* that are self-contained in various types of foreign confict behavior (Wright 1942; Denton and Phillips 1968; Farrar 1977; Most and Starr 1976). Third are the foreign policy *mood cycles* which may affect foreign conflict behavior (and in turn are affected by it) but do not index that behavior (Schlesinger 1986; Elder and Holmes 1985; Klingberg 1952; Schlesinger 1949). Possible overlaps and reinforcements between power cycle theory and these other currents of research have not yet been much explored. For instance, the insights of power cycle and long cycle theories may usefully be brought together in the context of background systemic conditions for overall growth.

Finally, and most importantly, confusion surrounds the different assumptions and implications of the various theories for order maintenance. Hegemonic stability and long cycle theories conceive of world order as controlled from above by a dominant state. That assumption is based on conditions which arose *after the collapse of world order in massive world war*. It is an assumption arising out of the *failure* of peaceful change rather than successful peaceful change. Power cycle theory, which was derived from a study of the efforts by statesmen after each of those failures to develop a more viable order maintenance, asserts that the mechanics of world order are neither devised nor maintained by such hegemonic dominance. On the contrary, the dilemma of peaceful change can have no resolution unless order maintenance is recognized as a shared responsibility. Only thereby can a just and stable equilibrium prevent a collapse into world war during systems transformation.

THE GOAL OF CUMULATIVE UNDERSTANDING

Power cycle theory abstracts from history to a model of the dynamics of relative power in the international system, enhancing understanding of systems structure in two ways. It enables the analyst to determine a direct and immediate effect of the system on state foreign policy behavior, namely, how systemic membership impacts on the very timing of critical changes in a state's political development. Conversely, it demonstrates how the dynamics of the many individual state power cycles create system-level changes in structure, most importantly, the massive changes known as systemic transformation. Power cycle theory thus enables the analyst to cross levels of analysis in a way not heretofore articulated.

Power cycle theory is not offered as the "correct" theory replacing other "incorrect" ideas. On the contrary, the theory asserts that each theory is a correct perception of the problem of systemic change and war causation *within the constraints of the perspective* it brings to the subject. By seeking theoretical formulation of the full dynamic of the state cycle of political development, and by examining the state and systemic changes simultaneously, power cycle theory offers a framework within which the varied perspectives might obtain greater focus. It seeks to contribute greater specificity of understanding to these long traditions of scholarship. If anything, at issue is the "power" of alternative paradigms (Vasquez 1983, Smith 1987).

Joseph Nye (1988a) argues that the "power" of a theory (robustness) is a function of both parsimony and "good descriptive fit." Parsimonious theory that does not explain very much is easy; descriptions of reality that are not parsimonious but go into enormous historical detail are common. By descriptive fit, Nye means that the theory ought to "encompass more corroborated empirical content than their alternatives," and that seeming anomalies ought to find some sort of plausible accountability in terms of the theory (p. 583). Much of what passes for theory is not well enough specified to be testable. Likewise, descriptive fit is not mere description but carries the implication that it contains a deep explanation of cause. Historical description can usefully illustrate the underpinnings of theory. But the essence of the difference between description and explanation is that the latter addresses causation while the former may not. Causal explanation is deeper, harder to conceptualize, and more important to the advancement of interpretation.

If international relations is a mature field of social inquiry, developments in theory must be interactive (Russett 1983; Lakatos and Musgrave 1970). The most precise causal explanation of the question under study, let us call it "truth," may be thought of (to borrow the idiom of abstract mathematics) as the "limit point" of investigation which is approached through such cumulative theoretical under-

15

standing. Each analysis involves a unique perpective with its own constraints and advantages. Hence, each analysis defines a "neighborhood" around the limit point which is as large as are the irrelevancies and imprecisions and other weaknesses of the perspective. The very subjective values and unique paradigms that stimulate theoretical insight also constrain analysis and restrict the potential validity of the theory as the most appropriate reflection of the reality being studied.

On the other hand, there is "some truth" to each perspective, and each neighborhood contributes a fuller understanding of the reality. By seeking the bridges and commonalities between various analytic efforts, the researcher will be able to get ever closer to that limit point, creating smaller and smaller neighborhoods of fuzzy understanding. Thus, theoretical insight accumulates as a sequence of partial sums ever approaching the "true" or best causal explanation of the question under study. Such cumulative growth virtually assures that the resulting understanding will be both more encompassing and more focused, the dual requirements that must guide the researcher in every theoretical undertaking.

Part 1

DYNAMICS OF STATE POWER AND ROLE: SYSTEMS STRUCTURE

1 WHAT IS POWER CYCLE THEORY? INTRODUCING THE MAIN CONCEPTS

The Preface, with broad strokes, captures the main ideas and arguments of this book. The Introduction provides analytic perspective, unravelling deceptively similar concepts and arguments that may obscure that panorama. This chapter sets the focus for understanding, delineating the parameters of the analysis and the steps by which the theory is developed and the policy conclusions derived. From its inception, power cycle theory sought to integrate the great conceptual opposites of international politics: actor versus system; absolute versus relative power; static versus dynamic structural analysis; complementarity versus competitiveness; and state interests versus capabilities. The problem of peaceful change demands holistic assessment.

1. Power cycle theory explains the *evolution* of systemic structure via the *cyclical dynamic* of state rise and decline. It is thus a theory of the international political development of the nation–state in the modern system *and* a theory of changing systemic structure. For the "power cycle" concept *encompasses both the state and the system in a single dynamic*, generalizable across states and across periods of history, which expresses the structural change at the two levels simultaneously. The power cycle can be analyzed on each level by means of a variety of approaches, from the facts of history and an understanding of international political behavior, to mathematical analysis and quantitative empirical assessment.

The foundation of state power which the power cycle traces is national capability *relative to that of other states in the system at that time*. Indeed, relative power itself cannot be fully understood outside the context of this dynamic (see 3). National capability can be indexed so that relative power can be "measured" via a "standard yardstick" and subjected to empirical test. These data depict graphically what heretofore history has traced only vaguely: the specific path of a state's rise and decline in relative power as indexed (chapters 2, 3, 9). Each state can be studied individually in terms of its *cycle of international political development* as it evolves over time, from its well-defined past towards

19

a projected but yet-to-be-determined future. Changes on the state power cycles are part of broader "cumulative patterns of social, political, and intellectual novelty" emergent in the historical period (Doran 1971, p. 6). Taken independently and in the aggregate, the various state cycles constitute the changing structure of the system.

2. The power cycle *unites the structural and behavioral aspects of state international political development* in that single dynamic. The cycle must be analyzed holistically as a "cycle of state power *and role.*" It incorporates changing state interests within the dynamic, and shows how power and interests can get out of sync. Future projections of power and role are embedded in the cycle, enabling analysts to examine each period of history from the clearly specified "international political perspective" of contemporaneous statesmen, preserving direction of causation both perceptually and operationally. Moreover, since role reflects the state's *relative power*, its *aspirations*, and the *system's acceptance of them*, two distinct types of disequilibrium or dissatisfactions identified in the rank disequilibrium literature are encompassed by this dynamic. Power cycle theory explains the conditions underlying structural disequilibria, and it asserts that these sources of threat have their greatest causal impact at certain unique times in the power cycle dynamic.

3. Analysis of the *full dynamic* of the state power cycle (chapter 3) is required for understanding the dynamic of international relations. Whether the system itself is expanding, in stasis, or contracting, a single actor growing faster than the systemic norm initiates *momentum of change* on state cycles throughout the system. But the system establishes its own upper limit for how much structural change driven by single actors it is capable of tolerating. The rise of a state must be viewed as nonlinear "logistic" growth which itself ultimately feels the constraints of an upper asymptote resulting from the limited number of systemic shares. The natural constraints on a state's *relative* growth are completely distinct from (can even run counter to) factors limiting or stimulating its absolute growth. They are no less important than the differential rates of power growth among states in determining the power cycle dynamic. The theory demonstrates that relative and absolute change often contain conflicting messages, and that these confusions hinder efforts to assess economic and strategic variables in historical interpretation and in the formulation of current policy.

This uniquely international political dynamic captures the international political concerns of statecraft. It resolves supposed puzzles of history resulting from the traditional balance-of-power focus on short-term shifts in the balance and an incomplete understanding of structural change. The most important aspect of a state's process of rise and decline as a major power is that it contains *critical times* at which the state's *perception of its future suddenly changes*. At four critical points on the cycle, the state experiences a complete *inversion* in the prior trend of its future power and security projections: the more farsighted the policy planning, ironically, the greater the error of judgment that suddenly confronts the decision maker. It is at these points that the tides of history change for the state and, by inherent structural association, for the system as well. With the anticipations of the state and system suddenly countered by a new structural reality, everything in the environment suddenly takes on great existential significance, so focused and yet so far-reaching.

4. These critical points, where foreign policy expectations are reevaluated by state and system, are *causally related to increased threat and uncertainty leading to major war* (chapter 4). When the future role projection of a major state changes abruptly and dramatically, the structural anchors for decision are cut adrift. Uncertainty prevails about whether the state will become or will remain a member of the central system, whether alliances will cohere, whether status will diminish, and whether the state will be able to play the type of role to which it previously could aspire. In the atmosphere of uncertainty, anxiety, and reevaluation that prevails at a critical point, *other sources of instability may become more salient*. Domestic instability, having its own origin, may impinge upon foreign policy decision making in a way that might at other times on the power cycle be minimized. In particular, a status disequilibrium (however defined), which may exist for the state at many times during the history of its foreign policy conduct, suddenly increases in salience at a critical point because *the state's expectations regarding future role and security become highly inelastic*. The "generative cause" (Dessler 1987) of major war subsumes both structural and behavioral aspects of state interaction in a dynamic context that can help explain not only why those wars occurred but, as well, their *timing*.

5. Since the system evolves according to changes on the various state cycles, sudden inversions in the prior trend of expectations regarding future power and role by several states, indicating massive structural change, exacerbate uncertainty and fear throughout the system (chapters 5 and 6). If these states are also highly disequilibrated *vis-à-vis* their power and role, the system suffers from an unstable disequilibrium, *increased inelasticities regarding future role and security lead to an inversion of force expectations throughout the system*, and massive system-wide war becomes more likely. The five historical attempts at

21

so-called hegemonic control of the system by force are instances of *disequilibrated systems transformation*.[1] Prior assumptions regarding role and future foreign policy options are suddenly shattered, and states throughout the system seek redress or redefinition of the systemic equilibrium according to their own perceived condition of internal disequilibrium. The *rational decision-making calculus breaks down* as anchors of structural certainty disappear, and the seemingly rational mechanism of inverted expectations may lead decision makers into run-away escalation. The underlying generative cause of these behavioral responses is a *structural disequilibrium straining the entire system*.

6. Power is sometimes regarded as antithetical to morality, yet power cycle theory invites a conception of *public morality* that is complementary to, yet constrains, notions of power (chapter 7). "The survival of the international system may depend on the ability of member states to raise the status of justice and lower that of efficiency as elements of the principle of competitiveness" (Doran 1971, p. 6). Unless governments in decline are prepared to relinquish some role (responsibility and status), difficult though this may be for them to do, and unless governments on the rise place some constraints on their hunger for (or their reluctance to accept) greater role and status, international equilibrium is very difficult to achieve. On the other hand, neither rising nor declining states have the right to challenge the vital security interests of other sovereign states. Thus implied by power cycle theory is a well-defined conception of minimum public morality that does not contradict other core values, and that indeed is presupposed by them.

Underlying this invitation is the concept of *general international political equilibrium* proposed as a guide to order maintenance. At issue here is whether a potential belligerent ought to be confronted with force so as to enhance security, or whether the prospect of force use will only elicit a further belligerent response. The dilemma is whether accommodation will lead to the integration of a belligerent into a peaceful framework of international relations, or whether accommodation will only be thought of as appeasement and regarded as a sign of weakness and therefore as an invitation to aggression.

We maintain that this dilemma of peaceful change has a rational solution in the dynamic of the power cycle. But the solution is not possible outside a concept of general international political equilibrium in which the *power and role* of each major state is considered in

---

[1] Wars of the Spanish–Austrian Habsburg Complex ending in the Thirty Years War (1585–1648), Louix XIV's wars (1672–1713), the Napoleonic campaigns (1792–1815), and the First and Second World Wars (1914–19, 1939–45)

terms of *position on its cycle*. The classical balance of power is inadequate as a guide to equilibrium and hence as a solution to the dilemma of peaceful change because it considers power only, leaving out much about which states fight. But to be truly just, and to succeed in both the short and long-term, the strategy depends very sensitively on correct *timing*.

7. *Assessments of "grand strategy" must include awareness that relative power trends change even when the absolute trends continue unabated* (chapters 8–10). That present trends are likely to continue is a valid assumption most of the time, and strategic analysis must assess the implications of such straightline extrapolations into the future. But, the success of "grand" (long-term global) strategic policy depends at least as much upon recognition that *an inversion in the prior trends of relative power will occur* at some time for each state in the system, for, otherwise, the strategies of order maintenance may perversely become the cause of new instability (Doran 1971). This thesis also appears in Edward Luttwak's (1987) analysis of how "peace can be the origin of war," an example of the dynamic consequences of the "paradoxical logic" of strategy (pp. 58–73). Power cycle theory explains why linear logic cannot work in long-term strategic policy. Competition in a finite system proceeds linearly only for a limited time period. Then the linear trends which compelled that logic undergo an inversion, and a new strategy becomes necessary based on an entirely new set of future structural conditions.

Power cycle theory demonstrates (a) that exactly *when* that inversion will occur cannot be determined in advance, but (b) the very complexity of the nonlinear dynamic of rise and decline in relative power adds both simplicity and definiteness to the analysis of realistic scenarios with which statesmen in the future may have to contend. The theory provides a framework for such long-term global strategic analysis, analysis whose purpose is to help guide governments through the traumatic, unsettling period of systems transformation that will *someday* occur.

8. A fascinating related question concerns the *degree of determinism* associated with movement along the power cycle (chapter 9). Are rise, maturation, and decline inevitable, or is there a large amount of room for choice and decision flexibility involved with future position on the cycle? Can governments affect their future power position and foreign policy role, or are they essentially prisoners of some hopeless web of predetermined variation? Can strategies be devised to *manage* change on the cycle, to manage systems transformation. Strategies inappropriate to the dynamical setting could worsen both economic health

23

and systemic security. Awareness of the full dynamic of relative power – of the conflicting messages of absolute and relative change, of the distinctly different economic and international political factors contributing to movement on the cycle – is necessary to both economic and strategic policy planning.

9. There is much complementarity in the field of international relations as analysts work toward a common albeit multifaceted understanding of systems transformation and major war. A declining hegemon, a redistribution of capabilities, a scramble for leadership, a power transition, an achievement discrepancy, a status disequilibrium – each is an accurate assessment regarding causes of major war, but each also suffers from varying degrees of incompleteness or misspecification. A hegemon is declining for a long period of time; deconcentration of power, power transitions, unfulfilled expectations, and power–interest gaps are so frequent that random distribution effects cannot be discounted.

For more accurate *specification of cause*, all of these perspectives ultimately require a foundation in the full dynamic of the power cycle as is attempted here. All require careful integration of state and systemic level. All must integrate structure with behavior to explain "how preferences [for war or peace] are shaped and change over time," and "how the compression of time" may magnify the "effect of nonrational factors" (Nye 1988a, pp. 586, 590). All require analysis that can distinguish periods of high likelihood for instability from periods of stability, and these distinctions must be identifiable in terms of the perceptions and the psychology of the statesmen during those times. All require precise delineation of variables so that empirical analysis can proceed to verifiable tests of the central hypotheses.

Power cycle theory will undoubtedly be one of many attempts to bring analysis of these issues into sharper focus. In particular, its proposal for managing peaceful change must be assessed from a variety of other perspectives as well. For this reason, we will try to present the logic of power cycle theory carefully and completely, and we will attempt an equally detailed and sensitive examination of its assumptions, concepts, and hypotheses.

IS POWER CYCLE ANALYSIS RELEVANT TO THE NUCLEAR AGE?

Governments with second-strike nuclear capability now are beginning to recognize that in contrast to the logic of a Bismarck in the Franco-Prussian War, no government can today go to the highest force levels, on behalf of any positive foreign policy objective such as additional territory or economic aggrandizement (Bracken 1983; Miller ed. 1984; Ravenal 1982; Allison, Carnesale, Nye eds. 1985). Nuclear weapons continue to have deterrent value, and defensive value, but for defensive purposes only. Does this change in force outlook render the dynamic of the power cycle a less significant explanator of major war, perhaps because major war itself has become less likely, and because the decision rationale for such war has become anachronistic?

While the overall probability of major war may have declined in the age of ICBMs and thermonuclear weapons because no rational government facing second-strike nuclear capability can contemplate going to the highest force levels to obtain any foreign policy objective other than deterrence or defense for itself and its allies, the risk of nuclear war has not disappeared. Moreover, the logic of the power cycle as an explanation for major war is perhaps more trenchant than ever, since it demonstrates *abnormal* force use in critical intervals. Power cycle theory accentuates the security crisis arising out of massive structural uncertainty at critical points in a nation's history and at intervals of critical systems transformation.

By examining the rational basis of decision making and role projection during normal periods of foreign policy conduct, the power cycle explanation accounts for behavior that precipitates major war when the structural controls on force use disappear, when the rational becomes the nonrational in foreign policy decision making. This explanation for *how and when the rational can become the nonrational* is the only circumstance in the modern world where war using thermonuclear weapons can become thinkable. Thus, because the power cycle explanation for major war deals with the collapse of structural certainty and inversion of normal force expectations, it is unusually well-placed to account for major war in a world of armed nuclear states, notwithstanding the theoretical and empirical basis of power cycle analysis in security crises of the pre-nuclear period.

STRUCTURAL CRISIS, RISK ASSESSMENT, AND FOREIGN POLICY DECISION MAKING

Foreign policy decision making involves rational choice on the part of government concerning the ends and means of foreign policy. Strategy is the art of rational choice. It links the ends to the means. Rational choice is possible where the number of decision variables is limited and where the framework of decision making is relatively closed (Simon 1957). Rationality in theory requires that all possible alternatives be considered. However, in practice only a few alternatives will be considered because of limited resources and time (Levi 1986). Yet these choices will often be sufficient, where a ranking of priorities becomes feasible, and where a utility can be assigned to the alternate means and objectives so that a "satisficing" strategy may emerge (Wright 1985).

Rational choice necessitates implicit or explicit calculation of risks. Risk is the calculated likelihood that an outcome will occur based on information and experience. Some actors are inherently risk-averse, others more risk-acceptant. Where risk can be assigned a probability of occurrence, the quantitative assessment of that risk in decision-making models is rewarding (Vlek and Stallen 1980). Whether decision makers consciously make decisions according to such a process is less important than that the conditions of rational decision making will have been met, and that the analyst is able to evaluate the decision process with some conviction concerning the validity and reliability of the assigned probabilities and utilities, and concerning the decision variables selected.

For the most part, foreign policy decision making *is* a rational process. This does not mean that nonrational elements of decision will not, even under normal circumstances of foreign policy conduct, enter the decision equation. Foreign policy calculation based on essentially external political criteria will be constrained by nonrational elements in the psychology of the individual statesman, by the impact of domestic political preferences, and by the interpolation of bureaucratic, cultural, and ideological factors which prevent a government from pursuing its best interests. But the elements of uncertainty that enter the decision process should not be exaggerated with respect to average foreign policy circumstances.

Uncertainty is the antithesis of rational decision making. To appreciate this, *risk* and *uncertainty* need to be differentiated. Risk involves known or estimated probabilities of outcome. Choice depends upon how strongly preferences (utilities) are felt (weighted). An individual can maximize utility where outcomes and probabilities are subjectively known. But where these foreign policy outcomes are unknown, or where probabilities of outcome or preference cannot even be subjectively estimated, uncertainty may become a large problem for the foreign policy decision maker. Structural uncertainty leads to complexity, namely, incompatibilities between goals that can presage tragic decisions (Steinbruner 1974).

Uncertainty can arise in a variety of different ways (Sylvan and Chan eds. 1984). The decision maker may not be able to envision the possible alternative outcomes, or to assign subjective probabilities to the outcomes even though the outcomes themselves can be identified. He may not be able to assign utilities to preferences with any degree of confidence because of lack of information about those preferences or because of inability to aggregate them. Risk is only a part, sometimes a rather small part, of the total universe of uncertainty with which the decision maker must contend (Kahnemen and Slovic eds. 1982).

There has been much controversy surrounding the notions of rationality and irrationality in decision making, and over the question whether structural change causes decision uncertainty that makes a difference. Power cycle theory confronts both these questions directly.

How structural uncertainty catalyses war at the critical point

An important article by Bruce Bueno de Mesquita (1978) asks whether structural change leads to decision-making uncertainty. It correctly assumes (a) "that uncertainty results from an inability to anticipate the likely consequence of one's actions," and (b) "that decision makers are capable of learning to discern patterns of action and reaction from their own and others' behavior." It likewise makes the correct conclusion that "so long as the system's structure does not change significantly, learned patterns from prior behavior will aid decision makers to anticipate the likely consequences of similar behaviors under similar circumstances" (p. 245).

That logical statement of assumptions and conclusions challenges the static view of structural uncertainty wherein a given systemic structure, bipolar or multipolar, would be more or less conducive to uncertainty and, accordingly, to more or less warfare. Equally important, it correctly establishes the decision-making dilemma associated with radical change in structure (non-similar circumstances) wherein "learned patterns from prior behavior" *no longer* enable decision makers "to anticipate the likely consequences of similar behaviors under similar circumstances." The dynamic view of structural uncertainty recognizes that "*if* the system undergoes substantial changes, then decision makers probably experience considerable uncertainty" (p. 245; Bueno de Mesquita 1983).

The article therefore hypothesizes that substantial structural change would foster foreign policy uncertainty *if such change could be found*. And since its author was unable to identify any structural change that could become problematic for the foreign policy decision maker, he concludes that no such substantial structural change is possible. This last conclusion stimulated a number of "impossibility theorems" regarding systems structure and power itself as cause of major war (Bueno de Mesquita 1981; Hussein, Bueno de Mesquita, Lalman 1987). But that conclusion is in error; the mistake is to accept the null hypothesis of no substantial structural change when all possibilities could not logically or empirically have been exhausted. Indeed, critical points on the power cycle are a type of structural change creating monumental structural and decision-making uncertainty. Structural change cannot be dismissed as an important cause of major war, and the decision-making calculus involves more than the estimation of subjective probabilities and utility calculations by more or less risk-acceptant actors (Anderson and McKeown 1987; McGowan 1989). Structure provides the material conditions that both "enable and constrain" state behavior, behavior which in turn "reproduces and transforms" the structure (Dessler 1989, pp. 466–67).

The structural constraints affecting decision-making behaviors can only be determined within the context of the full power cycle dynamic. At momentous times in the evolution of a nation's foreign policy, structural uncertainty does indeed become problematic for decision makers *for the very fact that it undermines such "learned patterns from prior behavior."* At these times, which correspond historically to the critical points on the nation's power cycle, the decision maker's linear projections of future foreign policy role and security suddenly undergo a complete inversion from the prior trend. At these points of sudden, massive structural change, all the conditions of foreign policy uncertainty of the most grievous sort are met. The government's former expectations about foreign policy role, status, and security, accurate over the long prior interval, suddenly are proven wrong. And all the familiar rules of diplomacy suddenly appear contestable.

Hence, in a critical interval, where monumental uncertainty suddenly replaces long-held certainty, *risks can no longer be adequately estimated.* Massive structural change causes the decision maker to miscalculate the strength of established expectations in the face of evidence which runs counter to them (Steinbruner 1974; Jervis 1976). The state discovers these mistakes about its future role projections but fails to adjust to them, and, in the process, it tends to miscalculate the role projections of rivals. The probability of incorrect interpretation of communications is more frequent during crises (Snyder and Diesing 1977). That is why Germany in July 1914 could delude itself (chapter 5) that if it used massive force, the members of the Entente would support it militarily, while at a minimum England would remain neutral. Nowhere else on its power cycle would Germany have been so likely to misconstrue the behavior of its rivals, their own structural priorities, and, in turn, their response to what Germany regarded as a "safe" course of military action.

The sudden, massive increase in an uncertainty that holds such high foreign policy stakes for the state also affects foreign policy behavior through increased stress and anxiety. "Hot" processes of emotion and motivation shape perception and therefore judgment (Lebow 1981). The capacity to think in terms of a sequence of causal logic during stressful intervals may become blurred (Smoke 1977). An increase in the mere volume and complexity of foreign policy issues can cause stress (Holsti and George 1975; Falkowski ed. 1979). Others have argued that the lack of information (certainty) is the primary decision-making element causing stress (Kahn, Wolfe, Quinn, and Snoek 1964). Governments accustomed to fairly predictable foreign policy behavior based on a set of structural circumstances with which they are familiar are simply unable to cope with structural conditions that provide too much uncertainty and insufficient information upon which to ground foreign policy action.

When the uncertainty occurs in a crisis setting or involves highly valued interests, the effect on the decision maker is even more pronounced. When extremely stressful conditions arise, cognition is disrupted, thinking becomes simplistic, memory fades, and the probability of wrong choice among strategic alternatives increases substantially (Janis and Mann 1977). In crisis intervals, communications problems within governmental decision processes lead to confused, unintended, or incorrect choices (Betts 1983).

In sum, while rational foreign policy decision making prevails under normal conditions, when known structural relationships in the international system facilitate the appropriate estimation of subjective probabilities and utilities, these conditions do not hold at the critical points on a nation's power cycle. Uncertainty tends to inhibit the calculation of risks. Strategy becomes confused as lack of information about future foreign policy distorts expectation, and anxiety stimulates belligerence and foreign policy over-reaction. Risk "acceptant" or "averse" become inappropriate descriptors for actors who can no longer estimate risk reliably.

Whether one characterizes this breakdown of the existing rational decision-making framework, and the state response to such monumental structural uncertainty, as rational or irrational is somewhat a question of semantics. The important question is how such monumental structural uncertainty alters that previous rational decision-making process, how decision makers react and respond to

29

such a systemic crisis. The answer of power cycle theory will be given later in this chapter after we examine two other conceptions which enter into that discussion.

GOAL-ORIENTED FOREIGN POLICY BEHAVIOR

As used in power cycle theory, *foreign policy role* is the encompassing demand aspect of state interaction. It reflects the goal aspirations and expectations underlying that "demand" on the one hand, and the extent to which the system accepts that demand as "legitimate" on the other (the extent to which the system actually demands or acknowledges that role). How foreign policy role changes as power changes over broad periods of history is key to understanding the power cycle dynamic.

National interest and security

The national interest is an assertion of the long-term goals of the state (Morganthau 1967). It emerges out of tradition, geopolitical situation, and culture, and may or may not be explicitly articulated. If not articulated, its manifestation is clearly deduced and understood by neighbors (Wight 1946).

For interests to become routinized in the discourse and behavior of nations, they must become legitimate. Legitimate interests are interests that are acceptable to the broad community of nations. Sometimes the legitimacy of interests is determined by how they are pursued or defended. For example, the desire on the part of the Soviet Union for access to warm water ports is legitimate if it is pursued via treaty purchase or international integration. If the access is obtained by the use of force, it would not be a legitimate state interest. Normally the defense of security interests is considered to be legitimate if that defense occurs on the territory or in the territorial waters of the home country or of an ally. The key to whether an interest is or is not a legitimate interest is whether other governments regard the interest and the manner of its pursuit or defense as legitimate.

International political role

Role amounts to more than power position, or place, within the international system, although role encompasses these considerations. Role suggests informally legitimated responsibilities and perquisites associated with position and place (Rosenau 1969; Holsti 1970;

Lieberman 1965). Role involves the extent of leadership or follower-ship, the capacity to extend security to others or the dependence upon external security; whether a state is an aid-giver or recipient, a lender or a net debtor; whether the state is sought after for counsel or is disregarded; and whether the state is an over-achiever or a com-parative nonparticipant in the affairs of the system. Role is determined not solely by power, or by the national capability that underlies power. It is determined also by the tradition of international political involvement and the record concerning how power has been used. And it is determined, in the absence of an actual exercise of power, by how other governments respond to the state because of its power and/or prestige.

Role involves such matters as the articulation and maintenance of international economic regimes, the responsibilities of mediation and peace-keeping, the functional responsibilities concerning inter-national environmental preservation and the protection of human rights, and the initiative taken in collective and organizational forums. The role played by the state is often partly the result of the status of the country as perceived by others, and is affected by internal electoral or regime strength as well as by how skillfully a government conducts its external relations.

Given a particular role, a state may be more or less able to pursue its own specific interest, although role and interest normally expand together. Saudi Arabia's role in the Islamic Middle East as "guardian of Mecca" and of the Muslim Holy Places, proscribes some of the diplomatic initiatives that Egypt, for example, might take. Canada's role as a rising middle power enables it to monitor its aid deliveries without being accused of "imperialist meddling." On the whole, however, a larger international political role for a state enables it to pursue broader, not narrower, interests and equates with greater systemic involvement, not less.

In that greater role correlates with greater interests, international political role reflects the set of foreign policy interests that a state has actually achieved. A state is able to assume this role, and to achieve those interests: (1) because of the relative national capability at its disposal; (2) because of its own aspirations regarding those interests; and (3) because of the willingness of other members of the system to let it obtain those interests. The concept of role encompasses these three interconnected aspects of foreign policy behavior.

In short, from the power cycle orientation, foreign policy role has special meaning. It is the encompassing notion that indexes the foreign policy behavior of the state over time. It is deeply normative. It

31

responds to incremental changes in power, yet it is conceptually distinct, and it in fact acts as a guide to the exercise of state power in broad terms.

Playing roles according to the victors' expectations

Postwar Japan has alternatively been described in the European and North American press as politically immature, pacifistic, interested only in amassing collective wealth, or unwilling to assume leadership responsibilities. Postwar Germans have been described as malleable, with no cultural core or sense of societal direction, because of their docility in accepting political regimes of lesser or greater authoritarianism or democracy. In each case, these political characteristics have been attributed to underlying cultural traits, but each of these interpretations entirely misses its target. Rather, they highlight the centrality of role and role expectations in international politics.

Like other defeated hegemonic states in history, postwar Japan and Germany have been playing roles, roles they believe the international system expects of them. These roles are carved out of a set of images each country believes the victors had of themselves and of idealized foreign policy conduct. Designed to please the system, this role became self-reinforcing, for it enabled the defeated states to be reintegrated into peaceful and productive relations in the system. By choice, they did not diverge from this role and seek to express their own foreign policy identities.

No two states in reality have stronger *Gemeinschaft* and *Gesellschaft*, to use the German terms for institutions and society, than Germany and Japan. No two societies are more highly motivated. Historically, none has been more interested in obtaining a major international political place on the world stage. But survival in the present international system required, according to the self-appraisal of each, a new more quiescent, pliable, and humble foreign image. Each has nurtured and played this role with such conviction, and it has been so well-received by the system it was designed to please, that even its architects began to believe it was permanent.

But all "role playing" exercises at some point come to an end. If the rejection of this postwar role occurs suddenly, Germany and Japan may be accused of nationalism and worse. They may in fact lurch toward another extreme out of repugnance for the "subordination" that some may feel was unfairly expected of them. Better a movement toward a more realistic place in the international political hierarchy, gradually, and without guilt or malice, than a sudden "role-reversal" that is as troubling to the actors themselves as to those other governments who will then rashly be called upon to adapt.

THREAT, POWER, AND STATUS DISEQUILIBRIUM

While the logic of increased salience during a critical interval and the process of inverted expectations are explained more intuitively in chapters 4 and 7, the remainder of this chapter uses an analytical framework that may enhance understanding of the complicated structural and decision processes.

Power cycle theory asserts that war breaks out at a critical point on its power cycle because a state is confronted with a totally new foreign policy "world view" and future security situation. The state either perceives this new world view to be threatening, or, in response to changing foreign policy circumstances, acts in a way that threatens others. Threat is the intermediate variable between changes of power and conflict behavior (Boulding 1962).

At the critical point, this sense of severe foreign policy threat stems from: (1) the shock of abrupt, unanticipated change in relative power; (2) the nature and ineluctability of the associated change in the projection of role; (3) the high stakes involved; (4) the increase in uncertainty associated with decision making; (5) the raw military strength at the disposal of major rivals, and (6) the presence of power-role gaps now suddenly the focus of foreign policy attention. When several states undergo such critical changes on their power curves at about the same time, the level of threat in the system becomes excessive. At those times, the need for adjustments of foreign policy interests becomes glaring; the system itself is said to be in disequilibrium (Mansbach and Vasquez 1981).

The power-role gaps express the degree to which adjustment is required for each individual state. The sense of threat associated with the mere presence of such power-role gaps is akin to certain ideas in the literature on rank disequilibrium. Although interpretation of the origin and nature of the threat varies greatly, these studies share a concern with how threat emerges out of disparities of power and/or status, and/or a state's expectations or aspirations regarding them. Power cycle theory does not assert the truth or falsity of any of the particular hypotheses in that literature. Rather, it argues that such disparities of power (or status or expectation) are most likely to become an issue, to be perceived as a serious threat, at the critical points on the power cycle. The disequilibrium suddenly becomes highly destabilizing for state and system.

The various rank disequilibrium hypotheses thus should be examined from the perspective of the state cycle of political development on the one hand, and systemic-level equilibrium on the other. A short piece entitled "'Equilibrium' and Rank Disequilibrium" showed that the rank disequilibrium hypotheses are lacking in an explanation for "degrees of inelasticity" (as explained below): *when* a rank disequilibrium is likely to produce a conflict outcome (Doran 1972). It proposed a resolution of this problem in the context of the dynamic of relative power and role. Once put in this context, the different types of "disequilibrium" can be assessed simultaneously, yielding a more encompassing notion of the requirements for equilibrium.

A first step in the power cycle reconciliation is to show that the rank disequilibrium literature addresses two very different types of disequilibrium. One type of disequilibrium involves *a single indicator*, namely, relative power, which we will call Type A disequilibrium. Another type of disequilibrium derives from a comparison of *two distinct indicators* (power versus status), and is called Type B here (Gleditsch 1970; Doran 1974a). These two very different types of disequilibrium can be synthesized in a single model because they are different aspects of a single phenomenon, the state cycle of power and role. In chapter 5 we dissect this cycle into its power and role components to explore the complex interaction of these two sources of threat perception. Here we briefly show how these two variants of the rank disequilibrium paradigm are illuminated by the power cycle dynamic.

Consider, for example, models referred to as "status disequilibrium" or "power inconsistency," which highlight the difference between achieved power and ascribed power for a state (Galtung 1966; Midlarsky 1969; Wallace 1973; Davies 1969). Our two categorizations do not include status ambiguity models, in which status disequilibrium results from uneven scores across indicators of capability (high on some such as size of territory, population and army, but low on others such as per capita income, military spending, and GNP). Models in which the status disequilibrium results from the reluctance of the system of states to give a newly risen state the status and responsibility it has "achieved" by its growth in relative power are clearly Type B. In still other models, the status disequilibrium refers to a disparity in the aspirations or expectations of a government for more power or a larger role in the system and its actual capacity to achieve such aspirations (which may be Type A or Type B as explained below). Whatever the particular focus of the model, insofar as the aspirations or expectations of the actor do not match its capabilities, the actor may also be said to be suffering from "achievement discrepancy." Variants of this latter type of status disequilibrium are so-called relative deprivation (Gurr 1970), systemic frustration (Feieraband, Feieraband, and Nesvold 1972), and relative gratification (Muller 1972).

From the power cycle perspective, insofar as the achievement discrepancy involves a "discrepancy" on a single indicator – a gap between the state's actual relative power score and that relative power score which it had anticipated or to which it had aspired – the associated sense of threat derives from the dynamic of that single indicator itself (Type A). In this example, the state feels stress because its relative power has not changed in the way it expected or hoped. The sense of threat thus derives from a frustration or insecurity regarding *the way its dynamic of relative power is proceeding*. Such variants of rank disequilibrium involve an assessment of the dynamic of the power cycle itself. This Type A version of "achievement discrepancy" is conceptually distinct from those variants which highlight the sense of threat associated with *a gap between power and status* (Type B). The Type B variant is conceptually akin to the power-role gap as developed in power cycle theory. The power cycle dynamic thus encompasses both of these very different types of "disequilibrium" identified in the rank disequilibrium literature as sources of threat.

Operationalized in a variety of different ways, the rank disequilibrium model is a compelling expression of the situation where governmental needs and aspirations are allowed to get out of line with its actual capability and become a source of grievance and sense of threat to the disequilibrated country, and thus a source of threat to other countries in the system as well. Each variant of status disequilibrium explains some source of threat in the system, but each is not independent of the other. To fully analyze the threat component of status disequilibrium requires a general "covering theory" incorporating all the relevant variables (Doran and Ward 1977).

Threat in each of these interpretations is an intermediate variable between power and war. Threat is viewed independent of actions or events of a threatening nature, and is due solely to the fact of power or of status disequilibrium. If that sense of threat is high enough and power is available to back up the threat, governments may be drawn into war to eliminate the threat or prevent its worsening.

Power cycle theory takes the threat equation one step further. It probes into that causal realm of actions and events of a threatening nature held constant in assessing power levels and rank disequilibrium. It answers the question why these gaps between achieved and ascribed power (and likewise these threatening high levels of power), which are present most of the time, lead to war only at certain times in the nation's history. Its answer is that a critical change on its power cycle will suddenly force the state to view its future security with uncertainty and fear. Power cycle theory attempts to explain why all of these sources of threat perception become focused for the state in single identifiable intervals of its political development.

FROM DISEQUILIBRIUM OF STRUCTURE TO DISEQUILIBRIUM OF BEHAVIORAL PROCESS: INELASTICITIES AND INVERTED EXPECTATIONS DURING CRITICAL INTERVALS

Although the power cycle interpretation of status disequilibrium has by no means been derived or "borrowed" from economics, the analogy between power and role on the one hand, and supply and demand on the other, is stimulating in terms of the mechanics of interaction. But beware. Both in graphical depiction and in meaning, the occurrence of disequilibrium is very different on the power cycle than in economic supply and demand. Nonetheless, similar "mechanics of interaction" are operating across concepts as diverse as demand and supply (economics), status disequilibrium (sociology), predator–prey models (ecology), Richardson arms race equations (international relations), and power cycle theory. The commonality of interaction, albeit regarding different behavioral settings and purposes, perhaps will more fully be recognized through the mathematics of dynamical systems analysis.

Power and role are the principal elements underlying the power cycle. How the interaction between power and role changes at a critical point on the power cycle becomes crucial to a more fully articulated explanation for major war. To tighten the analogy with economics, the "good" exchanged is the perception of "role."

Illustration of equilibrium between State A and the System is depicted in Figure 1.1. On the y-axis is the probability of conflict. On the x-axis is the percentage of systemic power and role at time t. Both power and role are relative concepts. The essential relationship depicted in Figure 1.1 is that between the power that State A obtains and the role that the System is willing to ascribe to State A.

Assumptions: (1) Equilibrium occurs when the percentage of power for State A equals its percentage of role. (2) In normal times equilibrium is the preferred condition. If State A moves toward equilibrium, so will the System. If State A moves away from equilibrium, the System will as well. (3) Elasticity is defined as a function in terms of the impact that a given change in percent of role (power) has on the change in the probability of conflict (Doran 1972, 1974a).

36

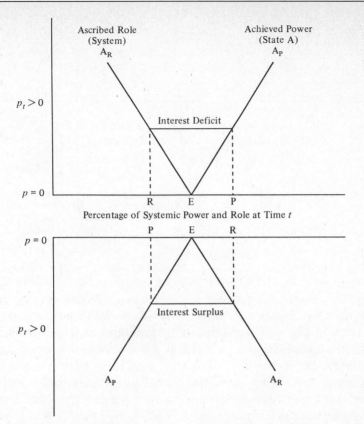

Figure 1.1 Equilibrium on the power cycle for State A and the System

Givens: (1) At time t, State A has a percentage of power P and the System is prepared to ascribe a percentage of the total foreign policy role R to it. (2) At time t, the willingness of the system to ascribe role to State A is $A_R E$, and the propensity of State A to increase its power is $A_P E$.

Figure 1.1 (upper) illustrates the situation in which an interest deficit for State A occurs. Achieved power for State A exceeds the role that the System is willing to ascribe to State A. Equilibrium is obtained when State A reduces its power by PE, inducing the system to increase its share of role from R to E. When the international system is in equilibrium, both State A (and all other states) are in a situation in which their percentage share of total systemic role equals their share of systemic power.

Figure 1.1 (lower) illustrates exactly the opposite situation in which an interest surplus occurs because the role ascribed by the system (at

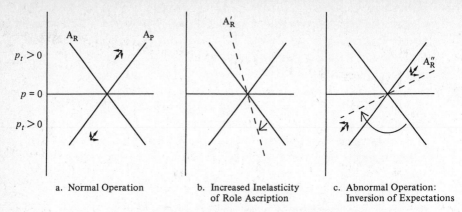

a. Normal Operation   b. Increased Inelasticity   c. Abnormal Operation:
of Role Ascription   Inversion of Expectations

Figure 1.2 From disequilibrium of structure to disequilibrium of
decision process: the mechanics of crisis during systems
transformation

the cost of some other state or states) exceeds the power achieved by
State A. This creates a situation in which State A has more interests
than it has power (over-extension). Equilibrium is obtained when
State A increases its power by *PE* and the System decreases the role
ascribed to State A by *RE*.

At most points in a state's history, that is at most points on its power
cycle, this type of adjustment occurs between foreign policy role and
power. Of course, slippage can take place in role relative to power over
time, a situation that may further complicate these basic relations and
which is likely to be discovered when the state is under the glare of
international scrutiny as it passes through a critical point on its power
cycle. But, for the most part, an effort by State A to return to
equilibrium is matched by a positive and reinforcing response from the
system. The elasticities of the achieved power and ascribed role curves
reflect this general atmosphere of flexibility and responsiveness on the
part of state and system. Security and peace are the consequence.

In Figure 1.2a, the interest deficit and interest surplus examples are
combined in a single graph. Suppose that the structural circumstances
underlying diplomatic conduct begin to harden. Governments compromise less willingly regarding high stakes matters. Alliances rigidify. Diplomats characterize such periods as "worsening atmosphere."
This circumstance is reflected in the curves as increasing "inelasticity"
or steepness. For example, increased inelasticity of State A's Achieved
Power curve means that movement away from equilibrium, either in
the direction of an interest deficit or an interest surplus, automatically

38

yields a more rapid increase in conflict probabilities. Similarly, greater inelasticity of the System's Ascribed Role curve results in a corresponding increase in the probability of conflict as the System becomes much less tolerant of demands by State A for a larger role. Increasing inelasticity of either State A's Achieved Power curve, or the System's Ascribed Role curve, can occur with a direct impact upon stability. Hence, structure is explicitly related to the probability of conflict in this model, and anything that increases the inelasticity for either state or system increases that probability further.

According to power cycle theory, such increased inelasticity for State A and the System are likely to occur when State A experiences a critical point on its power cycle. At that time, the State and System must confront a completely new projection of future power and role, and any existing status disequilibrium becomes an issue demanding adjustment. Note that the size of the interest surplus or deficit which existed in the normal diplomatic setting with probability of conflict P will have a higher probability of conflict in the critical point setting of increased inelasticity. That perceptions of threat do not correlate highly with status disequilibrium during normal periods was supported in Doran, Hill, Mladenka, and Wakata (1974).

Within the critical interval, this hardening of the diplomatic atmosphere can lead to disequilibrium if impediments to adjustment emerge, freezing interest deficits and surpluses throughout the central system. But the normal and anticipated outcome is for equilibrium to be restored in terms of cooperative actions and responses illustrated by the vectors in Figure 1.2a.

A situation in which disequilibrium is endemic, however, is depicted in Figure 1.2c. Here the System's Ascribed Role curve cuts State A's Achieved Power curve from above rather than from below. This corresponds to a situation of "inverted expectations" discussed briefly below and more extensively in chapters 4 and 7. For example, as State A's Achieved Power decreases in search of an equilibrium point, the System's Ascribed Role decreases even more rapidly, thus preventing equilibrium from occurring. This is the kind of circumstance that epitomizes negative action and response in the critical interval where perceptions become distorted as structural uncertainty mounts. State and system enter rounds of competitive brinkmanship that involves an inversion of force expectations and rapid increases in conflict probabilities. Most importantly, disequilibrium is lasting and irreversible, until the structural inversion of Ascribed Role (and possibly Achieved Power) return to normal. This is the type of disequilibrium that is most likely to precipitate massive war in a critical interval on the power cycle of one or more leading states. When many states are experiencing critical change, and when these states also have severe power-role surplus or deficits which demand adjustment, the international system is undergoing a disequilibrated systemic transformation and the probability of massive world war is greater than at any other time.

SYSTEM TRANSFORMATION: MODES AND MECHANISMS

The process whereby one type of mature international system disappears and another emerges is system transformation. In the broadest sense, system transformation involves "the evolution of real systemic novelty" which "is largely dependent upon patterns of long-term changes in relative war potential" (Doran 1971, p. 2). Statesmen must experience that "systemic novelty," and it must uniquely affect their international political outlook. This section provides a conceptual link between that general definition and the specific definition of system transformation in terms of radical structural change (chapter 5).

Modes of change and *mechanisms* of change underlie the transformation process (Doran 1980a). Modes of system transformation are anticipatory, productive, interventionary, and strategic. They are the substance of change, that which is being acted upon during transformation.

The anticipatory mode reflects the projections of governments about where they expect to be in terms of power relationships and security in the future. It involves diplomatic recognition and non-recognition, exchanges and communications, and coalitional information. It is the first to pick up the signal of ongoing system transformation.

The productive mode is next to feel the winds of transformation. It reflects changes in competitiveness, commercial behavior, trade flows, and international financial consideration. In the 1970s, important changes in the productive mode occurred with the collapse of the fixed exchange rate (Bretton Woods) international financial system, indicating that the US economy could no longer compensate for sustained balance of payments deficits. The interventionary mode involves the use of force outside the borders of a state for various purposes. If the locus of peacekeeping activity and of opposition to territorial aggression begins to shift from the top of the systems hierarchy to regional actors (or vice versa) or to new entrants to the central system, systems transformation is becoming more advanced.

The strategic mode is the last to show characteristics of system transformation both because the dominant polities have a decisive lead in the innovation and deployment of weapons technology, and because they place a high priority on retaining that lead. In nuclear strategic terms, the system is likely to remain decisively bipolar well into the next century.

Mechanisms of system transformation act upon and condition these various modes of transformation. The mechanisms determine the rate of emergence of novelty. One of the most important mechanisms of transformation is that which accounts for the past association between critical system transformation and major war. This mechanism is the *inversion of force expectations* which helps explain the manner in which a normally functioning international system suddenly is beset with cataclysm. The inversion of force expectations leads to a situation of international systemic collapse.

In brief, inverted expectations are the short-term response to the monumental uncertainty created by inversions in the trend of prior projections of power and role which occur at critical points on the power cycle. Inverted expectations are the response to a loss of "normalcy" in the environment, to a situation in which seemingly "rational" behavior leads to responses that afterwards appear "irrational." Itself an irrational response to a suddenly abnormal environment, inverted expectations initiate an abnormal decision making process which accelerates into greater crisis and war. Decision makers believe that each step is a rational choice as the sequence of events unfolds. Joseph Nye (1988a) quotes Charles Maier (1988) regarding the First World War: "From one point of view the war was 'irrational,' risking national unity, dynasties, and even bourgeois society. Many of the European statesmen ... claimed to understand that such long-term stakes were involved ... they did not think they were in a position to act upon these long-term forebodings. Rather, they saw themselves confronted with decisions about the next step." Nye's conclusion is in agreement with our own: "Although each step may be rational in a procedural sense of relating means to ends, the substantive outcome may be so distorted that one should refer to it as irrational" (p. 588).

According to power cycle theory, this abnormal environment is the period of critical systemic transformation. And at the heart of this breakdown of normal response in a critical interval is the fact of systemic disequilibrium between achieved and ascribed power, for it expresses what is at stake.

In the language of game theory, the inversion of force expectations

41

involves a situation in which actors change the "coefficients" *during a given game*, causing a transformation from one game to a different game. Redefining the coefficients changes the slopes of the equilibrium lines, and the new slopes change the system from a stable game to an unstable game (Boulding 1962; Zinnes 1976; Doran 1980a). Why does the system not revert to the normal condition of stable equilibrium? In theory, it may revert to normalcy, or it may alternate between phases of stable and unstable equilibria; or movement from unstable to stable conditions may not be symmetric with movement from stability to instability (Mansbach and Vasquez 1981).

Rigidities to reversion may prevent transformation to normal conditions from occurring. To revert back to normal, actors in a crisis must break out of a "negative cycle" in which a nation "sharply overperceives the hostility of another and substantially underestimates the hostility conveyed by its own intentions and plans" (Bobrow 1972, p. 54). Examining the crisis setting at the outbreak of the First World War, Nomikos and North (1976) observed that actors could not be guaranteed that conciliatory responses will be rewarded and reciprocated, implying that reciprocation may be denied and hence the determinism of the "known game" broken and perhaps reversed. Once inverted force expectation sets in, a stable game moves asymmetrically into a new game tending toward instability and a crisis environment. The literature on crisis decision making, and on decision making under uncertainty, provide further understanding of the mechanism of inverted force expectations (Jervis 1976; Holsti 1972; Russett 1983a; Anderson 1983).

Of course, the relationship between systemic transformation and major war is at once more complicated and yet less deterministic than this model may suggest. Yet the situation of inverted force expectations most aptly describes the essential conditions under which an international system may collapse in structural terms during transformation. A key conceptual question is how long-term movement on the power cycle gets transmitted into the short-term translation of the role ascription or power achievement curves such that an inversion of force expectations takes place in a critical interval (Doran and Marcucci 1990). Ascribed role reflects the state-complement's trajectory.

System transformation in the past understandably has been tumultuous. It is a traumatic and difficult exercise for governments accustomed to the politics of balance, nuance, signalling, and posture on the so-called "chessboard" of short-term strategic calculation. When confronted with the makings of an entirely new system with new participants, new projections of power and foreign policy role, new problems of order-maintenance, and new vulnerabilities for governments in leading positions, the members of the central system may be overwhelmed with the complexities of the new structural situation. The lesson of history which power cycle theory emphasizes is that it is changes occurring on the vertical hierarchy of power and role that will eventually determine the character of an emergent international system and that therefore must be dealt with directly to avert war and to construct a new stable world order. Major war is not an inevitable accompaniment of system transformation even though systemic transformation is an inevitable consequence of historical change.

2 MEASURING NATIONAL CAPABILITY AND POWER

"After 200," writes historian J. M. Roberts (1983), "there are many signs that Romans were beginning to look back on the past in a new way. Men had always talked of golden ages in the past, indulging in a conventional, literary nostalgia. But the third century brought something new, a sense of conscious decline" (p. 272). What was this Roman perception of conscious decline, and why was it "new"? Why was it that Romans as a polity could perceive that their power was in decline, and that historians, despite the intervention of centuries, can identify a precise interval when this sense of decline dawned on the contemporary Roman? Such contemporaneous perception of power, and of sudden change in the trajectory of power, is what any index of state power worth formulation must capture.

The goal of this chapter is to develop an index, or standard "yardstick" to "measure" a state's political evolution as a major power in the more recent historical past. Such a yardstick for power would have to be broad-based so as to encompass a variety of foreign policy leadership functions, and it would have to counterbalance actualized capabilities with those latent capabilities necessary for the state's continued long-term growth. The indicators chosen would have to be so basic to international political relationships that relative changes in the yardstick would be readily discernable in the operations of statecraft. With such a yardstick, we could "measure" at various time points a state's position and direction of change as it would have been perceived, plot these scores on a simple graph, and observe the pattern over time.

If the yardstick is an appropriate indicator of power *vis-à-vis* foreign policy leadership, and if each state's graph reflects the pattern of rise and decline described in the Introduction, and if critical points identifiable in the data correspond with periods of critical change identifiable historically in the perceptions of statesmen, we will have an empirical demonstration of the generalized state power cycle. For this test to be valid, our yardstick must be built up from the most basic assumptions regarding power and foreign policy behavior.

44

A number of questions had to be addressed if power cycle theory (indeed, any power-based theory) were to be operationalized and tested empirically.

First, do governments know what power is, and is there agreement across informed observers about which governments hold less or more power? Definitions of power abound (Simon 1953; March 1955; Dahl 1957; Deutsch 1968; Baldwin 1979; Riker 1964), but critics point to the considerable variation in them as evidence that power cannot be known. A related question is whether power is strictly issue-specific or whether it can be usefully employed in aggregate, structural terms. The issue-specific thesis corrects the over-generalized concept of power as omnipresent and capable of explaining all activity in world politics (Keohane and Nye 1977). In focusing on core values such as prestige and security (not marginal issues), however, the aggregate approach to power analysis may be more important, perhaps essential, because these are the purposes to which aggregate power is most effectively devoted.

Second, is the concept of national capability – the material base of power – internally consistent and able to be quantified? The concern is whether national capability is such an amorphous concept, and must include so many subjective elements, that it contains no core components. Furthermore, no basis of comparability exists across components, so that aggregating them is like adding apples and oranges. Is indexation a possible solution?

Third, does national capability in fact act as the substantive base of power as assumed? The notion that change in national capability is equated with change in the capacity of a government to implement a foreign policy is fundamental to the understanding of world politics. This relationship must be conditioned regarding *outcome* by the comparative *utility* of the disputed objective. Goals are no less important than means in examining the origins and outcomes of major war. National interest conditions how power is used. Despite the difficulty of defining foreign policy interest, analysts must assess how interests and power come together in stable foreign policy as well as foreign policy that goes awry.

The utility of objectives thus cannot be ignored conceptually for it accounts for much of the uncertainty in prediction involving power. In disputes such as the Vietnam War, where at least one actor uses much less than the full capability at its disposal, and where the two actors value the disputed objective very unequally, the outcome of the dispute is likely to be very difficult to predict in advance. The fault lies not with the inapplicability of power as an aggregate notion, but with

45

the extreme variability of predictions resulting from the unequal valuation of the disputed objective and from the perhaps consequential inequality in the magnitude and way in which power is applied by the two governments.

The fourth question concerns the origin of threat perception in international relations. Is all power corrupting and therefore threatening? How is power, and change in power, related to the sense of threat experienced by society and decision-making elites?

We approached each question analytically. Most serious was the widespread concern that power is an ephemeral concept about which there is little definitional or perceptual agreement. We asked samples of knowledgeable respondents in four countries (the United States, Japan, Canada, and Finland) to rank states in terms of the respondent's own definition of power (Doran et al. 1974). Not only were there very high correlations within samples (r above 0.9), but very high correlations across these quite different cultural groupings as well. Our conclusion perforce was that perceptions of power in international relations are well-delineated and broadly shared. Regressions of an empirically developed power index on these perceptions of power in turn showed that such an index captures as well the bulk of the variance in commonly held state power rankings.

Our conclusions regarding the four questions influenced the development of our research design. (1) Power is a concept understood by observers and readily applied by them to international politics. Perceived power can be conceptualized and states ranked accordingly. (2) National capability is an internally consistent concept, and multiple and broad components of the material base of power can be identified, analyzed quantitatively, and indexed. Notwithstanding the issue-specificity of power, within certain limits, one type of influence can generate others and act as a substitute. *In this sense*, power is fungible, and it is subject to augmentation, diminution, aggregation, and diffusion. But it is easy to confuse diminution of power, or inability to aggregate power, for example, with lack of such fungibility. Periods of reduced coerciveness, such as the later 1980s, should not be mistaken for premature diffusion or ineffectiveness. Likewise, not all power is equally fungible, and not all governments are equally skilled in the use of power or are willing to assume risk. The capacity to translate one type of power into others, at some cost and not without slippage, is nonetheless important in international politics. When the origins of the generation of power from inputs is correctly assessed, and the power index is properly composed, the state power cycle becomes operationalized.

(3) Regarding inputs generating power, about 60% of the variance was explained by a complex of *size* variables (military spending, armed forces, population, and GNP) and another 25% by a *wealth* variable (GNP/capita). Indexes of national capability do predict to perceived power with a high degree of reliability (and, we believe, validity). In terms of both additional growth in overall capability and actualizing a greater fraction of military potential, greater economic size enables a country to accomplish more; and economic size accounts for more of the variance in overall capability than other indicators. But it cannot be used to the exclusion of the other indicators. If two polities have the same size (large) GNP, but one has a much larger military capability, most analysts would agree that the state with the high scores on both indicators is much more powerful. GNP alone would fail to differentiate the power of the two polities. Similarly, purely military variables would fail to reflect the extent to which a state had over-actualized its latent base and hence would not be able to sustain that power in the long run. With multiple indicators, all the relevant variables underlying capability are more likely to be included, and the greater impact of the confluence of high scores for a single state is captured as well.

(4) Perceptions of foreign policy intent condition whether power is viewed as highly threatening or highly non-threatening. And perceived power is a better predictor of threat than status disequilibrium in normal periods (Doran, Hill, and Mladenka 1979).

ACTUALIZED AND LATENT CAPABILITY

A distinction with a difference for the theory of the power cycle is that between actualized and latent national capability (Knoor 1970). Latent capability changes incrementally and continuously over time as determined by a host of long-term factors, none of which is amenable to manipulation by government in the short term. An example is population or GNP. Actualized capability is subject to short-term policy intervention and, despite limits to governmental action, will tend to vary much more strikingly from year to year. Examples are military manpower size and budgetary spending.

This distinction is much like that in international economics between the short and long-term. The distinction there is whether a host of endogenous factors like information and technological change are held constant or allowed to vary. In terms of demand and supply, the distinction asks whether movement is up and down the supply and demand curves (short-term price fluctuations), or whether a translation of the curves left or right takes place (long-term effects). The

47

distinction between actualized and latent capability rests on whether in the short term the component of national capability is subject to policy choice and manipulation or is largely determined by factors out of the reach of the policy maker (Kegley and Wittkopf 1976).

Without this distinction guiding the construction of the power cycle index, mistaken conclusions are likely to be drawn on the basis of overall capability alone. For instance, some analysts have been impressed with how close Germany came to winning in the Second World War even without the acquisition of nuclear weapons (Renouvin 1969; Taylor 1963). In 1938, Germany had actualized its capability base to such a high degree that it was several years before all of the allies *collectively* would equal its level of munitions output. But by 1943, the far greater latent capability of the allies was totally outstripping Germany's latent base. Early actualization ratios were misleading. Germany could not have overwhelmed Europe once the latent capability base of the allies was exploited.

The actualized/latent dichotomy reveals that national capability is somewhat elastic. The advanced industrial states in particular have extensive room for shifts between latent and actualized capability. Shifts towards military actualization involve cutbacks in welfare for the present, but also involve tradeoffs over time. It is possible for a state to mortgage the future for the present, for example by sacrificing funds for education, medical care, and research and development. It is possible to starve the basic industries of reinvestment capital. Short-term actualization of power thus can be purchased at the cost of long-term growth in the latent capability base of the state power cycle.

The relationship between actualized and latent capability involves a kind of equilibrium between expenditures for security versus economic and welfare considerations. Many explanations have been given for the phenomenon of disproportionate defense spending whereby, during peace time, the larger and richer states spend more on defense, the smaller and poorer states spend disproportionately less. Whatever the explanation, a type of homeostasis may exist within the system that affects this pattern. When a state in either category moves significantly away from the norm for its group, the homeostatic tendency is to bring that level of spending back into the norm. Military spending, regardless of the ideological orientation of society or regime-type of the government, is in competition with other forms of spending for growth and development purposes, and across the system these opposite political pressures bring military expenditures as a percent of GNP into line around a norm. Governments very high on the list of military spenders are likely to be driven downward on the relative level of their expenditures; governments low on the list are likely to move upwards. The qualification is that these are expenditures during peace time and are relative to the economic size and wealth of the country.

Hence, the construction of the power cycle index must take into account two sources of dynamism that affect the evolution of relative national capability over long time periods. First is the impact of actualized on overall capability that may introduce great volatility into the series immediately prior to, during, and immediately after a major conflict, but is actually an aberration (noise) in the trend. Second is the homeostatic relationship between military expenditure and social and political expenditure that sets limits to the extent to which either type of expenditure can crowd the other; it is a dynamic which tends to drive each type of expenditure (per GNP levels) toward a mean for state and system. This homeostatic tendency provides underlying statistical stability (and inertia) to the overall series captured by the power cycle index.

YARDSTICK FOR POWER IN INTERNATIONAL RELATIONS: RELATIVE NATIONAL CAPABILITY

International relations badly needs measuring sticks and barometers (Singer, Bremer, Stuckey 1972). Yardsticks and metersticks are standards of measure that can be applied to variables or indicators central to the understanding of the discipline. These measuring sticks have several characteristics: (1) they are somewhat arbitrary measures, but (2) have been generally accepted as reliable and valid by the profession, and (3) are nonelastic measures of data used to index essential concepts in the field. Barometers provide early warning of oncoming storms and, while not infallible (they evince more false positives than false negatives), they are indispensable instruments when sailing the ship of state.

In economics, GNP is a principal yardstick. It is generally understood to measure the total goods and services within the economy. It is invaluable because it indexes an absolutely critical concept, the size of a national economy. It is applied consistently across time and across states. Its rules of measurement do not vary according to circumstance but are rigidly defined. It is not a perfect measurement; for example, it arbitrarily omits the contributions of household work, and it fails to overcome the problem of qualitative improvements in technology. Yet it is accepted as a valid and reliable measure of a central variable (total goods and services) and of a central concept (economic size).

49

National capability is a measure of the underlying substantive and material base of power. Like GNP, it is an aggregate measure, and like GNP, it is not a perfectly inclusive measure: it does not incorporate the more subjective qualities of power such as national will or national cohesion. National capability as a variable and concept is no more goal-oriented (issue-specific) or less goal-oriented than GNP. Both are underlying indexes of a concept or notion central to the field of inquiry, namely *the totality of the material base*. Less aggregate indexes of capability may be more useful in certain analytic circumstances, just as is true in economics of gross domestic product or national income. Data on national capability, once collected and collated, can be used for a variety of analytic purposes wherever the overall size of a state's capability base is relevant (Ferris 1973, Stoll and Ward eds. 1989).

But there are constraints. First, regardless of whether other fields are (or think they are) actually measuring an underlying behavioural reality like the total goods and services in a national economy, the scholar of international relations should have no misgivings admitting that national capability is a *concept* that can only be *indexed*. Direct measures of national capability are impossible because no quantifiable medium of exchange undergirds and interrelates the entire field of behavior and attitude in international relations in the way money does for economics. But even if such a quantifiable medium of exchange did exist, the problems which economists often skirt such as price inflation, exchange rate incomparability, and the impact of qualitative changes such as technological innovation, would plague international relations, committed to the study of long time periods, even more than economics. But insofar as national capability is recognized to be only an *index*, yet an index that contains many of the properties of a direct measure such as quantifiability, much progress can be made.

Second, power and national capability are not identical. National capability, as the underlying material stratum, ought to include the bulk of the variables of which power derives its essence. And while more subjective and secondary variables such as national will, or national cohesion, or patriotism are not included in the yardstick, they must always be *included in the interpretation* and, if satisfactorily indexed, could be added later to the empirical exercise itself.

Third, there is a certain arbitrariness in the standard measure or index. An index must be reliably constructed and be valid as a quantitative characterization of the concept. It must be recognized as an approximation or contrivance, albeit a very useful universal within the field. Part of the value of a yardstick is its inflexibility. Everyone knows its shortcomings, but by using the yardstick, the resulting research is expressed in the same units of assessment so that everyone knows exactly what is being studied. The fact that a field is able to agree on the index, despite unavoidable arbitrariness, indicates that it has become sufficiently mature to reach some consensus on its conceptual universals and most important standards.

The field of international relations thus must decide the following if national capability is to fulfill the tasks sought for it here.

(1) How much conceptual scope is national capability to encompass? The yardstick must encompass both economic and military components of state attribute and behavior. It also must encompass the two underlying dimensions of power previously identiifed, a *size* dimension and a *development* dimension (Doran et al. 1974).

(2) Which variables adequately cover the scope of the analysis, are defined at the appropriate conceptual level, and are neither conceptually nor empirically (colinearly) redundant? Neither too abstract nor too specific is the rule for variable formulation. Neither too many, nor too few, is the guideline to variable selection.

(3) What is the correct functional relationship among these variables? To achieve the proper blend of generality and inclusiveness, national capability must include very diverse units such as numbers of people, BTUs of coal, square miles, and dollars of expenditure. Since the yardstick is regarded as being composed of variables which *index* but do not directly measure national capability, it is able to encompass that diversity. Via indexation (assuming the problem of satisfactory weighting of the variables can be solved), "apples" can be combined with "oranges" to create the notion of "fruit" at the appropriate level of conceptualization.

Operationalizing national capability

In addition to criteria regarding scope, further guidelines stemmed from our particular analytic questions: how to index the international political development of a major power. Our national capability yardstick must (4) be sensitive to both latent and actualized capability, and (5) not be overly sensitive to any one activity such as war or economic control. Our resulting choice of indicators representative of national capability in the post-1815 period (until the early 1950s) follows:

> *size*: iron plus steel production, population, size of armed forces
> *development*: energy use in the form of coal production, urbanization

Although GNP was not included because of the aforementioned problems of exchange rates, uneven inflation rates, and qualitative technological change over long time periods, our index of economic performance (iron plus steel production) correlates very highly with the best collection of GNP data currently available for the nineteenth and twentieth centuries (Bairoch 1979). Only the U.S. level is significantly underrepresented by excluding oil and gas production from the energy use index. Otherwise, the *pattern* of relative power change over time for all the states is not affected by such index modification.

For the post-1950 period, high technology and nuclear capability make urbanization and armed forces size inappropriate indicators for the yardstick of national capability. These accordingly are replaced by GNP per capita and defense spending respectively, yielding:

> *size*: iron plus steel production, population, defense spending
> *development*: energy use, GNP per capita

The new set of indicators is congruent with the former in terms of the pattern of the cycle, but yields a more realistic fit in terms of power level.

The five indicators for the pre-1950 period encompass all but one of the COW indicators, military expenditures. Military personnel is sufficient to reflect military strength in that period, and it is not hampered by problems of exchange rate vacillation and inflation over the long time span covered. Moreover, inclusion of military expenditures would give too much weight to actualized military potential and hence the fluctuations due to a state at war, distorting the true latent potential of the state power cycle. Conversely, after 1950, military personnel is insufficient since defense preparedness becomes increasingly capital-intensive (e.g., missile transport and thermonuclear weapons). Dale Copeland (1988) has described military fluctuations as shorter cycles around the curve of latent potential represented by the power cycle. Short-term balance-of-power calculations must include those fluctuations as well as the trend of the power cycle.

Throughout, the yardstick must counterbalance the somewhat arbitrary choice between a number of equally appropriate variables with the strict requirements regarding conceptual validity. The yardstick appropriate for one period of history may not be appropriate for another unless qualitative changes occurring in the underlying material basis of power, with respect to both economic productivity and military strength, are adequately indexed with different but parallel indicators (Marchildon and Doran 1991).

What about the *future* international system – the appropriate yardstick for a state's ability to wield a variety of leadership functions, and the applicability of the power cycle itself? Qualitative changes in the substance of power do occur, just as the outputs may vary. Fungibility, aggregation, and diffusion are all a function of time and place. But what is claimed here, without qualification, is that changes in terms of power inputs and power outputs *do not* alter the contour of the power cycle appreciably. A new source of political power such as the acquisition of nuclear weapons gave to the United States a brief increase in influence (an upward translation of the cycle occurred) while the monopoly lasted, yet as the events of the Korean and Vietnam wars showed, the local conventional force balance remained very important. New indicators of capability may underlie the power cycle, but the evolution of the state power cycle continues unabated.

Alliance impact

Although *alliance formation* may also augment the power of the nation–state, it is not a component of national capability since it is a factor external to the state and often occurs *in lieu of sufficient national capability*. It is an offset to insufficient capability in the face of an expansionist threat and, hence, is not appropriate for an index of the state's long-term political evolution as a major power. Greater power acquired through alliance is more problematic than internally generated power since it is conditional and can be withdrawn.

A pathbreaking contribution to the analysis of power that stems from coalition formation (Shapley and Shubik 1954) attributes behavioural power to the "pivotal member" of a "minimum winning" coalition of states. While it captures important thought processes of governments struggling with alliance association in balance-of-power logic, its assumptions of randomness do not totally conform to international political reality.

First, the minimum winning coalition formulation assumes that there are no "strings attached" to certain conceivable alliance combinations. But for reasons of opportunity, domestic preference, traditional enmity, or a host of not always identifiable factors, certain alliance combinations in practice may be foreclosed to governments. Within a committee structure or even a parliament, such political strings are less problematic than within the more unkind environment of world politics.

Second is the thorny matter concerning actors that devote only a fraction of their resources to a particular confrontation. Weights assigned to capability become somewhat arbitrary when only a fraction of capability is employed, a fraction not knowable in advance of a conflict and even difficult for historians to unearth with the advantage of hindsight. Randomness is violated here because, had strategy evolved in a different way, alternate levels of actualized capability might have been used, yet the rules for delineating the plausibility of such alternate scenarios are not at all clear from the perspective of a calculation of a minimum winning coalition.

Operationalizing power: relative national capability

If the essence of international politics is power, the essence of power is the concept of *relative*. Yardsticks of power must capture the notion of relative position within the hierarchy of the system, and the change in that relative position, to convey the heart of what the statesman understands to be important about world politics.

The term relative denotes a comparison which operationally can be either a signed difference or a ratio of the things compared. Analysts often use these operational variants of relative capability as though they were equivalent. Although the *difference* between two national capability scores (for states or coalitions) is quite meaningful for understanding their actions or expressions of power *vis-à-vis* one another (balance-of-power calculations), it is too coarse a measure of interstate relations.

The *ratio* of State A's national capability to the aggregate national capability for the "system" reflects the percentage of this total "systemic" capability which State A holds at that time. This operationalization of "relative national capability" enables the analyst to compare all of the states in the system against one another with a single score for each state. Expressed in percentage terms, capabilities can be compared in an intuitive sense across years as well as across actors. As noted in the Introduction, this operationalization for relative national capability is *the* meaning of "systemic structure."

Regarding aggregation of component indicators, neither an empirical nor a theoretical argument could be found to give the indicators other than equal weight. Thus, for each state, its relative national capability at a given time is its percent share at that time of the total capability of all the major powers then in the central system, averaged across the five indicators.

This yardstick of *Relative National Capability* (or national power), call it *RNC*, incorporates (1) a particular set of capability indicators and (2) a particular "system" or set of states. Theoretically, a "meterstick" utilizing individual indicators or a different set of capability indicators is also conceivable if a less broad-based notion of power (more slanted towards economic assessment or *machtpolitik*, for example) is also

54

sought. However, to be a standard unit, the measuring stick must necessarily involve a fixed set of national capability indicators. When an analyst speaks of a state's *RNC* in the system, everyone knows exactly what indicators of power are involved. On the other hand, the state or the analyst is able to define his system, restricting and defining the relevant domain of actors according to the question at hand. This attribute of the yardstick is as important and useful as its frozen set of indicators (see chapter 3).

The yardstick for national power was conceptualized broadly, as a likely measure of a state's political evolution as a major power. It will be used to test war hypotheses tied directly to that dynamic of power and role.

Choosing the relevant system

Neither the statesman nor the analyst always compares the state to the same group of actors. "Relative to whom?" is the essential question. In international politics, a state compares itself to its major rivals, meaning states with sufficient capability to affect its power adversely. To study the fuller diffusion of power, the referent may be the international system as a whole. Or a state's single principal rival may be its most important referent; the "system" is then composed of those two states.

Power cycle theory deals with the select group of systemic leaders distinguished by a substantial threshold of power and foreign policy interactivity. Although sometimes criticized for either arbitrariness or the opposite, too rigid categorization, the concept of major power or central subsystem is an essential element of the reality of international politics. For the most part, the leading players compare themselves to each other as a set, rather than to the system as a whole. Entry and exit from that system, according to the criteria of political capability and intent to play a role as delineated by Singer, underlies the dynamics of world politicis. But does sudden entry and exit introduce discontinuities and/or distortions into the index and hence the analysis (Thompson 1983; Mayer 1983)?

The difficulty operationally is to determine when power is sufficient, and when foreign policy is enough affected by internal and external factors, to make entry and exit certain. Exit occurs automatically when a state possesses less than 5% of the capability in that system. Entry is likewise determined by both power level and commitment to an active role, but the date is somewhat judgmental here. However, we show, whether one is five or ten years premature or late affects the statistical (and the historical) interpretation very little.

Consider U.S. entry into the major power system. Before entry occurs, the United States must not only have at least 5% of the subsystem total, it also must have significant foreign policy inter-actions with the other major powers. Although the U.S army and navy were among the largest in the world in 1865, and the U.S. economy was continuing to grow at a consistently high rate, these factors were not of consequence to the major power subsystem centred in Europe until perhaps the Spanish–American War of 1898. Hence the United States "entered" the central system in about 1898.

But does this date of entry create a great "discontinuity" in the index since the United States "entered" with far more than the requisite 5%, indeed with a greater power score than any other member? While this entry may be a "discontinuity" in the sense of creating a sudden decline in the scores of the other members, that discontinuity is a fact of history which the other members "felt." While the United States and Japan, separately and for reasons of concentration on internal development and other isolationist preoccuptions, remained essen-tially indifferent to politics in the central system, the role and status of the members of the European system was supreme. In contrast, U.S. participation in the First World War and its leadership at Versailles reflected its new participation as the leading great power.

Furthermore, as chapter 3 demonstrates, that sudden impact on the scores of other members of the system does not create a distortion (empirical verification). Nor does it create critical points, which are determined by comparative rates of growth after entry (mathematical proof and simulation). Indeed, not to capture that discontinuity would be a severe "distortion of *history*." The emergence of the United States and Japan, and the decline of Austria-Hungary and Italy, are historical facts. The point is not *whether* states move up and down the state hierarchy, and in and out of a central system that is slowly changing in composition. The point is how the analyst can capture these move-ments analytically in a valid and reliable fashion.

Based on these criteria, the subsystem of major actors, 1815–1985, varied in composition as declining states exited the system due to loss of capability and role and/or rising states began to assume major systemic roles.

1815–1985 Britain, France, Prussia/West Germany, Russia/USSR
1815–1914 Austria-Hungary
1860–1943 Italy

1894–1985 Japan
1898–1985 United States
1950–1985 China

Most analysts considering security as well as economic concerns have arrived at this same composition, and dates of entry and exit, for the post-1815 period (Singer and Small 1972a; Waltz 1979; Levy 1983a,b). Studies whose purpose was to analyze war omit Germany and Japan as major powers after 1945.

HOW TO USE "MEASURING STICKS" FOR RELATIVE NATIONAL CAPABILITY

How do relative power scores differ from absolute power scores? Relative power scores take their values in a bounded as opposed to an unbounded set, with all values falling in the range 0 to 100%. Furthermore, a state's relative power score contains information not only about itself. That one number tells as well how it compares to other members in the system at that point in time. Together the relative power scores for states in the system tell the distribution of power in the system – the systems structure. But is there anything else about systems structure that the analyst might "measure" other than the comparative standing of the various states in the system?

While a measuring stick may be defined in terms of the particular indicator or aggregate of indicators which is taken to capture the essence of power in the international system, it may also be distinguished according to that which it seeks to measure about relative power, whatever index is chosen: the hierarchy of states in the system; the difference between two states' scores; the degree of concentration in the system; whether or not a transition occurs; the rate at which a state's relative power score is rising or declining; whether that increase or decrease is accelerating, constant, or decelerating; and so on.

And while all of these measurements utilize relative power score, not all of them are measuring something unique to the perspective of *relative* power, of systems structure. Not all of them tell something about the *effect* of systemic structure that could not have readily been obtained from the absolute scores themselves. The analyst must ask: Is there anything unique, new, or surprising in the measurement obtained that illuminates what it means to be constrained by membership in the system?

If the systems structure truly *affects* the reality of international

57

political behavior, some "measurement" involving the relative power scores should register this unique effect by some clearly identifiable *difference* from what one would expect when examining the absolute scores in isolation.

Consider first the distribution of shares in the system – the relative power scores for the individual states – taken at a single point in time. The position in the hierarchy is the same in the relative and the absolute scores, although information is gained by expressing the proportional share of the system held by each state in the hierarchy. In and of itself, relative scores at a single point in time yield no "surprises" about the meaning of systemic participation. The *static measuring stick* gives no clue to how systems structure *uniquely* impacts on international political behavior.

Short-term changes in relative power scores – the short-term effects of differential growth rates – are measured in traditional balance-of-power calculations. The *short-term measuring stick* enumerates differences in the scores for two nations (or groups of nations), and whether that difference is converging or diverging. In the balance-of-power framework, the short-term focus puts emphasis on the absolute size of the difference between two scores, and it is concerned with convergence or divergence only because of the issue of possible transition. Once again, these two "measurements" could also be readily obtained from the absolute scores; no new information is obtained regarding the nature of "relative" itself. Transitions occur in the absolute and the relative scores at the same time. And deconcentration processes are just as easily attainable from the absolute scores. The short-term measuring stick gives no clue to how systems structure affects the foreign policy behavior of its member states.

On the other hand, when relative power is considered dynamically over lengthy time periods, the unique *effect* of systems structure on the nature and behavior of the units is finally able to be measured. The *dynamic of relative power over lengthy time periods* is the only measuring stick which is able to capture that which is unique and determinative about systems structure. As we will demonstrate, the individual rates of growth for the states comprising the system, together with the finiteness of systemic shares, determine the unique properties of relative change for the component states. The fundamental and very important difference between absolute scores and relative scores lies in the nature of their trajectories over long time periods. The true impact of "systems structure" on international political behavior lies in the full dynamic of the state power cycle.

3   THE CYCLE OF STATE POWER AND ROLE

Over lengthy time periods, the power of a state relative to others follows a curve of rise and decline with unique properties, and of specific consequence for security and peace. The state cycle of power and role is the truest expression of relative change in the structure of the international system. It is the gist of that dynamic: changes on the state power cycles and changing systems structure are codeterminative. Without a comprehension of the full dynamic, as this chapter argues, the most significant aspect of systems structure – the bounds it places on international political opportunity and behavior – is obscured.

Intuitive recognition of the difference between absolute and relative power change, and of the importance of relative change for foreign policy conduct, permeates the assessments of statesmen about the future of their own statecraft, the speculations of diplomatic historians about the causes of war, and the analyses of scholars of international relations about the changing structure of the system. Yet, in these discussions, the concepts of absolute and relative are often juxtaposed and misconstrued when dealing with that which is most *different* about the two concepts, namely, the *nature of their respective trajectories*. Consequently, the foreign policy meaning is lost in contradiction. For an intuitive recognition of the difference between absolute and relative power change is insufficient to an understanding of the very peculiar nature of relative power itself.

Germany, and the origins of the First World War, illustrate both the contradictory messages of relative and absolute power change, and the importance of a correct understanding of relative power change as a clue to German belligerence. It is therefore also a clue to order maintenance in a system subject to change and challenge.

LONG-TERM TRAJECTORIES OF ABSOLUTE AND RELATIVE CAPABILITY

The power cycle is actually a dynamic coefficient that changes slowly across lengthy time periods. The power cycle coefficient is a ratio of change in the power of the state relative to the change in the power of the system. Analysis can begin either with the numerator or the denominator of the ratio, that is, either with the state or with the system.

If we begin with the system, the relevant conditions are expansion, contraction, and stasis. Performance of a state on its power cycle, set against each of these systemic conditions, is somewhat unique, judged by historical as well as theoretical criteria.

Moreover, each of these conditions can be taken to mean two very different manifestations of power change, although the impact on the power cycle of the state may in practice be quite similar. The first manifestation of systemic change involves the *internal organic change* composed of an aggregate of population numbers, economic size, wealth, and military capability of states (Doran 1971). As state power "grows" for the states that comprise the relevant system, there is a clear impact on the denominator of the power ratio for the individual state. But a second manifestation of system change also exists, namely, *state entry into or exit from* the central system. Very real in historical terms, the entry or exit of great states establishes a new norm for systemic change. It affects the contour of a state's power cycle as much in terms of actual state behavior as in terms of internal organic change.

System expansion.   When the system is expanding rapidly, the economic climate tends to be very positive, and, other things being equal, "non-zero sum" cooperative solutions would seem to be very feasible because resources seem less scarce, and shared solutions to problems appear more attractive, or should appear so. For the individual state, an expanding system in either the internal organic or entry sense is, however, like a moving escalator. The rising state is walking up a down-escalator and must walk all the faster in order to get anywhere. Acceleration of the power cycle is impeded. Conversely, when the state is already on the declining side of its power curve, expansion of the system is like walking down a down-escalator. The pace of change is simply much more rapid. The awesomeness of both Germany's rise and Britain's decline in the late nineteenth century is due in part to system expansion.

System contraction.   In a world economic depression, such as that after 1929, or in a period of actual population contraction, such as during the Black Death of the fourteenth century, circumstances are reversed. Accelerated growth for an individual state becomes theoretically easier, and accelerated decline becomes less troublesome for the state because the system is slowing down too. But in practice this means that critical points will be reached earlier than on average on the ascending side of the curve and later on the descending side, as systems change tends to augment or resist the respective trends. A contracting system may impart a pessimism of its own to world events, but it is far from clear that such a mood in and of itself necessarily worsens the problem of major war.

System stasis. In a system that is barely changing, the power cycle of the state may be most clearly, symmetrically, and even predictably etched. Whatever momentum is imparted to movement on the power cycle is momentum that stems from the internal organic change within the corpus of the state itself. Change is not accelerated or decelerated by influences beyond the perimeter of the state. Systems stasis does not ensure that critical points will hold reduced impact for overall systems stability. But what stasis does imply is that whatever shocks occur internationally from the power cycle dynamic, the shocks emanate from the state's own behavior, neither impeded nor magnified by change in the system. Likewise, systems stasis does not guarantee that other individual members of the system will not simultaneously pass through critical points on their power cycles; that is a matter of comparative levels and rates of growth.

Most components of national capability, such as GNP, population size, and military spending, have followed an upward-bending curve over time (Figure 3.1 upper left), increasing for most states in a fashion that is faster than linear (Landes 1981; Kuznets 1966; Rostow 1978). Limits to growth such as depleting resources, or diminishing marginal returns to investment or production because of environmental degradation or crowding, may slow that growth down for a time (Barnett and Morse 1963). But in the longer run these "limits" have always been transcended by means of resource substitution and technological innovation (which indicators of national capability must capture), so that the level of absolute capability of the nation–states has not decreased historically. Even population growth, which reaches an asymptotic level in societies with high literacy and wealth, may continue to increase again as new societal preferences shift the asymptote outward (Oliver 1982). Analyses positing an S-shape or even a downturn for a state's absolute capability curve are in fact dealing only with a portion of that curve.

In contrast (lower left), relative capability change involves asympto-

61

tic behavior that *cannot* be transcended because the system establishes *bounds* to growth and decline. The limited number of systemic shares (100 percentage points of relative power) establishes an absolute constraint on relative power growth. Of itself, such a constraint will put brakes on a state's capacity to collect more and more shares. Of itself, such a constraint will determine the occurrence of an inflection point in the state's ascendancy (and its decline) within that system.

In absolute power terms, governments come to expect certain results from a given growth rate. Early in the growth phase, a constant absolute growth rate produces an even larger increase in growth *relative to others in the system.* Governments accustom themselves to such results and see no reason why the same performance should not continue. Why should they not do as well in the future as they have in the past? They fix their eyes on the amazing absolute growth increases, translate those into accelerating increases relative to rivals, and are thus confident of the continuance of their surging strength. Suddenly, the relative rate of growth begins to fall off. This happens *in spite of* absolute growth that remains at the same steady growth rate. What has occurred? The state has crossed the first inflection point on its power curve. It has passed a critical point where everything changes *regarding capacity to shape future role* (pp. 95–8).

Above the first inflection point, even more strange and seemingly counterintuitive behavior occurs. The same rate of absolute growth produces less and less increase in power position relative to rivals. Eventually governments acclimatise themselves to this reality. For them, the important fact is that absolute power increase does translate into an increasing position of relative power within the system. So great is each annual increase in absolute level of power that they tend to forget an even more important fact: the rate of relative power increase is actually falling off. (Today everyone focuses upon the phenomenal increases in Japanese economic growth level without noting that its rate of growth in relative terms is sharply declining). Without warning, suddenly, and with grave consequences for their security and expected future status, the relative increases end. Absolute power increase continues but to no avail. Its relative power has peaked, and it has entered relative decline. The same rate of absolute power growth seems futile in terms of capacity to generate an improving overall position of relative power within the international system. The state is now on a downward relative growth path and does not know why, or what it has done, to have earned such a strikingly different and negative outcome. All that has happened is that momentum has shifted on the power cycle at a point of non-linearity.

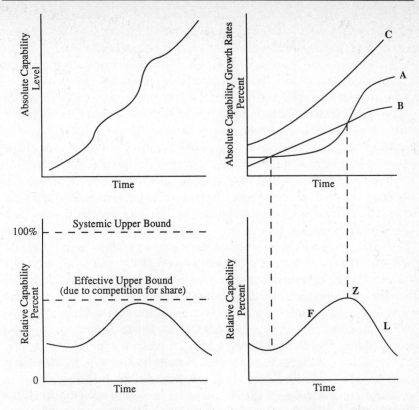

Figure 3.1 The dynamics of absolute and relative capability: principles of the power cycle

Source: On the right is a disaggregation of the figure in Doran (1971, p. 193)
Legend:
Curves of absolute growth rate: A, for the major power system; B, for State B;
 C, for the entire system.
Critical points: F, first inflection point; Z, zenith; L, last inflection point.

The same logic applies to relative power dynamics on the downward side of the power cycle. Translation of absolute power growth
into relative power change is full of surprises, both shocking disappointments and unanticipated opportunities. This is the lesson of
the power cycle.

Figure 3.1 (right) depicts the first principle of relative power change
discussed in the Introduction (proof in Appendix, p. 263). The key to
whether a state is rising or declining in relative power in a given
system is whether its rate of absolute growth (curve B) is greater or less
than the "systemic norm" (curve A). The figure shows increasing

63

absolute growth rates over time (an expanding system): a state's decline in relative power is not tied to declining growth for the state or for the system. For a more static system, the systemic norm is a flatter curve (imagine the intersecting lines twisted clockwise); a contracting system is depicted by a still further twist of the line pair. Curve C depicts a faster growth rate for the entire state system, corresponding to the reality that faster growing states outside the great power system become candidates for entry.

Graphs of growth rates tell much to the analyst familiar with the dynamics of relative change (Rostow 1978). A graph of the growth rates for an actor and the system to which it is comparing itself readily identifies the periods of its relative rise and decline in that system. The effect of systemic bounds is captured by the varying degree to which the state's own rate of growth contributes to that systemic growth rate.

Why should states follow this general pattern? Why do they not rise through many bumps before peaking and entering decline? Why should there be an inflection point? States may go through many bumps on the way up and down the power cycle. But within a certain period of that growth, the state is able to transcend bumps on the curve with greater ease (prior to inflection). As argued above, after some point, the state discovers that it is having greater difficulty transcending similar bumps; at that time it has experienced the first inflection point. Future security and role suddenly look different.

Certain of the disaggregated indicators of power are smooth, such as population growth. Others such as armed forces size (or budgets) are much more stochastic. But together they interactively reinforce a momentum that captures the inertia of changing power and that takes it in a particular direction. Small aberrations in the flow of power change are overtaken by the robust dynamism in the overall aggregate of indicators moving together. Over long time periods, the policy maker forms a perception of the trend in the growth or decline of state power. By a "smoothing out" of the "data" of perceptions, the policy maker comes to know this trajectory of the state's power growth in the major power system. It underlies the state's strategic outlook.

When a state discovers that it is at a critical point, why can't it reverse the new trend of relative change and revert to the prior one? Reversal is theoretically possible but extremely difficult to bring about. There is so much inertia in the power cycle in part because big decisions, and equally monumental actions, are required to offset an established trend. The difficulties are even greater at a critical point because prior rates of absolute growth do not yield the same returns in relative power; the state feels the systemic bounds via an ever worsening of those returns. After the critical point, the state can reverse the momentum of decline (in rate or level) only by *accelerating* its absolute growth. It must change suddenly its entire prior growth pattern. Thus, the state "knows" that a critical point has "occurred" when it sees that its prior absolute growth rate no longer has the same payoff regarding relative growth. It "knows" that the critical point is *irreversible* when it realizes it cannot accelerate absolute growth to alter that new relative power trajectory.

A critical point that seems irreversible may, albeit rarely, prove to be only a "temporary" critical point in that either (1) the state is finally able to accelerate growth sufficiently to overcome the systemic bounds, or (2) other states suffer a decrease in absolute growth rate.

SEEING IS BELIEVING: COMPUTER SIMULATIONS OF THE "SINGLE DYNAMIC"

Thought experiments like those that suggested the principles of the power cycle have recently been simulated by computer (Doran 1990a,b). A series of four simple simulations clearly depict the thesis that state and system are part of a single dynamic. The dynamics of systems structure *is equivalent to* the individual state cycles comprising the system.

In each simulation, the only input is a given hierarchy of states and their rates of absolute growth. In simulations I, III, and IV, "everything remains the same" in terms of absolute growth rates throughout the system. Simulation II interrupts simulation I at three time points to show what happens when absolute growth rates are altered during the process.

The simulations unambiguously reveal the nature of nonlinearity on the state power cycles. They demonstrate the two principles of relative change, in particular that the occurrence of inflection and turning points is intrinsic. They show that the mathematical properties hypothesized for the state power cycle express change in a finite system, and are not peculiar to the international system or to any particular index: firms and industries compete for *relative* "market share."

Simulation I. One state with faster absolute growth rate (Figure 3.2, upper left). If all states have the same rates of growth, the relative power trajectory for each state will be a horizontal line, reflecting no change in systemic share (see proof in Appendix, p. 263). The system is in dynamical equilibrium. If one state's absolute power begins to grow at a rate faster than the systemic norm, that state will begin to

65

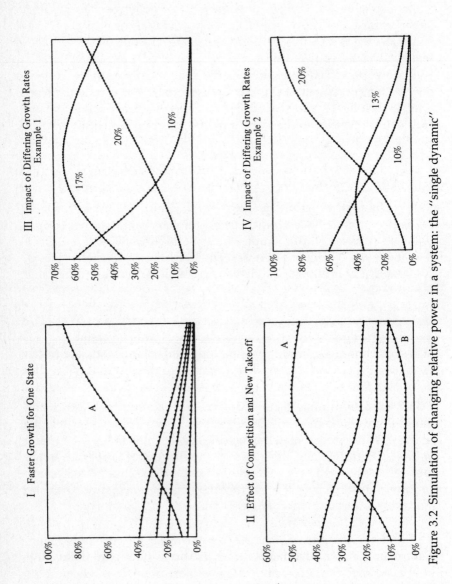

Figure 3.2 Simulation of changing relative power in a system: the "single dynamic"

rise in relative power, automatically creating a decline in relative power for all the other states. So long as this rate difference continues, the one state will continue rising and the others declining.

Simulations III and IV. Differential (unequal) absolute growth rates (Figure 3.2 right). These two simulations start with an equivalent hierarchy and involve three states growing at three different rates. The growth rate of the middle state differs in the two cases. Completely different state and systemic dynamics result with only one growth rate altered.

Note. In all three simulations, even though no state changes its rate of growth during the entire simulation, suddenly (at different times on the various cycles) "everything is different" in terms of each trajectory of relative power throughout the system.

In simulation I, the faster state initially gains shares at an accelerated rate; suddenly the rate of growth in relative power increasingly slows down. The sudden reversal in the prior trend at the so-called inflection point is *intrinsic*. It is a necessary aspect of change in a finite system, due to an absolute upper bound to growth in relative share. The curve which *resulted* for each state has the form known as the logistic.

Likewise, in simulations III and IV, without any change in the absolute rates of growth within a period of 85 time-units, the states experienced complete inversions (critical points) in their relative power curves. In fact, in each case, a rising state peaked and fell into decline. The *direction* of relative power change was reversed.

The maximum and minimum and the points of inflection are clearly visible on the curves, and readily identified in the printout of the data by calculating the "change in relative power score" at each time point. When the trend of ever increasing "change in score" suddenly becomes a new trend of ever decreasing "change in score," the point of inflection has occurred. This "change in score" reflects the slope (also called the rate of change) of the relative power curve.

Simulation II. Competition and new takeoff prevent absorption, induce decline (Figure 3.2; lower left). In simulation II, the declining states seek to avoid absorption by increasing their growth rates in phases 2 through 4:

Phase 1.   State A 2.0 times as fast as all other states (as in simulation I).

Phase 2.   State A only 1.5 times as fast as all other states.

Phase 3.   State A same rate as all other states.

Phase 4.   The smallest state 1.2 times as fast as all other states.

During Phase 2, State A continues to rise because its rate of growth is still greater than the systemic norm, but that rise is much less rapid. During Phase 3, all the states have a horizontal trajectory – no state is rising relative to any other. For this interval of time, the system is in dynamical equilibrium – no state growing at the expense of the others. During Phase 4, the smallest state in the sample suddenly achieves a rate of growth faster than the others – experiencing a "take off" of economic development. This slight increase in growth rate for the smallest state is sufficient to pull the other states into decline. The greatest effect is registered on the largest state in the system.

These simulations illustrate how the power cycles of the individual states are the resultant of the dynamics of systems structure. Set in motion by rates of change within the individual units, the dynamics of systems structure in turn shapes the individual state power cycles. Necessary aspects of that shape – that generalized cycle – are the inflection and turning points.

GENERALIZED ASYMMETRIC LOGISTIC, AND DYNAMICAL SYSTEMS ANALYSIS: TWO MATHEMATICAL "MODELS" FOR THE DYNAMICS OF SYSTEM CHANGE

Conceptualization of the mathematical form of the relative power dynamic provides fuller understanding of both the conditions affecting the trajectory of relative power growth and the peculiarities of that dynamic. Theoretical analysis indicated (and the simulations demonstrated) that a state's rise on the power cycle is a process homologous with asymmetric logistic growth to a maximum, and that its decline on the power cycle is likewise asymmetric logistic growth. The state's relative power trajectory is due to differential rates of growth between states *and* to the systemic constraint of a limited number of shares.

The generalized asymmetric logistic fits the criterion of this situation exactly. Refer to the equations in the Appendix (p. 264). The dynamical equation for the logistic – the logistic differential equation for its changing rate of growth – is the product of two terms, one term representing exponential growth and another representing the factors retarding growth. The associated integrated form (the solution of the differential equation) is the logistic curve depicting a state's rise in relative power to its peak, or its decline to a minimum. The generalized asymmetric logistic represents constrained growth in any limited system: it is a natural model for the analysis of change *within* a system and, hence, *of* a system as well. It is theoretically and methodologically essential to understanding structural change at both the state and the systemic levels.

The logistic has also been at the center of important developments in mathematics regarding the dynamics of nonlinear systems. Those developments underscore the uniqueness and centrality of the critical points in nonlinear dynamics. The structure of the logistic differential equation parallels that of the corresponding difference equation, and the critical behavior of the former equation reflects the source of dynamic complexity in the latter. Studying the finite difference form of the logistic, expressed as an iterated mapping, mathematicians discovered the effect of a too rapid rate of growth on the dynamic *vis-à-vis* the inversion in the trend of slope: namely, instead of stabilizing and entering equilibrium in the asymptotic limit, the dynamic "breaks down" and enters a period of wildly fluctuating change that has been labeled "chaos." The effect long observed in ecology in which a rapidly growing population suddenly "bumps" against the limits of its environment was one of the examples stimulating research in that area (May 1975).

The inflection and turning points are contained in the relative power scores and can easily be calculated by examining the trend in level and rate of change in relative power. The perception of the state's trajectory that has entered the consciousness of the statesmen of the time can be captured without curve fitting. But knowledge of the functional form highlights the effect of systemic bounds in creating the surprises of the critical points.

HISTORICAL AND EMPIRICAL EXAMPLES OF THE CYCLE FOR LEADING STATES

Despite the variation in power cycles across the states in the system, the striking characteristic is the cycle's imperturbability and generalized pattern. From the beginning of the modern system, states have become ascendant, peaked in power terms, and declined relative to peers and competitors. We hypothesize that the times of the nadir, zenith, and points of inflection in a state's international political development are identifiable in the perceptions and behavior of contemporaneous statesmen.

Several countries have passed through the entire cycle in the major power system. In the sixteenth century, the Habsburg family complex dominated Europe from the Spanish and Austrian thrones. Following the religious wars and the peace arrangements at Westphalia, Spain

69

lay exhausted, never to recover politically, while the lesser Austrian branch remained a highly significant political actor in Europe for another two centuries. At the other extreme regarding period is the leadership role Sweden played for some seventy-five years before retiring to a peripheral stage.

Holland's ascent was also particularly rapid (Boxer 1965). Starting from a very small territorial base but a propitious geographic location at the mouth of one of Europe's largest trading rivers, Holland became a commercial and financial center with few peers by mid seventeenth century. Its maritime and colonial trade was large, as was its naval fleet. In international politics, its primary contribution was financing the allied opposition to Louis XIV's aggressiveness. Dutch power and prestige rose throughout the seventeenth century during Louis' four long wars, only to peak near the end of the century and plummet in the next. By mid eighteenth century, Dutch ascendancy within the system was but a memory. The per capita wealth of the country remained high as did the productivity of its people, but its small latent capability was overshadowed by the much larger industrial power of its neighbors. From the Thirty Years War to the mid eighteenth century, Holland must have passed through the entire power cycle virtually as depicted by the idealized curve. Although at no point in this period was it the preeminent state in the system, the trajectory of its relative power curve was unmistakable to contemporary statesmen and subsequent analysts of history.

But we are not limited to qualitative assessment of the rise and decline of states in history. Using our "yardstick" for "foreign policy leadership capability," we collected data on national capability for the nine countries that since 1815 either have, or presently do figure, significantly in the major power subsystem. The resulting relative capability scores are the data points in Figure 3.3

All nine countries reveal at least a portion of the generalized cycle during the 170 year interval. In general, each state falls into one of three developmental categories on the power cycle, each category defining different opportunities and limits for foreign policy role: young states recently independent or emergent, mature states near the top of their power cycles, and old (not chronological age but international political age) states in advanced decline relative to other members of the system.

Of this sample, *France* was probably the first to acquire the characteristics of the modern, centralized, bureaucratic nation–state (Burckhardt 1967; Wedgwood 1962). Building on the territorial consolidation of Richelieu in the face of Huguenot opposition, and the

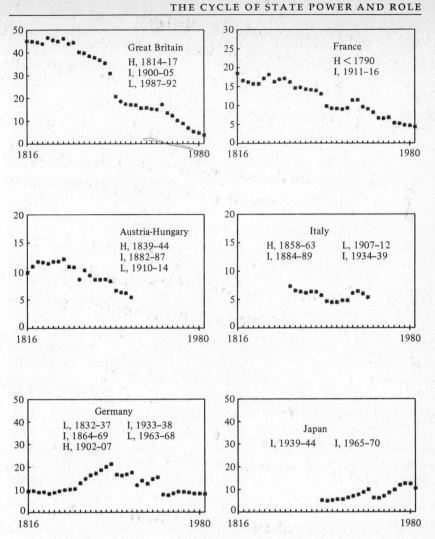

Figure 3.3a Relative power of the nine major actors,
1815–1985

continuing effort to undercut the fissiparous activities of the regional aristocracy under Louis XIV, France emerged first among equals in the late seventeenth century. No small share of the credit goes to (and was raised by) Colbert, the financial minister who eliminated internal tariffs, rationalized the transportation system, and created an efficient method of collecting taxes. Its rapid rise began to slow down, and at some point after mid-century, in advance of the French Revolution (which is often depicted as stemming largely from the bankruptcy of

71

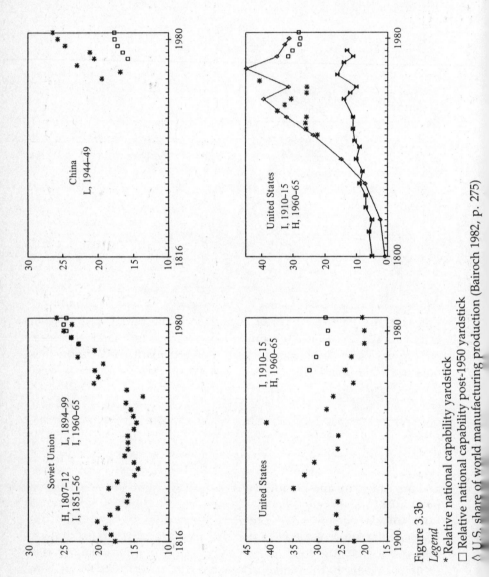

Figure 3.3b
Legend
* Relative national capability yardstick
□ Relative national capability post-1950 yardstick
◊ U.S. share of world manufacturing production (Bairoch 1982, p. 275)

72

the state), French power relative to its rivals tapered off. Analysis of our data suggests that French power peaked in advance of the Napoleonic Wars, not after or because of them.

Already in decline by the Congress of Vienna (1815), French relative power continued, slowly but inexorably, downward for the next 170 years. Fluctuations down and then up occurred after each of its major wars. Yet despite the incidence of depressions and booms, wars and recoveries, the trend line of French power was decidedly downward: from about 20% of the total power in the central system in 1815 to less than 5% by 1975. How could Napoleon, with such a modest share of systemic capability, become a threat to all of Europe? He was able to actualize the French latent capability base through his mesmerizing skills, not once but twice, to a very high degree, and he used the capabilities of allies, clients, and conquered peoples to a far greater extent than is commonly realized (Lefebure 1953).

Britain was the most powerful state in the system in 1815, with perhaps 40% of the capability in the central system on this index. The large share may to some extent reflect the "artificial collapse" of the Continent after the French Revolution and the Napoleonic wars. More positively, Britain had benefited from application of modern industrial technique to the cottage industries in textiles and elsewhere in the economy (Lewis 1978; Hobsbawm 1969). With the advent of the steam engine, coal could be more easily obtained from the flooded mines of England and Wales. With more cheaply available and abundant coal, Britain could become the center of the iron and later the steel industries. Both the steam engine and abundant iron production ushered in the railroad era which sustained British power for a time, but also undermined it as other countries rushed to adopt the British advances. Naval power and the great sailing ships were the backbone of the British armed forces in 1815, but the Dreadnought did not give Britain the same naval comparative advantage late in the century. The most precipitous change in British fortunes came in the 1890 to 1905 interval when the German industrial effort was still growing rapidly and the American and Japanese entries into the central system became unavoidable (Friedberg 1988).

British relative power declined more rapidly than French power, but it was also a larger fraction of the power of the total central system. Perhaps because of the industrial revolution and inputs from its colonial empire, Britain had succeeded in actualizing a larger fraction of its capability base than France. When the decline began to set in, however, British power for the very reason of its higher ratio of actualized to latent capability began to drop off more rapidly especially when Germany, the United States, and Japan began to accelerate industrialization.

British and French trajectories look remarkably similar – in 1816 the most powerful, in 1980 near equals on the lower fringe of the central system. Even if one attributes more salience to a colonial empire as a continuing source of power, the trend lines would have been the same, with perhaps more precipitous decline late in the period (Porter 1975). Given the costs of the empire and the responsibilities of defense and administration, empire is a virtual wash in terms of long-term net benefits to either state in power terms despite the reality that empire had great value regarding status and visibility in the nineteenth century and before.

It is also interesting that the upsurge in British colonial interest at mid nineteenth century in Africa, the Middle East, and Asia occurred after the decline in British power had begun, not before or at the peak when presumably it might have been more readily implemented and administered. Perhaps colonial activity had little to do with intra-European comparisons of power and more to do with the absolute levels of capability available to the European state. When this capability had grown to a certain absolute threshold, the technical capacity to project power further became possible. This point happened to coincide with the point of considerable relative decline for both France and Britain but also was prior to the significant rise of German power. In any case, the relationship between British national capability and colonial empire is not one which would alter very much the conclusions about the decline of British power during the two centuries.

With the restoration of the so-called *ancien régime* in international relations after the Congress of Vienna, *Austria–Hungary* enjoyed a considerable increase in visibility under the diplomatic leadership of Metternich (Kann 1974). This interim ended with the collapse of the Austrian throne and the flight of Metternich during the Revolutions of 1848. Our data show that the sustained level of Austro-Hungarian power assisted Metternich in his endeavors, and the rapid decline of Austrian fortunes after mid-century mirrored his diplomatic fate. Austria–Hungary had a large territory, population, and army, but its industrialization was belated.

The data also reveal that Austria–Hungary was in abject decline before the onset of the First World War and became virtually a non-member of the central system as measured in strict capability terms. Internal problems of maladministration and poverty in the face of dynamism elsewhere in Europe were part of the cause. Versailles was presented with a genuine problem of what to do with an

Austria–Hungary in such advanced decline. In systemic political terms, Austria–Hungary was a forerunner of the problems other members of the central system would experience some thirty years later.

Italy and Germany are somewhat more complex examples of the declining polity. *Germany* is the only state in the sample to pass through the entire power cycle during this interval. Although the Prussian state under Frederick the Great had established a reputation for military prowess, it was the Napoleonic Wars that gave the German principalities a sense of nationhood (Thomas 1952). German reaction to French nationalism and administrative procedure created German nationalism and the modern German state. A steadily accelerating rise in relative power occurred between 1835 and 1865, slowly diminishing thereafter until a sudden peak around 1905 (see next section). Never had Europe witnessed such a consolidation of national authority as under Bismarck, nor seen such an efficient exploitation of industrial method.

Because German history is so broken by warfare, the descent of Germany from the center of the world stage was not smooth. Yet the data reveal that, despite the extreme efforts to actualize German capability prior to each of the world wars, the overall trajectory for the period is downward. For Germany more than for most states, it was a reluctant decline following on the heels of a too-rapid ascent. It stabilized at a low-point greater than the combined shares of Britain and France.

Italy follows a pattern that is equally nonlinear but puzzling. In the 1860s, the Italian state was created out of the nationalism of Mazzini and the adroit diplomacy of Cavour (Smith 1954). It entered the system with power nearly equal to that of Austria–Hungary, and thus had an immediate impact diplomatically and undoubtedly boosted Austria–Hungary's push toward industrialization. Faster growth rates throughout the system forced it onto a declining trajectory for forty years. Its recovery from relative descent after 1900 shaped Italian attitudes toward society and foreign policy in a way typical of youthful states. Italy rediscovered the external dimensions of nationalism, identifying with the expansionist tendencies of Germany and paving the way for the jingoism of Mussolini during the 1930s. But the relative ascent of Italian power was short-lived. It ended with the events of the Second World War, which for practical purposes removed Italy from the circle of states that would conclude the Peace at Yalta.

Italy's turbulent diplomatic course is typical of the comparatively small state that is buffeted by rivals. Italy has also had an ambivalent social experience, with the unevenness of economic development and severe social class stratification leading to extremes of social preference, internal party fragmentation, and political polarization. This societal unease is reflected in its foreign policy and its structural role in the system. Always brushed aside, always on the outskirts of the central system, the Italian role has always been poorly defined. Italy has been influenced by structural change emanating from the system more than it has been a source of influence upon the system.

Japan and the People's Republic of China conform to the dynamic of the "youthful" state in international political terms. Both were recent arrivals into the central system.

Japan epitomizes the ascent of a country that is disrupted by major war but within a decade or so returns to exactly the same trend line of growth. Japan has continued its meteoric rise, driven not by resource wealth or military spending but by trade-oriented economic growth. More than any of the other major polities, Japan has made the world market place work for it. It is the prototypical ascendant country in that the variance around the upward trend line on relative capability is very small. In this respect, the upward paths of Germany in the late nineteenth century and Japan in the late twentieth are quite similar.

The dynamic of Japanese ascendancy has taken place against the backdrop of small territorial size and too few natural resources. Japan has found a formula in terms of internal discipline, constrained openness to the world economy while making use of that economy for exports, and dependency on others for expensive security arrangements, such that Japan so far has been able to surmount the asymptotic effect on growth experienced much earlier by other states with similar internal constraints.

There is reason to believe that this Japanese "miracle" cannot go on forever and that Japan like other polities will begin to feel the constraints of its natural limits (as well as the systemic asymptotic limit), albeit at very high absolute levels of power, in the early twenty-first century if not before. First, Japan is more vulnerable than other polities to resource scarcity, as the interval of relative energy scarcity in the 1970s showed. Second, Japan is very dependent upon a benevolent international trading system that until now has been willing to accept a surplus of high-quality Japanese goods even if Japan was willing only to accept largely raw materials and agricultural goods in return (Allen 1981). New protectionism and a much tougher view with respect to trade balances will not bode well for the Japanese capacity to keep its own market as closed as before and to rely on trade alone. Other trading partners will expect Japan to expand its internal market more and to rely less on the external trading system for job creation and economic growth. And Japanese trading companies will have to become much more like other multinational companies that invest abroad. But by investing abroad in lower productivity countries, Japanese growth itself will fall off (Yoon 1987).

Third, because of homeostasis regarding military spending, Japan will begin to provide more of its own security. An increase of defense expenditures will add to the overall power of the Japanese state, but by shifting from the economic to the military component of capability, something will be lost in terms of the multiplicative and accelerative aspect of growth. Military expenditures are like unilateral payment since they cannot be reinvested. Even research and development is not as efficient as in strictly civilian areas. Japan has been so competitive in leading civilian technologies because its firms have invested more capital on their projects relative to American and European firms.

Finally, the Japanese population is aging and will demand more welfare expenditures while also declining somewhat in its capacity to contribute as productively as in the past (Vogel 1963; Reischauer 1977). For all these reasons, Japanese growth in power is likely to continue to tail off. The precise apex is indeterminate. The Japanese employ a linear projection of future possibilities, projecting the present growth rate in power far into the future. Chapter 10 discusses the security implications of this dilemma.

China, the most recent entrant to the circle of major powers, is in many ways a peculiar case (Fairbank 1986; Brown 1982). It is the only developing country of Third World origin. It has a very low per capita income. Its military capability is still primitive despite its acquisition of nuclear weapons. Its large and growing national capability results from its huge population and large territory and economy. Its manpower base gives it a huge if poorly equipped army. Its geopolitical location adjacent to the Soviet Union, and its history that contests borders with the Soviet Union, India, Vietnam, and Outer Mongolia, create for it an active role in the regional and to some extent global power balance. The extent of China's accomplishments in economic and security terms and the increased stature it has enjoyed in the world community are unmistakable.

China has shown a persistent if somewhat erratic pattern of increase in relative capability since 1945, suggesting the difficulty with which the inertia of its enormous population can be moved. Given the large variance around the trend-line, and the substantial problems confronting its developmental effort, very little can be said about China's likely future trend. The momentum of Chinese growth has not been great. Yet the capacity to sacrifice and to discipline itself is well-established, and the 6 percent and 7.8 percent growth rates in real GNP for 1986 and 1987 respectively indicate what internal diligence and reform can mean for the material base of power. Severe recession, governmentally induced, after the Tienanmen Square incident, show how quickly momentum can be reversed. In contrast to the growth paths of Germany and Japan, the Chinese path may be more variable, and hence the steepness of its rise less easy to predict. Nonetheless, given its huge base and all of the polities which Chinese decisions directly or indirectly affect, China has carved out an unquestioned place in the central system.

China possesses size but not development. China is capable of virtually excluding the superpowers from much of a role within its own region but currently has little capacity to project power outside of its region (Barnett and Clough, eds. 1986). Its substantial navy is solely a coastal fleet. Its army has no rapid deployment feature. China influences superpower diplomacy by influencing the Soviet Union. If China leans toward the Soviet Union, it puts pressure on the United States; if China leans away from the Soviet Union, it puts pressure on the Soviet Union. The China Card is not so much a card played in Washington or Moscow as a card played out of Beijing. Until the international political deck is substantially reshuffled, Beijing will continue to weigh heavily on the global international balance.

The growth in power and structural dynamism of the young states in this sample are in marked contrast to the power dynamic of the old European states. Power in the 1980s was drifting away from Europe to Asia, or, more accurately, Europe no longer enjoyed a surplus of power and Asia no longer suffered a deficit. As the quintessential maritime state bordering the two oceans, the United States stands between these shifting tides of power as a broker more than does the Soviet Union which, because of its continental character, is itself directly drawn into the geopolitical power shifts internally.

The *United States* and the *Soviet Union* are mature states in the international relations sense of being at or near the top of their respective power cycles. Russia has been in the central system since the beginning of the period under study, and its cycle is somewhat more complex (Pokrovskii 1970; Liska 1982). It suffered a slight decline in relative capability in the nineteenth century when its larger man-power base could not offset the greater industrialization of the other European economies. But throughout the century, the trajectories of the two states have been roughly the same. Refined data provided by recent reevaluations of economic statistics (CIA 1989) highlight important differences.

The variance around the trend line of U.S. power is far greater than that of Soviet power everywhere along the curve but most strikingly during the world wars. The United States tends not to actualize its power militarily to the same extent at each point of the development process. Indeed, the United States tends to cut back military spending and army size in peacetime, and it has an enormous capacity to actualize its capability in a short time because of the flexibility of its economy and the ease with which it can mobilize human resources and capital. Furthermore, its foreign policy resolve and commitment to a world role may be somewhat less and may vary with administrations (Calleo 1982; Klingberg 1979). For all of these reasons the U.S. level of relative power has fluctuated more than that of the Soviets.

Although the United States appears to be a bit more advanced along the cycle, differential power levels still favor it. Also, the United States extracts far more power from its economic base than the Soviet Union, whose economy is far smaller. The Soviet Union draws its power from the large size and increasing sophistication of its armed forces capability. More will be said about the US and Soviet power cycles in Part 4.

The post-1950 yardstick yielded more appropriate power levels for the United States, the Soviet Union, and China, but the pattern of the cycle remains the same (Figure 3.3b). Data for the U.S. percent share of world manufacturing and of world trade generally follow the same track as the relative capability data for both pre-1945 and post-1950 periods. The pattern of the power cycle with identifiable critical points is evident in each trend.

PARADIGM SHIFT: FROM BALANCE OF POWER TO DYNAMIC STRUCTURAL PERSPECTIVE

The power cycles for Germany and Russia (Doran and Parsons 1980) have triggered much theoretical discussion among political scientists and historians, a discussion that has important implications for the understanding of statecraft in history.

Substantively, the debate centers around "the almost universal pre-1914 belief in inexorably increasing Russian power," to quote William Wohlforth (1987, p. 380). The questions are three-fold. (1) Why did decision makers throughout Europe foresee great relative gains in power for Russia? What was it that they were perceiving about power relationships? (2) Were the statesmen correct? What changes in power actually took place, and do the perceptions correspond to them? (3) What were the implications of rising Russian power for Germany, and hence for German behavior?

The curves for Russia and Germany were provocative for several reasons. On the one hand, they accurately captured the pre-war trend (perceived and real) of Russia rising from the lowpoint on its power cycle and Germany near the peak of its relative power in the system. On the other hand, Germany peaks in relative power well *in advance* of the war, counter to accepted historical interpretation and "common sense." The power cycle argument that *expectations*, and hence *behaviors*, are based on an extrapolation of existing trends became a focus of debate. Wohlforth emphasized the importance of combining perceptual and structural explanations. But, just as he seemed ready to accept the full implications of his findings – namely, that contemporaneous statesmen realized Germany's leveling out of relative growth – he did a *volte face*. He accepted the arguments put forth by Paul Kennedy (1984) that the contemporaneous perceptions of rising Russian power were "misperceptions" and that Germany was still a rising power prior to the war.[1]

We argue that these issues of historical interpretation are in fact deeper *conceptual* issues involving fundamental aspects of (1) absolute versus relative power, (2) the short-term balance of power versus the long-term trend of relative power, and (3) the static conception of "system" versus the "dynamics of systemic change." Moreover, the structural, perceptual, and behavioral aspects of causation must be assessed holistically for a full paradigm shift to the dynamic view to occur. The perceptions of statesmen accurately reflect the reality of power trends, and the unique concerns of statecraft.

"Russia is rapidly becoming so powerful." Was this vision of the contemporary statesman right, or was it obscured by mistaken perception? This was the question Kennedy (1984, 1985) addressed. His answer was the "giant–pygmy" thesis: Germany's power was so much greater than that of Russia, and its yearly increments were so much greater, that surely Germany did not consider Russia a threat. Kennedy examined production data on steel, coal, and other manufactures. So obvious was Germany's superior strength, and so obvious did the continued rise of Germany's relative power seem, that the contemporaneous statesmen must somehow have "misperceived" reality. He thus posed two puzzles which historians must seek to explain. *Puzzle 1*: "Why was Russian power before 1914 so absurdly

---

[1] In a personal letter in 1983, Kennedy asked whether I was certain my findings were not in error.

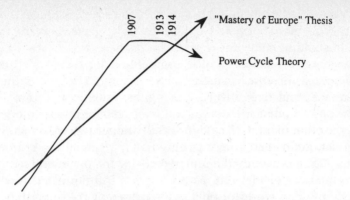

Figure 3.4 Contrasting interpretations of Germany's relative power trajectory in the European System: 1870–1914

overrated? . . . Did they not see that Russia, despite its lurch towards industrialization, was a military colossus but an economic pygmy?" (1985, p. 28). *Puzzle 2*: "Which power, Russia or Germany, was *objectively* the most likely to alter the existing order in Europe?" (p. 29).

"Russia is rapidly becoming so powerful that . . . " What were the implications of Russia growing so rapidly, albeit from such a low level? Figure 3.4 depicts the two diametrically opposite interpretations of the contemporaneous statesman's perception. Russia is rapidly becoming so powerful . . .

> *Power Cycle Theory*: that its increase in relative power will force Germany into relative decline.
>
> *Mastery of Europe Thesis*: "That some Germans worried about the Russian 'threat' is undoubted. But what is also undoubted, as A. J. P. Taylor acutely pointed out some 30 years ago, was that: 'Their fears were exaggerated. . . . In fact, peace must have brought Germany the mastery of Europe within a few years.'" (Kennedy 1985, p. 29)

The giant–pygmy argument and the mastery of Europe thesis are based on the traditional balance-of-power concern with the size of the difference between power levels (absolute or relative) for two states or coalitions of states, and with short-term shifts in the balance. Given that focus on the difference in power levels and short-term strategy, the assertions seem indisputable. But, when examined from the power cycle perspective of long-term changes in relative power, the giant–pygmy argument and the mastery of Europe thesis are shown to be wrong. From the power cycle perspective, the perceptions of contemporaneous statesmen look neither distorted nor incongruous.

81

The key to the paradigm shift is understanding how the pygmy forced the giant into relative decline. Viewed alternatively, the key is understanding how the giant's huge increases in absolute power could be overwhelmed in the competition for systemic share by the very small increases gained by the pygmy. The key is the deeper meaning of relative power, of changing systemic structure.

In one of our earlier simulations of changing systemic structure, namely, simulation II's (Figure 3.2) thought experiment in which competition comes from a pygmy newly rising at the bottom of the hierarchy, we already demonstrated how the pygmy forced the giant into relative decline. But, as opposed to the simulated world, what about the real world of politics? What about the "objective" power indicators which Kennedy looked at? Can we prove that the giant's huge increases in absolute power were overwhelmed by the small increments of the pygmy?

CONFLICTING MESSAGES AND DISTURBING SURPRISES OF RELATIVE VERSUS ABSOLUTE CHANGE

So obvious does the continued rise in German relative power in the European system seem, that any study claiming otherwise is "obviously" wrong. Conversely, any study asserting the continued rise of Germany makes a claim to historically documented correctness. This, indeed, is what has occurred within the field.

A recent study on the balance of power (Niou, Ordeshook, and Rose 1989) argued the superiority of its complex index of power on the grounds that it was able to show a continued rise in Germany's relative power, in agreement with A. J. P. Taylor's judgment on the matter. They noted that our yardstick agreed with theirs in showing Germany's rise except for some "data points that deviate inexplicably from the trend at the end of the period" (p. 301). Graphs for Germany's *absolute* power on four economic indicators were included to show those trends, and no comment was made in that study about the trends of the *relative* scores on those indicators. Were the relative scores calculated to confirm their continued rise, the "obvious" message deduced from the absolute trends, and the judgment of historians?

Similarly, again trusting in the "assumed fact" of continued rise in German relative power in the European system, analysts have tried to explain the supposedly mistaken empirical conclusion in the data used herein. They have variously attributed the peaking of Germany's relative power as due to supposed flaws or errors in the yardstick, in the choice of system, in the mathematical method, or the theory of the power cycle itself: (1) that it somehow is peculiar to the particular aggregate index used; (2) that it is due only to U.S. and Japanese entry into the system circa 1900; (3) that it incorporates the effect of the First World War (that somehow the future postwar data points are responsible for, and are used to calculate, the high point); (4) that this and all the other "critical points" are mere artifacts of the method used in curve fitting, namely, the logistic function; and (5) that the use of the logistic is *ad hoc* or invalid. No proof has been given for any of these criticisms, which often appear in a footnote (Niou et al., p. 301; Goldstein 1988, pp. 141–43), for sufficient proof lies in its "obviously incorrect" depiction of Germany's entry into decline prior to the war.

This section confronts, and eliminates, each of these concerns about power cycle theory by anchoring the analysis in the historical puzzles generated by the assumed historical facts. It examines the absolute and relative scores on those same production indicators which Kennedy interpreted, and which Niou et al. used as part of their complex index for power; the absolute scores are drawn from their own data source (Mitchell 1980).

We include the absolute and relative scores for two of the four economic indicators, steel and iron ore (Figure 3.5). In the graphs for the absolute scores (upper figures), the unambiguous message is the very rapid rise of Germany to a position of dominance over the other European states, indeed very great dominance on some indicators such as steel production, the indicator Kennedy emphasized most. These data reveal that for some ten years prior to 1914, Germany was the dominant economic power in Europe in terms of industrial production. Moreover, each year it registered greater incrememts of power than the previous year. Thus, the very large slope of the line for this "topdog" looks very threatening, evoking images of a dominance that would completely overwhelm all of Europe (be greater than all the others combined) in a short time. Such were the fears of many in Europe at the time.

But the absolute capability graphs conceal (indeed distort) important aspects of relative power change (lower graphs in the figures). It is true that on each of these indicators, Germany's relative power dominance in 1914 is quite sizeable. But when one examines Germany's relative power over this entire time period, a number of very astounding findings are immediately discernible in the very plot of the data themselves.

The core of these surprises is that, on each indicator, Germany's relative power clearly appears to have peaked! The very steep slopes

83

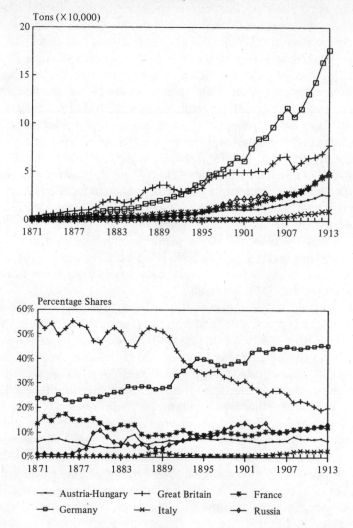

Figure 3.5a Conflicting messages of absolute and relative power *trends*, 1905–1913: steel and iron ore production

of large absolute power increase which are so apparent during Germany's period of dominance (the last ten years 1904–13) are not matched by a corresponding increase in relative power. On the contrary, on both indicators, the relative power curve shows a very clear flattening out. For *steel*, relative power growth has slowed down to a mere incremental size; during the decade 1904–13, when it was

Iron Ore Production, 1871–1913

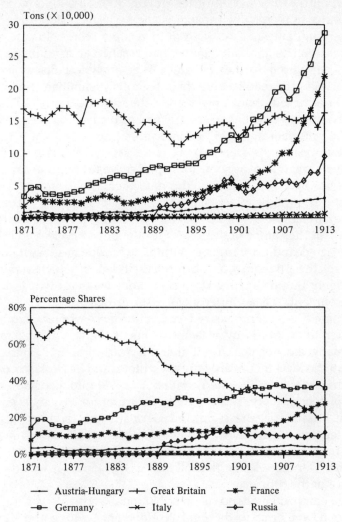

Figure 3.5b

registering the greatest absolute increases ever, its share rose less than 1%, in contrast to the increments of 10% and more in previous decades. For *iron ore*, relative share fluctuated around one value from 1903 to 1913, again in marked contrast to the rapid rise of more than 10% in each of the previous two decades.

Note carefully what has happened to Germany's relative power scores without any alteration in the trajectory of its absolute power scores. Whereas the very steep slopes for Germany's absolute power during the earlier period of its growth do correspond to periods of rapid rise in its relative capability, the very steep slopes for absolute power suddenly register *no gain* in relative scores. In other words, Germany's rise in relative power had reached an asymptotic limit.

As supported further by our earlier analytical discussion, these empirical data readily and unambiguously eliminate the first four concerns raised about power cycle theory's assertion of Germany's pre-war relative decline. Germany had peaked in relative power terms (1) on a number of individual indicators (the critics' data); (2) within the European subsystem; (3) on data restricted to the period prior to the war; and (4) not as some artifact of curve fitting (the turning point is in the data). In addition, the data themselves show (5) that the logistic asymptotic effect is not heuristic but is implicit in the relative power dynamic. The data points "deviating inexplicably from the trend" in the composite yardstick for the power cycle are visible here in the single indicator iron ore within the European subsystem. It is, of course, the phenomenon already discussed in which a population suddenly bumps against the upper limit to its growth in a limited environment. It is a property of logistic growth.

Kennedy also emphasized *coal production*, where Germany was greater than Russia by a factor of about eight. On that indicator, Germany did not peak until after the war, although it already had begun the leveling towards the asymptote, and its peak score was not much larger. But Kennedy failed to take into consideration the completely converse relation in the indicator for *oil and gas production*: there Russia was the giant and Germany the pygmy. Russia was greater than Germany by the enormous factor of about ninety (and that ratio continued)! Although much of Russia's production was for export, Germany knew that oil and gas production was the energy source of the future.

The empirical evidence is unambiguous: Germany was no longer a rising power prior to the First World War. Taylor's and Kennedy's only "support" for the contrary view was the much bigger absolute level of power held by Germany after the war, as before it. But because Germany was larger than the other European states individually, and even when several were combined, says nothing about the *direction* or trajectory of Germany's relative power, that is, *whether the size of its potential for supposed "mastery" over Europe was expanding or contracting*. The fact was, the German potential for continued rise was contracting, and Germany knew it.

In making the conclusion that the perceptions of statesmen about "inexorably increasing Russian power" were mistaken, Wohlforth drew upon Kennedy's "counterfactual (though well-researched) speculation" (p. 380) that even in the near-to-medium term, "the figures suggest that Russia would do well to maintain its position *vis-à-vis* Germany, let alone improve it" (Kennedy 1985, p. 30). But, as we have shown, the speculation was in error. The perceptions of diplomats of the period were not misperceptions but accurately reflect the reality of changes in relative power.

Kennedy asked historians to help resolve these puzzles. In putting my "disputed" graphs of Germany and Russia in *The Rise and Fall of the Great Powers* (1988a, pp. 240–41), he appears to have accepted the political scientist's explanation of the puzzles. But he does not mention the puzzles therein. He acknowledged that the graphs on relative power capture the trends of the period – Germany near its peak and Russia rising from its lowpoint after 1894. But he still questioned Stolypin's "boast" in 1909: "Give the state twenty years of internal and external peace and you will not recognize Russia" (p. 241). Moreover, in the Epilogue, he wrongly dismisses the debate among political scientists as one of "*theory* and *methodology*" (p. 536, his emphasis) rather than conceptual and historical accuracy.

The "puzzles of history" dissolve when one grasps the most important aspect of relative power change – the full complexity and significance of change in a finite system. Neither relative power nor the associated concept of the "rise and decline of states" correspond to the intuitive understanding. Once the full complexity is understood, the meaning of Stolypin's boast is likewise discernible: the significance to great powers not merely of comparative levels of relative power but, most importantly, of the *direction of its trajectory*. At issue is its *future* position and role in the system. Figure 3.6 depicts the relative power scores regarding steel production, Kennedy's major focus, of Germany and "the rest of the system" for two different systems. The upper graphs depict the European system, the latter the system consisting of Germany plus Russia. These two-actor "competitions" are examined for 1871–1913 and the postwar years 1920–40.

Despite Germany's meteoric rise in absolute capability on the index steel production, the percentage share relative to the European system, and relative to Russia in particular, had peaked a decade prior to the war. Then, in the two years prior to the war, the pygmy's increased rate of growth forced Germany onto a declining trajectory. The power cycles for the two actors in each competitive setting began to converge. The postwar period shows that the trends begun just before the war continued thereafter. Germany never again was able to

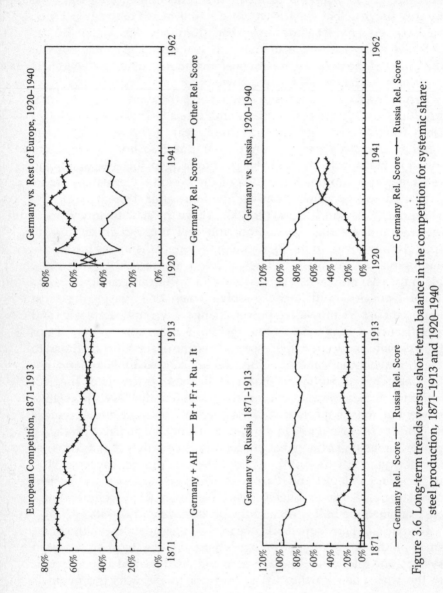

Figure 3.6 Long-term trends versus short-term balance in the competition for systemic share: steel production, 1871–1913 and 1920–1940

equal the level of relative power it had before 1913, even during its period of rapid acceleration after 1932. Within the Germany–Russia subsystem, the pattern is the same. After the setback of the Russian Revolution, Russia's steel production skyrocketed from about 2% of the Germany–Russia system shares to 50% some fifteen years later!

The true significance of the power cycle paradigm for the rise and decline of great powers lies not in the *post-hoc* depiction of the trends of history, but in being able to depict the trends – and the inversions in the trends – as they are experienced. It assists the analyst in the effort to get into the mind of the contemporaneous statesmen, to experience the conflicting messages and shocking surprises with which they had to contend as the very "data" (perceptions) year by year became registered. It seeks to help the analyst of history meet Collingwood's (1956) requirement of reenacting the past in one's own mind. Although we have been guided by conceptual and mathematical understanding of change in a finite system, it is the historical data themselves, not some mathematical concept, which convey the messages of critical change which led all of Europe into world war. Only if the analyst truly understands the unique international political concerns of the statesmen of the period can he or she properly interpret the normative options in foreign policy (Hoffmann 1984; Nye 1990).

A generation of scholars has continued to accept the "mastery of Europe" thesis, stated so strongly by A. J. P. Taylor in 1954. Taylor later expressed doubts about the war causation aspect of the thesis. "We still have doubts about what the issues were, whether it really was a conscious struggle for the mastery of Europe or of the world" (1979, p. 126). In preparing a comparative study on "how wars begin," he had already come to quite a different conclusion. "Wars in fact have sprung more from apprehension than from a lust for war or conquest. Paradoxically, many of the European wars were started by a threatened Power which had nothing to gain by war and much to lose" (p. 15).

How much more convinced of his latter conclusion about war causation might Taylor have been if he had realized that his other assumption about the 1914 period was also subject to reinterpretation, based on the application of international relations theory and on a more complete rendering of the historical data of relative power growth? Had Taylor realized that German ascendancy was not foreordained, that German relative power had already peaked on the eve of the war, he would have found the evidence needed to support his new speculation about the causes of the First World War.

Part 2
DYNAMICS OF MAJOR WAR AND SYSTEMS TRANSFORMATION

4 CRITICAL INTERVALS ON THE POWER CYCLE: WHY WARS BECOME MAJOR

There is a time at which the tides of history change. There is a time at which the nation–state suddenly becomes cognizant that a discontinuity with the past has occurred, that its long anticipated place among countries has been irrevocably altered, that its prior assumptions about role, status, and security have been proven wrong. This is the existential interval in which a government is vulnerable to entanglement in the most major wars. This existential interval is the critical point on the state power cycle.

The next three chapters weave conceptual and theoretical argument with historical evidence and empirical findings to develop the power cycle theory of major war and systems transformation. To emphasize generality, we begin at the theoretical level. Chapter 5 ties each aspect of theory to the real problems confronting statesmen, and their specific responses to them, in the early years of the twentieth century. As a prelude, we here include statements of the period which express something of the uncertainty and tumult felt at a time of monumental critical changes in the trend of history for all the leading states.

"The future belongs to Russia, which is growing and growing and is becoming an ever-increasing nightmare for us." The German Foreign Minister, long haunted by this reality, finally confronted it in August 1914 (Wohlforth 1987, p. 362). Awareness of the changing tide of German power was expressed in Berlin by profound angst. "The World will be engulfed in the most terrible of wars," screamed the Kaiser, "the ultimate aim of which is the ruin of Germany. England, France, and Russia have conspired for our annihilation . . ." (Tuchman 1962, p. 95). British and French diplomats were confident that Russia's huge resource base and population would enable her to overwhelm Germany in the not too distant future. Both Russia and Germany had passed through a critical point on their respective power curves. As these statesmen saw clearly, Germany had passed its peak in relative power, whereas Russia was just beginning its ascendancy.

But other major powers had also undergone critical points on their

93

power cycles in that same decade or the prior one. Most of the foreign ministers recognized that the future trend would be different, a turn for the better for some of the governments, a turn for the worse for others. Most of the heads of government were worried about their security and their place in the system. The time was ripe for military action and over-reaction, belligerency and counterresponse, where mere statecraft seemed to have failed.

Prior to every massive war, state behavior was marked by the same suddenness of discovery that "things had dramatically changed" in terms of power trends, and hence in future foreign policy role and security (Doran 1971). Abrupt structural change throughout the great power system was accompanied by similar systems-wide tension. The tension came not so much from mobility up or down in the systemic hierarchy, which occurs at all times, but from a government's sudden discovery that its projected future foreign policy role had dramatically and unexpectedly changed.

Contrast the outlooks of Charles V of Spain and Philip II in the sixteenth century. Although the Spanish–Austrian Habsburgs remained the dominant power in Europe for decades thereafter, Phillip II suddenly interpreted foreign policy negatively, even arguing that "God had forsaken" Spain, expressing paranoia and belligerance at the same time. Sweden and Holland enjoyed a meteoric rise, abruptly demanding a larger role. France under Richelieu began to consolidate its power. This massive transformation of structure and roles resulted in the Thirty Years War.

Similarly, in the mid seventeenth century, the passage of Louis XIV's France through a first inflection point, threatening slower growth for the first time in its development as a major power, led to confrontations with Sweden (an erstwhile ally) and Holland, each of whom had discovered that its relative power had peaked, thus creating severe problems of overextension. Meanwhile Prussia was rising in the heart of the central European system, and Britain had reconstituted itself to the extent that it was enjoying a renaissance of power growth by the end of the century, stimulating it to confront France directly with an army on the Continent. Once again, the wars of Louis XIV, ending with the Treaties of Utrecht of 1713, resulted from a systemic transformation that saw each of Europe's major players viewing its own foreign policy role in highly altered and more troubling fashion.

In each historical epoch of systems crisis, the existing system of maintaining order collapsed under the weight of arrangements whose structural foundations had long since been eroded away.

Major war is characterized by high intensity (battlefield deaths), long duration (months at war), and great magnitude. Magnitude is conceptualized here as the number of combatants weighted for their power and rank. The larger the number of combatants, the bigger the war; and the more significant the actor within the international system and the more power that actor is able to bring to bear in a conflict, other things being equal, the more serious the war. The frequency of war is not a preoccupation of this study, regardless of whether it tells something about the quality of world order associated with a particular system and era. Many diverse causes undoubtedly underlie the repeated occurrence of non-major war. Structural change on the power cycle has its greatest significance regarding major systemic distruptions.

Each index of major war reflects in a different way the extent to which the objective is deeply contested, yet they are also closely related. In long wars, the contestants are either rather evenly matched, or they are unable to bring the full brunt of their capability to bear early in the war. In either case, long wars tend to escalate, attract a larger number of participants, and grow in terms of battle deaths as well. Similarly, the number of combatants and the power rank of the combatants taken together escalate the size of a war very quickly as each variable itself increases. Thus, whereas powerful states do not always get involved in major war, major wars almost always involve powerful states. And whereas wars involving numerous states are not always large, major wars normally involve quite a number of states. A variety of indicators helps the analyst control for the counter-examples which prevent each separate index from being universally appropriate.

SHOCKS AND UNCERTAINTIES OF NON-LINEAR CHANGE AT CRITICAL POINTS

Can statesmen *perceive* critical points on the power cycle? We have seen that statesmen not only are able to perceive critical points, they are highly sensitive to their occurrence. That perception underlies the decision-making process culminating in major war.

Decision making and future foreign policy expectation

Regardless of where decision makers are located – in government, in the firm, in the stock market – the preferred and somewhat automatic decision model is a straight-line extrapolation of past

95

experience *because* this model will be right more of the time than the multitude of more complicated models conceivable. It is because straight-line extrapolation tends to be right more often than it is wrong that it is ingrained in the consciousness of the decision maker. This situation is especially striking for statesmen extrapolating future power and role capability in the system since such straight-line extrapolation will in general be correct *except at a few "critical points" during the state's entire history as a major power.*

What do we mean by straight-line extrapolation? In brief, linear extrapolation means a continuation of the past trend. Consider some econometric examples. The best predictor of next year's budget is last year's budget; the best predictor of future arms spending is the spending that has occurred over the last time period (Lindblom 1959; Wildavsky 1964). The more recent the time points used, set against a reasonable history of prior experience, the more sensitive this common mode of decision making will be. No forecast is likely to be better, other things being equal, than the last forecast undertaken (Ascher 1978, p. 214). Temporary fluctuations in the process are seen as such and indeed lessen the likelihood that decision makers will be able to predict real breaks from the trend.

The problem with linear extrapolation is that it is *not* able to predict real, incontrovertible breaks from the linear trend. An extensive study by the National Bureau of Economic Research on forecasting business cycles examined in particular whether turning points could be predicted; "The data as a whole suggest that forecasters have yet to establish their ability to detect turning points in aggregate economic activity well in advance of the event. What they do demonstrate is an ability to recognize turns at about the time or shortly after they occur" (Moore 1986, p. 407). The study also found that "both private and government forecasts have erred on the side of optimism more often than not" (p. 440). These striking conclusions about the most sophisticated research forecasting methods apply to at least the same degree to the less formal and non-econometric process by which decision makers project future trends and plan future policies.

All of these conclusions – the *overoptimism* in forecasts; the *inability* to determine a critical point *well in advance* of the event; and yet the *ability* to recognize a critical point suddenly *at or right after* the event – have great significance for the decision-making process leading to major war.

A critical point may be described as an inversion in the dynamic, or an inversion in the prior trend. At the critical points, the slope of the line drawn tangent to the relative power curve suddenly *changes direction* from the previous trend. Perhaps the clearest way to "see" the abrupt, unanticipated and ineluctable "inversion" occurring at the critical point is by observing the direction of movement of succeeding slopes over time. The slope of the power cycle at a given time is the basis for the state's linear extrapolation of past and present experience into the future, and a critical point suddenly breaks the pattern of that prior trend.

But why does it matter if an inversion in the prior trend suddenly occurs? Governments are concerned about changes in power because those changes translate into a change in role, in future role, and changes in future foreign policy role affect security and status. In an atmosphere of certainty, adjustment even to unpleasantness is comparatively easy, since the past is considered "prologue," and linear extrapolations of past experience provide a pretty good guide to future expectations. What is projected at each point along a state's power cycle is *its future foreign policy role and security position*. At a critical point, the state's view of its future long guiding policy is suddenly proven wrong. The assumptions about future statecraft carried possibly for decades, and rewarded year by year in actual outcomes, suddenly lose credibility. The tides of political momentum have suddenly shifted. The critical point thus introduces sudden uncertainty regarding future foreign policy possibility and expectations.

It is easy to see the change in direction of the slope at the maximum and minimum (turning points). Less easily observed is the change in direction at the inflection points. Indeed, the casual observer may regard change at the inflection points as "gradual" and rather undistinguished, and because apparently so gradual, impossibly evocative of violent conflict. Yet the inflection point is the start of something very different and very new for the conduct of the state's foreign policy.

Consider (Figure 4.1) the slope drawn just prior to the inflection point and the associated projection of foreign policy expectations – projected as far ahead as the decision maker wishes to speculate. The farther ahead one speculates, the more striking the judgment that prior assessments of future position were wrong, catastrophically wrong. The slope of these role projections is now tending in the *opposite direction* from what was most recently concluded. The state's future foreign policy expectations projected over one decade leave it with a sizeable disparity compared to what it previously had anticipated; projected over two decades, the disparity is much greater. Thus, at the inflection point, a very small change on the state's power curve changes completely the direction of expectations. The further

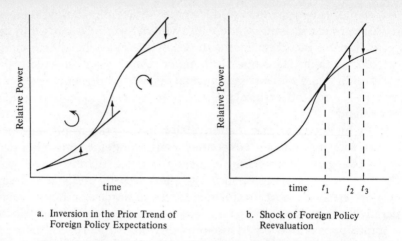

a. Inversion in the Prior Trend of
   Foreign Policy Expectations

b. Shock of Foreign Policy
   Reevaluation

Figure 4.1 Crisis of foreign policy expectations at first inflection point.

one looks into the future, the larger the suddenly realized error in those future foreign policy expectations. The inflection point is a unique point in the dynamic, the point where the acceleration has peaked and begins to decline. Acceleration is no less important than velocity in a dynamic process, and the impact of an inflection point is *a priori* no less nor more troublesome than passage through a turning point.

The essence of critical change is an inversion from the prior trend of the curve, taking the state farther and farther away from past expectations. (Graphs of level, velocity and acceleration in the Appendix depict these aspects of the dynamic.) Figure 4.1a shows this inversion graphically for the first inflection point. When the curve rises at an ever increasing rate below the first inflection point, the slope or role projection at successive points turns ever upward – counter-clockwise. Above the first inflection point, however, the curve suddenly begins to rise at an ever decreasing rate; hence the slope of the line drawn tangent to the curve (projection of future power and role) at successive points abruptly begins to turn increasingly downward – clockwise. At the critical point, and only at this point, the slope of the line drawn tangent to the relative power curve suddenly *changes direction*, in this case from counter-clockwise movement to clockwise movement.

Hence, at the first inflection point as at each critical point, an abrupt inversion in the expectation of future role and security outlook has occurred. The whole sense of "where the state is going" is fundamentally and drastically changed. This is why the critical point on the

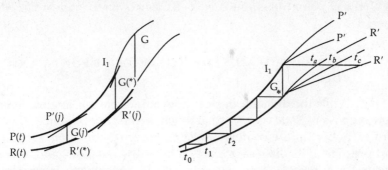

a. Increasing Slippage (Slope Difference):   b. Uncertainties Arising at I_1
   Widening Gap due to Lag Alone

Figure 4.2 Disequilibrium between power and role: crisis of the first
inflection point

Legend
$P(t)$ = Relative power at time t
$R(t)$ = Role at time t
$\bar{T}$ = Time of high point of relative power curve
* = Time of 1st inflection point on relative power curve
I_1 = 1st inflection point on relative power curve
$G(*)$ = Power–role gap at time of inflection
$\bar{G}$ = Maximum size of gap assuming isometry, at time $\bar{t}$
$P'(j)$ = Slope of relative power curve at time $t = j$
$\bar{P}^1$ = Upper projection of relative power at I_1
$\underline{P}'$ = Lower projection of relative power at I_1
Case of rising state: $P(t_i) < P(t_{i+1}) < P(\bar{T})$ for all $t_i < \bar{T}$
Interests lag behind power by $\triangle t$: $P(t_i) > R(t_i)$ and $P(t_i) = R(t_{i+1})$
for $t_i < \bar{T}$
Differences in projection depend upon concurrent slopes:

$$P'(j) \approx R'(j); \text{ but } P'(*) >> R'(*)$$

Gap increases to maximum size beyond I_1, and then diminishes until
highpoint of curve: $G(j) << G(*) < \bar{G}$; $\bar{G} > G(k)$ for $\bar{t} < k < \bar{T}$
In Figure 4.2b, gap made up eventually:
$$P(t_i) = R(t_{i+1}) \text{ for all } G_i < G_{i+1} < \bar{G}$$
Without isometry, time for making up gap increases until $\bar{G}$ is attained:

$$\triangle t_i < \triangle t_{i+1}$$

Uncertainties arising at I_1:

$\bar{P}' - \underline{P}'$ = Uncertainty re. projection of power
$\bar{R}' - \underline{R}'$ = Uncertainty re. projection of role   } Actor/
$t_c - t_a$ = Uncertainty re. time for gap $G(*)$ Redress } system
                                                              response

99

power curve is such a fundamental source of trauma and uncertainty. At a critical point the entire *Weltanschauung* of state interest has been altered.

EQUILIBRIUM AND THE DYNAMICS OF POWER AND ROLE[1]

While the dynamic of state power and role is a single dynamic – encompassing *state interests* (that to which the government aspires in foreign policy) in the context of *relative power* (the national capability and prestige at its disposal for achieving these interests) and *systemic foreign policy role* (the interests the state has achieved, or expressed differently, the interests which the system has allowed or encouraged the state to obtain – it is useful to dissect the dynamic into component parts in order to understand better the structural and psychological causes underlying the movement to major war.

Components of general equilibrium

We begin with the too formal assumption of *perfect isometry* between relative capability and role attainment, an assumption not totally unrealistic since indicators are chosen to reflect capability to implement policy broadly.

Visualize two congruent curves, one mapping a state's relative power over time, the other mapping its foreign policy role (interests obtained). The *slope* of the power curve (indexed by relative capability) traces the rise and decline of the state over the broad expanse of history. The *slope* of the curve at a point, represented by a line drawn tangential to the curve at that point, measures the rate of growth of relative power at that time, and thus also represents the government's current *projection* of future relative power. The same analysis applies to the role curve, where the slope represents projection of future role attainment.

At four points on each curve (lower turning point, first inflection point, upper turning point, second inflection point), the slope of the curve undergoes a sudden violation of the prior trend. This means that the projection of relative capability, and likewise the projection of future interests and role, has been drastically altered. Assuming isometry, the state thus faces maximum *uncertainty regarding its future place in the system and regarding its fundamental security interests* at the congruent point in the dynamic where it faces maximum *uncertainty regarding its continued relative power growth*. This uncertainty about its

---

[1] This section originally appeared in Doran (1989c).

100

future position and role increases the probability of major war. Causality moves from abrupt changes in power and projected foreign policy role *at the critical points on the relative power curve* to greatly increased probability of involvement in major war.

But is isometry a valid assumption, and, even if it is, is the *occurrence* of the critical points on the two curves simultaneous? Are the respective times of "maximum uncertainty" of projection simultaneous, and is the uncertainty regarding future role position perhaps more complicated than the uncertainty regarding future relative power? Answers to these and other issues regarding the dynamic of power and role must begin with the observation that state role at any point in time is a function of many diverse elements – e.g., the state's own aspirations, its relative capability, its own actions, and the systems' response – each of which varies over time. However, one can analyze the role dynamic as though it were a dummy variable.

The relative capability dynamic for the most part determines foreign policy outlook and function: it is a determining and a limiting condition for the possibilities and the requirements of international politics. But there is a great deal of inertia both in the underlying processes affecting power change and in the government decisions responding to such power changes. Consequently, *the change in foreign policy role across long time periods lags behind the change in power*. Note that abbreviated phrases such as the "interest–power lag," "power–interest gap," or "equilibrium of power and interests" are always restricted to *relative* power and *attained* interests.

How does this interest–power lag affect the idealized role curve? As state power increases on the ascendant side, the state and system find an increase in the state's interests difficult because *these interests must come in part at the expense of other states in the system*. This is true for interests that are legitimate as well as interests that directly challenge another state's sovereignty or security. Thus the system acts as a drag on the capacity of the state to expand its role. On the declining side of the power curve, overextension tends to occur, fueling further decline. Again changes in foreign policy role lag behind the change in power. Elites within the state oppose the contraction of interests and the attendant loss of prestige (Chan 1984). Other states in the system, including allies and those involved in power balancing, also hinder the declining state from revising its interests and commitments downward.

Second, this lag of interest behind relative power results in a *gap* between a state's relative power position and its foreign policy role. But one state's gap must be offset by a gap (or gaps) between interest and power elsewhere in the system. A state's *surplus* of power over interests is a *deficit* of power *vis-à-vis* role for another state or states. The gap is in effect a measure of the extent to which the state's systemic role does not accurately reflect the interests of which it is capable relative to the other members of the system.

Disequilibrium of power and interests for a state occurs when a large gap emerges between its relative power and attained role in foreign policy. Large gaps are likely to develop in an interval when the rate of growth of interests obtained differs from the rate of growth of relative capability. Even with isometry, the lag of role behind relative power results in an *increasing* gap prior to the first inflection point of the power curve because the ever-increasing slope of relative power in that segment is always greater than the slope of the lagged role curve (Figure 4.2a). This widening of the gap is called *slippage*. The greater the lag, the greater the slippage in that interval, and the longer the interval after the inflection during which the gap will continue to rise. In addition, assuming non-isometry, a further difference (or greater similarity) in growth rates between the two curves could make the shape of the role curve in the preinflection interval become increasingly (or less) different from that of the relative power curve, creating even greater (or less) slippage between the two curves. They get out of "sync." The greater the difference in rates of growth (slopes), the larger and more rapidly developing will be the slippage and the resulting gap between interests obtained and relative power.

These gaps between interest and power develop slowly, and they are not always or immediately evident to state and system. When they do become apparent, the state and/or system will want to correct that failure to match role with capability (Levy and Collis 1985). The gaps become most evident at the critical points on the power cycle where the state is forced to review its overall foreign policy situation. Internal elite criticism and external pressure for adjustment by opponent states force the state to address the gap so as to protect these not-yet-obtained interests from being denied it because of new projections at the critical point. Together, an inversion of the dynamic at the critical point and a power–role gap introduce a new element of uncertainty, further increasing concern for future role and security.

The greater the slippage (slope differences) and hence the greater the resulting gap and disequilibrium of interests and power at a given time, the greater the difference between the *projection* of future power growth and the *projection* of future role at that time. The difference in projections results in a high degree of *uncertainty regarding the actor and/or system response to the accompanying disequilibrium*. At critical points of relative power change, this uncertainty regarding responses is added to the uncertainty and anxiety already surrounding projections of power and role. Regarding the state itself, will it try to close an interest–power gap at the expense of the system – by using force to obtain legitimate interests suddenly perceived as vital and at risk, or by claiming interests that are illegitimate such as control over the high seas or sovereignty over the territory of others? Regarding other members of the system, *what slope* will they hypothesize in projecting the state's future *role*? Will the system respond to the inversion in the trend of projections of power by further increasing the gap, denying the state the role it has been (and continues at present to be) capable of achieving (Figure 4.2b).

An ideal *equilibrium* of interests and power for a given state is therefore likely to take place when (1) the gap between relative power and obtained role is nonexistent or small, and (2) the rate of growth of relative power at time t is approximately equal to the rate of growth of interests obtained at time t. In other words, both the actor and system have been responsive to adjustment needs arising from vertical changes in relative power. Equivalent growth rates for relative power and role in turn imply that uncertainty regarding future role attainment is no greater than uncertainty about future relative power growth. When the power–interest gap is not large, and when the uncertainty in role *vis-à-vis* relative power change is minimized by equal slopes, the inversion of slope for relative power change (accompanied by an equivalent inversion in role projection) is not as shocking as it otherwise would be, and it will be more easily managed by state and system. Thus, a corollary of power cycle theory is that the absence of disequilibrium of power and interest at the critical points may ease the adjustment, by both state and system, of massive changes in the relative power dynamic conjointly occurring.

A logical policy implication follows: an important path to international political stability is the elimination of aggravating gaps between state capability and role. Conversely, at a critical point on the power cycle, the discovery or acknowledgment of a sizeable gap between relative power and role occurring *at a critical point in the power cycle* is important in influencing the probability of major war.

This analytic conclusion was tested before planning an empirical test of power cycle theory (Doran et al. 1974, 1979). Status disequilibrium (a discrepancy between levels of power and role as indexed by diplomatic respresentation) does predict to levels of threat among states viewed as hostile, but levels of power are much more robust in explaining threat perception. Hence, the cycle of relative power is a

103

primary predictor of the likelihood of major war, and the role dynamic can then "filter out" false positives from that prediction.

THE MECHANICS OF DISTURBANCE AT THE CRITICAL POINTS

We now turn to the dynamics at each of the critical points on the power cycle to illustrate how complete is their destabilizing character for the state and system. All of these states are clustered in the "top" layer of the international system hierarchy. Each power cycle reflects the state's rise and decline relative to the other members of this small group of "great powers." A state near the low point on its power curve is thus a great power wielding much influence in the international system, a possible candidate for eventual "topdog" state in the hierarchy.

(a) Lower turning point (birth throes of a major power). Power of the youthful polity grows rapidly. Sudden discovery of its dynamism encourages states to adopt an aggressive foreign policy. The state uses its newly discovered dynamism to consolidate its territory. Extreme nationalism invites wariness and a sense of threat on the part of neighbors who fear borders are insecure. Its foreign policy imprudence thus causes other governments to regard it as a threat to the stability of the system and it, in turn, to fear retaliation from more powerful states capable of intervening against it. Over-reaction and belligerence are the marks of its response to its neighbors whom it regards as constraining its international political opportunity and refusing to confer upon it the status and role it feels it has achieved capability-wise. Its power exceeds its interests as permitted by the other actors in the system.

(b) First inflection point (trauma of constrained ascendancy). For the first time in his historical experience, the state discovers that, relative to its rivals, although its level of power continues to increase, its heady growth rate abruptly and without warning declines. This decline in rate comes as a shock. The state now cannot achieve its projected future role as quickly as supposed, or perhaps at all. It begins to question its whole place within the hierarchy. If its interests and responsibilities have lagged behind its phenomenal growth in power, the disappointments and doubts are compounded. Other actors in turn are increasingly reluctant to yield in foreign policy matters to an ascendant state that appears aggressive. Threat and

104

counter-threat in this situation of uncertainty and stress increase the probability of a major war over power position and security involving core values of a number of major states. Aberrant foreign policy behavior can emerge from circumstances where the dual shocks of discovering structural decline, and perceived interest deprivation, tend to reinforce each other. Combine these conditions with a sense that the foreign policy stakes are enormous and one has a recipe for massive instability.

After the trauma of this critical point is passed, this phase of the state's power cycle is extremely dynamic because the state's relative power continues to grow in terms of level. It is a phase of ebullience. Greater attention is paid to interests and power as an equation.

(c) *Upper turning point (trauma of expectations foregone).* The state discovers that its relative power has peaked. The problem is no longer just that of declining rates of relative growth. For the first time in its systemic experience, the level of relative capability itself is in decline. The state has entered a phase of rectification (Liska 1990).

The discovery is extremely disheartening for the actor bent on a world role. Its potential for a larger role in the system has been foreclosed by its declining relative base. A government strongly committed to a larger world role may trigger a war in order to try to reverse this decline and fulfil its aspirations for leadership. This situation is all the more traumatic for the state if it had been denied a larger world role throughout its period of ascendancy, so that it suffers from a sizeable power–interest gap when it crosses its upper turning point.

Also, a state whose role did increase with its increasing power may worry about the recently discovered disparity between its global responsibilities and its declining relative capability, perceiving a situation of over-extension. A failure to make timely adjustments may draw the country into conflicts over the delineation of these interests and responsibilities. A tendency to try to hang on to status and power will also entice rivals to look for weaknesses and vacuums, further stimulating the state's own paranoia about its increasingly tenuous foreign policy position. The role-equilibrated state at the apex of its power feels threatened because of the burdens it is no longer easily capable of defending, but is unable to discharge because internal elites resist, and external dependants implore.

(d) *Second inflection point (hopes and illusions of the second wind).* At this critical point, the improvement in the rate of decline drags the state's foreign policy in one direction while the continued

105

decline in the level of relative capability drags it in another. In terms of strict power considerations, the state continues to fear more powerful rivals attempting to dislodge it from interests and responsibilities. Yet the improvements in the rate of decline encourage it to believe it can rescue its fallen status and position in the system if it adopts a more assertive role. It believes that it can participate once again as a full member of the inner circle of states.

This new assertiveness, combined with actual continued decline, makes the state an extremely unpredictable ally. It also becomes a likely target for rival foreign policy behavior probing to determine sources of weakness. Feeling that it has a new international political lease on life, and no longer is in a position where it must continue to make concessions to other states in the system, it is actually a source of disequilibrium because of the growing gap between its retained interests and declining power. But the dynamics of the second inflection point embolden the state not to admit this reality and instead to see its improvement in rate of growth as a last chance for increased world role. Hitler (1961) argued in 1928 that if Germany wanted a place "in the future order of world states" so as not to end up as a "second Holland or a second Switzerland" (p. 158), it had to act quickly for "with the American Union, a new power of such dimensions has come into being as threatens to upset the whole former power and orders of rank of the states." When Germany passed through its second inflection point of improved rate of growth, epitomized by its early recovery from the Great Depression, this desire for increased role seemed imminently attainable.

This momentary stiffening of its political and military spine could not come at a worse time for the state, since it is no longer in a position to play this kind of challenging role. Yet, over-confident of its abilities, the declining state takes the steps that ironically are likely to ensure its continued decline thereafter.

Once the trauma of critical change has passed, the state enters a phase of retrenchment. Historically, states have accepted a more modest role in the system, established new relations with former dependants and future superordinate polities, and erased the discrepancy between interests and power. The state enjoys prestige but has less influence than other states in earlier phases on their cycle, and less than it had in the past. The state's foreign policy role is more constrained, yet it can enjoy considerable peace and security provided it has established the proper alliance relationships.

  (e) Lower turning point (throes of demise as a major power). Here the dynamics are superficially the same as at point a. The difference is that the lower turning point comes at the end of a long period of decline for the state rather than at the beginning of statehood or state entry into the central system. At *e*, unlike at *a*, the situation is of interest surplus rather than deficit. Efforts to try to rescue the last vestiges of a past role of high visibility may be stimulated by the recognition that the trajectory of power decline is beginning to level out. Things are beginning to improve for the state in structural terms. But the disparity between power and interest encourages the state to seek powerful allies that it can entangle in a dispute on behalf of the defense of its role and position, now largely an historical legacy. Instead of curbing belligerency and seeking accommodation in keeping with its reduced capability, instead of further curtailing its interests in keeping with its diminished power base, the state may attempt to manipulate the balance of power through external alliance formation to defend interests it alone can no longer defend. This substitution of short-term balancing of power for long-term adjustments to structure and role greatly increases the likelihood of major systemic war.

DECISION CALCULUS OF ESCALATION IN THE CRITICAL INTERVAL: INVERSION OF FORCE EXPECTATIONS

Although problems of adjustment caused by the sudden awareness of non-linear aberrations regarding state position and outlook, combined with the problems of coping with disparities of power and interest, have their own peculiarities at each critical point, the same decision characteristics tend to prevail – namely, shock, uncertainty, over-reaction, and exaggerated foreign policy behavior in the face of what is felt to be a massive crisis of security and opportunity.

On the surface what distinguishes conflicts in which force use is minimal from those in which it is aggravated is not only the availability of force and the high stakes. It is the matter of *control* (Osgood and Tucker 1967). In extended wars, force use is out of control. But why is it "out of control," and why does force use in extended conflict not obey the rules applied in other conflictual situations?

Suddenly confronted with the monumental structural uncertainty of a critical interval, governments are subject to perceptual aberrations and behavioral excesses (Fournari 1974; Solomon 1970). At other times and under other conditions, the government would react in much more conventional ways to the same set of hostile stimuli. The government addressing its problems of adjustment in the critical interval has a tendency to misread as threatening, signals that have no threat content (Kelly 1965; Montague 1968; Masserman 1963). But once this sense of threat from abroad has been internalized, the government then undertakes actions which are interpreted by *others* as threatening, because in terms of mobilization and other indications of aggressiveness those actions may indeed be bellicose. Hence the system in its turn responds in a way which is *in fact* very defensive and hostile. The government is then reinforced in its belief that other governments are planning collusive and coercive activity against it, and that unless it takes major steps to counter this aggression all will be lost (Mansbach and Vasquez 1981; Taylor 1967, pp. 11–26).

Such behavior, a kind of situationally induced paranoia, creates its own rationale and justification. No appreciable threat exists before the government imagines that threat. But once it begins preparing to meet the imagined threat, genuine justification for the fear begins to emerge as the system responds through mobilization and concerted action to constrain the now deviant state. This is the trigger that sets off force expansion and conflict diffusion throughout the central system. Once the government is convinced in its own collective decision-mind that war is inevitable, and that maximum force use will be used against it, it is ready to employ maximum force, albeit at first perhaps selectively and in very calculated fashion, against certain of its opponents that it deems most readily conquered.

There is a kind of all or nothing quality about extended war, a condition in which the government is incapable of discrimination and balanced interpretation. Instead, all mental activity is devoted to how to carry out a successful attack, preemptive or otherwise, rather than on how to determine whether an attack is in reality likely or being planned. The government assumes that the attack is inevitable and takes steps to assure itself of getting the first and heaviest punch in. Every action by its opponents is taken to indicate further evidence on behalf of the assertion that all-out war is inevitable. Given this predisposition to believe in imminent total war, and given the failure to discriminate, all-out war becomes possible.

Such abnormal behavior is not likely in other less anxious periods of the government's history. It inverts the assumptions of *normal* political behavior that governments will act with *prudence and restraint* when confronted by a credible power balance. Inside the critical interval, the abnormal becomes the normal, in psychological terms, and the irrational becomes the rational (Lamborn 1985).

These behavioral responses have a "rational" as well as a psychological basis. The decision maker continues to utilize a logical calculus and believes in the rationality of his actions. We thus review the logic, for both aggressor and defender, of force expectations in normal periods as compared to the critical interval.

Normal periods. (1) A potential aggressor is deterred from aggression during a normal interval of statecraft because the foreign policy gains from an aggression, whatever these may be (territory, status, economic benefit) are not regarded as worth the cost. Expectations concerning the massive use of force are that the utility of the objective does not equal the potential cost of aggressive action. Moreover, if force is used and war does break out, escalation does not go very far for essentially the same reasons (Russett and Huth 1984; Peterson 1986; Jervis 1979). Expected costs increase more rapidly than expected gains, and the conflict situation returns to the normal condition of stability.

(2) A defender in a normal interval of diplomacy likewise is not prone to escalate disputes because the presumption is that the defender cannot increase its security by an exaggerated force response. The presumption is that the prudent use of deterrence (and defense if necessary) will yield adequate security. Force expectations are that, if force is used against the defender and war does break out, the benefits of escalation for the defender do not outweigh the costs of escalation to the defender. The defender is aware that escalation may be matched by the aggressor, leaving the defender worse off than prior to escalation. Other solutions are sought to resolve the conflict, including the possibility of stalemate, and the situation returns to the normal condition of stability.

In sum, in normal periods of diplomacy, force use of course may occur, but this force use does not escalate into all-out war. For a potential aggressor, escalation does not occur because the perceived increase in the gains from force escalation do not equal the perceived increase in costs. For a potential defender, an exaggerated force response is not regarded as appropriate because such an attempt to escalate a dispute is not likely to lead to greater security.

Critical intervals. Inside the critical interval, the logic of force expectations is inverted (chapter 1).

(1) A potential aggressor suddenly believes, contrary to prior assumption, that escalation of force use, both horizontal and vertical, will yield great foreign policy dividends. Because the inversions of expectations arise in a crisis setting threatening existing gains, these

109

"dividends" or "benefits" to be derived from escalation of force at least initially are recognized to be in essence "necessary protection against otherwise irrevocable losses" of great magnitude and foreign policy significance. The escalation may be incremental, even veiled, but the inversion of force expectation is nonetheless clear.

In 1939, the government of Japan was warned by its top naval commanders that the Japanese navy could not prevail against the American navy (Storry 1983, p. 211). Yet Japan attacked Pearl Harbor in spite of rational military advice because, in the atmosphere of inverted force expectations, objective advice often gets ignored because it does not fit the preferences of the political leadership. Likewise, despite sanctions for such supposedly disloyal behavior, German military advisors warned Hitler of the perils of the Eastern campaign against the Soviet Union. Yet under the euphoria that can evolve out of inverted force expectations, Hitler chose to ignore the analysis of his top generals. Inside the critical interval, a potential aggressor is likely to exaggerate the gains from force use and to depreciate the costs, even when more objective advice is available.

(2) Inside the critical interval, a potential defender is subject to inverse force expectations as well. Exactly the opposite of the normal assumptions about force use prevail. An increase in force use is thought to yield gains that exceed costs because the defender is extremely frightened and convinced that nothing less than massive escalation will halt the aggressor. This is a problem with "launch on warning doctrines" (Graham 1979; Steinbruner 1981). As the defender escalates force use, counter responses from the aggressor reinforce the seriousness of the security situation and the need for the defender to escalate once again on a massive scale.

Why are force expectations inverted for both the aggressor and the defender in the critical interval? The answer lies once again in the actors' perception of future foreign policy reality. Suddenly, inside a critical interval on its power cycle, the state becomes aware that all prior assumptions about position and security are wrong. By extension, the other actors in the system, aware of the stakes and the sudden uncertainties, in turn are also called upon to make extraordinary adjustments and to cope with this unparalleled circumstance. It is the shock of foreign policy adjustment imposed by the discovery of nonlinearity, and of suddenly discovered (or admitted) power–interest gaps in future foreign policy outlook, that are mainly responsible for the inversion of force expectations (Brenner 1985).

Geoffrey Blainey (1973) explains major war in terms of involvements among the principal actors in the central system where conflicts

110

cannot remain isolated in bilateral dyads for long. That explanation does not account for the timing of major war. All kinds of disputes are going on among the members of the central system all the time. The mechanism of the inversion of force expectations inside the critical interval supplies an understanding of *how* escalation occurs, that is, of how a particular incidence of force use leads to systems-wide confrontation.

EMPIRICAL FINDINGS ON WAR INITIATION

A theory is to be rejected if the hypotheses underlying it are to be rejected, or, more formally, if the null hypotheses underlying it cannot be rejected. This assumes that both the null hypothesis and the research design correctly represent (do not misrepresent) the theory, and that the data used are valid for the task. In this section, we report the results of a very demanding series of tests of some of the most important assumptions underlying the power cycle theory of major war. To capture the full complexity of causation in power cycle theory, a research design would have to incorporate interests as well as power, examining the power–interest gap for each state throughout its systemic experience (see chapter 5). But here we examine the impact of the mere fact of passage through a critical point, the mere fact that the state experiences an inversion in the prior trend of its foreign policy expectations.

Our research design confronts a problem facing all events-data research, a problem inherent in the nature of behavior/perception and actor/observer relationships and not peculiar to this analysis. The problem is to encompass four types of theoretical variation: (1) objective change in relative power; (2) perception, perhaps anticipated or delayed, of objective change by the actor; (3) the behavioral response of the actor; and (4) measurement of the objective change and behavioral response as recorded by the analyst. Since perceptual data are not available, we collapse these types of theoretical variation into categories (1) and (4), yielding for purposes of discussion objective critical points (OCP) and empirically determined critical points (ECP). We recognize, however, that categories (2) and (3) may affect category (4) such that OCP and ECP do not always correspond, and our research design therefore directly addresses how this possible disparity would affect the statistical test of our causal hypothesis, as explained herein.

In addition to and irrespective of complexities of research design, many factors operate against statistical support of the theory applied

111

Table 4.1   *Germany 1885–1914*

Year of perception	Projected peak	
	Central System	European System
1885	>1930	>1930
1890	>1930	>1930
1895	>1930	>1930
1900	1900	>1920
*1905	<1900	>1910
1910	<1900	1910
1914	<1900	1910

to wars initiated by the state undergoing critical change. First, the theory asserts that a critical point increases the likelihood of major war at that time, not that all major wars for a state are the result of a critical point. Second, cases in which a state initiates war in response to another state's critical point are not included. Third, we test the relationships for all three indices of major war, which differ greatly in profile. War initiation is thus a very demanding test of the impact of the critical point on major war. We use Correlates of War war data.

Our empirical tests (Doran and Parsons 1980) did support rejection of the null hypothesis. The series of tests was repeated, based on newly calculated critical points, now treated as a five-year period. The retest thus provides a fine-tuning of the prior analysis.

The methodology and research design preserve direction of causality in both the calculation of the critical points and the hypothesized direction of causation in our war hypothesis. Critical points (intervals) were calculated by a variety of techniques to show that they are not an artifact of method but reflect a unique time in the dynamic when an inversion from the *prior* trend of slope suddenly occurs. Nothing in the future data is used to calculate that critical point. Although the analyst *post hoc* can clearly see the critical point because the future data so evidently depict the new trend, the decision maker sees nothing but the well-defined past and its projections for the future until, suddenly, the critical point occurs and challenges that projection. For instance, consider the differing perceptions of the contemporary decision maker observing the pattern of growth in relative capability for Germany at different points of time between 1885 and 1914 (Table 4.1).[2] Until 1900, the observer projected continued rise in German relative power into the third decade. After 1900, that projection suddenly foreshortened.

[2] These projections hold for disaggregated industrial indicators as well as for the yardstick. Yearly data supplement the five-year data as a further check.

In the central system, the observer was able to see that Germany had reached its high point only in about 1905. In the European system, Germany plateaued for about a decade before turning into decline in about 1913–14. According to Wohlforth's (1987) study of perceptions of the period, Germany was thought to have reached its high point in about 1907.

Three critical points from the prior test fall outside the range of newly calculated critical regions. Constraints in the prior technique had forced highs and lows outside the temporal range of the data to fall within it (Britain's low and France's high). One critical point was a temporary inversion in the trend (Russia's suspected inflection in 1821) rather than a true critical point (which occurred in the 1851–56 period). This situation suggests that a suspected critical point may likewise be conducive of major war; indeed, Russia initiated several major wars during the next decade. The two critical points for the United States based on the pre-1950 capability index are replaced by the one critical point based on the more relevant post-1950 index. This new set of calculated critical points provided even more significant prediction of major war in each of the tests.

To capture the impact of passage through a critical point on the initiation of major war, we first tested two separate definitions of a critical interval. A conservative definition of a critical interval consists of 16 years (one-tenth the 160-year period), ranging from 3 years before and 12 years after the midpoint of the critical period to compensate for measurement error (without adding more than a year to the earliest estimate of the calculated critical point) and the lag involved in actor perception and response. Time is required for the reality of the new foreign policy situation to sink in cognitively and in terms of action. Given the five-year averaging of the capability data, even measurement error may be a problem for intervals much shorter than a decade or perhaps even a decade and one-half. But the longer the interval, the more "type two" error is introduced; more years of low probability war initiation dilute the findings and lower the statistical significance. The two interval sizes selected thus appear like a plausible compromise minimizing these contending design problems.

The smaller, more restrictive definition of critical interval consists of only ten years, three years prior and six years after the midpoint of the empirically determined critical period. Using this smaller critical interval implies theoretically that both perception and behavioral response are abruptly sensitive at the critical points.

This test (Table 4.2) overwhelmingly supports rejection of the null

113

Table 4.2 *Extensiveness of wars initiated by major powers*

Group	No. of wars	Duration	Severity	Magnitude (Doran)
10-yr. critical interval	20	28.31	2,871,860	27.650
Remaining interval	57	20.23	295,026	12.631
		$t=2.18$	$t=6.19$	$t=5.54$
		$p=0.016$	$p<0.00005$	$p<0.00005$
16-yr. critical interval	29	28.36	2,296,672	23.828
Remaining interval	48	17.76	159,380	12.104
		$t=2.78$	$t=4.67$	$t=4.27$
		$p=0.004$	$p=0.00005$	$p=0.0001$

hypothesis for all three indicies of major war. The best results are for conflict magnitude, which here combines both size and number of states involved in a war and thus captures the essence of the big armed conflict.

A second statistical test makes use of the simple but very demanding idea that the further away from the critical point, the lower the probability of major war involvement. Suppose that markers locating critical points and dots locating war initiations are put on a time line, each color-coded to distinguish between nation cases. Also suppose that each dot is proportional in size to the size of each war as measured by an index of war extensiveness. According to this schema, the size of the dots of a given colour will diminish as one moves away from the preceding critical point marked by that colour: the size of the wars initiated are inversely proportional to the temporal distance from the preceding critical point (measured from the upper value of the five-year calculated critical period). This test requires that passage through a critical point has an almost immediate impact on behavior. It also does not incorporate a margin of error around the calculated critical period.

A simple linearized least-squares design was used. Several cases explored the effect of *lags*, and the possibility of a *counter-causal linkage* in which major war creates the critical point. The results again were overwhelmingly strong, supporting causation from critical change to major war initiation. All correlations were positive without lags and continued to be positive (though at a decreasing level) with lags of up to ten years, indicating that while some of the effect of the critical point may occur only after a delay of a few years, the impact of the critical point is in fact quite abrupt. The counter-causal hypothesis (using distance between a critical point and wars *preceding* it) was rejected for lack of statistical support. The size of wars initiated by states passing through a critical point is greatest as the state first confronts an uncertain and troubling change in its relative power and systemic role. The critical points do appear to be more traumatic for a government than other periods of its history.

The following facts underscore the parsimony (few independent variables) and robustness (high explanatory value) of the analysis. Only one predictor variable is involved, the occurrence of a critical point on the power cycle, and it is not concerned with comparative power levels or particular grievances of state dyads. Second, the power cycle itself indexes the capacity of a state to sustain a systemic leadership role, not *machtpolitik*. Of the five indicators of relative national capability, only one involves military size.

These facts also reinforce the correctness of the assumptions of the theory. First, the political development of the state as a major power contains in its own dynamic important structural (and associated behavioral) reasons for the increased probability of major war. Second, a yardstick of power in international relations does not have to focus on measures of aggressiveness, or the ability to wage and/or to win a war, in order to predict to those wars that are the consequence of power diffusion in the system. To put greater emphasis on military variables in the index of power is to lose the cycle of political development in the exaggerations and fluctuations of short-term actualizations of capability. A measure of power which emphasizes these short-term actualizations is likely to predict better to the frequency of major war.

CAUSES OF WAR IN THE CRITICAL INTERVAL: A REASSESSMENT

Interrelated in terms of process, yet conceptually distinct, at least three sources of instability are at work within the critical interval. First, suddenly discovered nonlinearity at a critical point on the state power cycle creates a foreign policy disjuncture which the state finds difficult to accept and to cope with in policy terms. Second, fissures long in the making between power and role come to the surface during a critical interval because the clash of interests both internal to the polity and external to it tear away the delusion that has half-concealed these clefts in the past. Third, war results from the inversion of force expectations inside the critical interval. Capability and role ascription become extremely inelastic to the point where force expectations become inverted and the nonrational (maximum force use) appears to

115

be rational. Escalation to enormous force levels is a probable result of this disequilibrated foreign policy situation.

Together, the three sources of instability reinforce each other in the critical interval, heightening the probability of major war. The theory of the power cycle tells us that all states sooner or later must face intervals where structural change within the international system is threatening and problematic. Not to acknowledge this reality is probably to precipitate the kind of instability that all rational statesmen want to avoid.

The individual state is not a pawn of history driven only by the dynamics of the power cycle. That war is more probable in one interval than across the historical average is not cause for desperate action. Each polity has the capacity to take effective control of its foreign policy and make the adjustments necessary, bureaucratic or otherwise, to see it through this (as any) difficult period of its history (Axelrod 1968; McGowan 1974; Hermann 1979; Wohlstetter 1962). The other members of the system can make this task of adjustment either easier or more difficult. The relationship between the power cycle and war must be placed in its largest and most general application at the systems level.

At critical points, the internal strain at the state level rises to the level of the system. Evaluation by statesmen of their changed future foreign policy position in terms of sudden new distributions of power (power ratios)[3] ricochet across the system, translating the strains internal to each state to the essence of structural equilibrium within the system itself. From state to system and back to state, the discontinuity precipitates tumult.

---

[3] Intuitive feelings of statesmen are reflected analytically in the variety of "ratio tests" recorded in the Appendix, pp. 265–6.

5 SYSTEMIC DISEQUILIBRIUM AND WORLD WAR

Changes in the interacting state units and changing systemic structure are inseparable (albeit different) aspects of a single structural dynamic. Here the systemic perspective provides a focus on historical and contemporary statecraft needed for articulation of general equilibrium.

STATE VERSUS SYSTEM AS A SOURCE OF CONFLICT EXPLANATION

Chapter 4 explored the relationship between the critical intervals on an individual actor's power cycle and the wars which that actor initiated. In this sense, the causation was direct, explicit, and one-to-one (albeit, as well, highly restrictive). To shift to a systems perspective regarding the origins of major war is to adopt the focus of the other actors with which the potentially disruptive actor must deal.

In strictly a negative sense, the old Rousseauian adage is true relating the decentralized nation–state system and conflict: wars happen because there is nothing to stop them, or despite efforts to stop them. If the individual state is the initiator of a conflict, the system is that which has permitted it to happen. The system can act with complicity or in opposition. It can strengthen or dampen the urge to use violence. It can create a setting in which expansionism is easy and encouraged or in which the use of force either is not sought or is unproductive. At the very least, the system determines the nature of the response to aggression. But the system may also be a catalyst or a direct cause of major war.

Problems with hegemonic leadership/dyadic competition causation

This view runs counter to a premise in the recent literature which obscures the role of the system of leading states in both order maintenance and massive war. That premise treats the system as controlled by a single dominant state (hegemonic leadership view), and considers systemic war as a fight for preponderance in the system between a dominant pair of states (dyadic view of systemic war).

Confusion arises in part because of ambiguity in the term "hegemony." Hegemony is actually a very old concept taken from the Greek notion of ruler and associated with the modern ideas of both leadership and dominance. In nineteenth-century diplomatic parlance, it means attempted preponderance of one or more of the great powers by military force, threatening the very sovereignty and political integrity of the nation–state. In recent international political economy, it means the dominance of the leading capitalist economy or of the "core state" in the system (Wallerstein 1974). While Marxists have borrowed the concept to denote the dominance of one social class over others, as in bourgeois hegemony (Gramsci 1977), other Marxist–Leninists have distinguished externally between imperialism and hegemony. The Chinese continued the pejorative usage of these terms by reserving the term imperialism for Western dominance while characterizing Soviet behavior as hegemonic (Griffith 1964; Jones 1985). For some liberal writers of international political economy, hegemony contains the purely positive idea of economic leadership and stability. For others, it implies manipulation of the rules of the international market place at the cost of states in the Third World, for example, and to the supposed advantage of the hegemon.

The hegemonic view of order maintenance finds part of its intellectual ancestry in the writings of E. H. Carr before and immediately after the Second World War. Carr is credited with establishing some of the principles of international political realism, with justification, even though he later expressed grave doubt about the future of the nation–state (Carr 1951). But he also left as legacy a perhaps unintended broader interpretation of history that has led to a conceptual confusion: 'The working hypothesis of an international order was created by a superior power ... The British fleet is no longer strong enough to prevent war ..." (Carr 1949, p. 232).

Carr made the assumption that a single state was responsible for creating world order in the nineteenth century, rather than the more plausible assumption that world order emerged out of a balance-of-power system of five states. He assumed that British naval force prevented war, rather than that the structure of the international system was primarily responsible for peace. Like colonialists of the age, he perpetrated the myth of Pax Britannica and tried mistakenly to extend it to the affairs of the central system. This myth projected forward has become that of Pax Americana wherein the United States is the arbiter of international order. The far more convincing view is that in matters of the central system, the system has been bipolar and the balance with the Soviet Union is its principal feature.

Our own data on relative national capability could be used to reinforce these distortions: Britain was by a considerable margin the most powerful state at the beginning of the nineteenth century, as was the United States this century. But how was this power used, and in which spheres did it extend? For Britain, power extended in trade and naval terms to the colonies and outlying areas of the system. The doctrine of "splendid isolationism" meant that Britain did *not* try to impose order on the Continent, that is, in the central system, and *instead* relied on a "balance of power" to prevent war there through shifting alliance relations. Likewise, the United States was never able to "impose its will" on the central international system, nor wisely has it tried to do so. This does not deny that it has assumed the costs and benefits of leadership in the West, nor that its preferences for policy were less likely to be challenged by other states which otherwise may have pressed harder for a different policy. The United States conformed to the great maritime (and air and space) power, the Soviet Union to the great Continental land power. A balance emerged that has served the system quite well for more than four decades. Because Britain and the United States had a larger share of power than other states does not mean that they were ever able to impose order at the heart of the system. That order has always emerged out of an equilibrium involving the interest and power of other leading actors.

The dyadic view of massive world war is a kind of anachronistic projection of the present bipolar competition backwards into other eras and other systemic contexts where it merges with the Pax Britannica interpretation of order maintenance. But, if Germany had been challenging Britain for hegemony instead of challenging European encirclement by several leading states, or instead of seeking a greater role in Continental policy, Germany would not have attacked France and then Russia, hoping that Britain would stay out of the war. Germany would have attacked Britain directly. Much more was involved in the structure of the international system, and in the causes of the massive world war, than a competition for hegemony.

The following qualifications to hegemonic leadership and dyadic warfare assumptions are essential, and they are compatible with the analytic purpose of each notion of hegemony today. With confusions about assumptions eliminated, problems of interpretation or extrapolation dissolve.

119

(1) No single state "dominated" any of these systems; no single state was a true hegemon who successfully imposed its power on the system by either military or non-military means. Hegemony always involved only a degree of dominance. Power was always pluralistic and shared.

(2) Any powerful state bent on hegemony would, as was said regarding seventeenth and eighteenth-century France, "always require the assembling of great international forces to contain it" (Roberts 1983, p. 578). Because the structure of each system was pluralistic, the system historically has always been able to prevent a single hegemon from using military force to impose its own singular concept of world order on the other members. In each case, the single hegemonic challenger – Philip II, Louis XIV, Napoleon, post-Bismarck Germany, Nazi Germany, and Fascist Japan – failed to conquer the system and to remake the rules of the central system in its own self-image. In each case, world war resulted when the pluralistic members of the system attempted to defend themselves by force and succeeded. But the "generative cause" of these world wars was not such a hegemonic attempt and the ensuing defensive efforts; the cause lay in the structural dynamic in the system and the disequilibrium that strained its further operation.

(3) The origins of world war stem not only from the actions of the "hegemonic contender" for systemic leadership, nor only from the interaction between a rising power and a dominant declining power. It would be reckless to consider declining Austria–Hungary or France any less important than rising Germany or declining Britain in the causes of the First World War. Nor does it matter whether the potential hegemon is second in power, nearly equal, or already the preponderant state, or whether a change in the power hierarchy has occurred or is considered imminent. The massive wars initiated by France under Louis XIV were the efforts of an already dominant state, still rising, to extend its hegemony further by force. The system is not led to massive war by a single pair of states.

Each state in the great power subsystem has both the threshold of power and the level of interaction which make it a "contender" for shares of systemic leadership. The desire for dominance is the extreme of the desire for "greater leadership," which can occur for major states throughout the systemic hierarchy. And the desire for greater leadership, if it is rational, suggests that *changes in leadership role have not kept up with changes in relative power* – a failure of systemic adjustment. The relationship between interests and power for all the members of the central system are important to systemic equilibrium, to security and

120

peace. With the broader notion of the equilibrium, massive world wars are seen less as a single state's aspirations for hegemonic dominance (or a rivalry among states for hegemony), and more as the system's failure to prevent a severe disequilibrium of power and interests for many of the leading states.

(4) Finally, following each historical case of massive warfare, no single state among the victorious so dominated the system that it "wrote" the new rules according to its own preferences in the absence of the consent of the other principal members. Such an interpretation is a distortion of the diplomatic reality of all of these periods of history. Rules and regimes have always been negotiated, not imposed.

Hence we emphasize the important impact that the *central system* has had on the character of future peace and future regimes, an impact which has been most evident after a major hegemonic war. Soviet–American and Club of Seven approaches to summitry reflect important post-1945 systems participation in decision making. The collective, not a single actor, is always determinative of the outcome.

Multiple critical points versus transition: towards increased specificity of war causation

Power cycle theory argues that the occurrence of multiple critical changes in a short interval (irrespective of levels) indicates an abrupt and extensive systems transformation. When there are enormous gaps between power and interests in the foreign policy profiles of the leading states, the system is disequilibrated. A critical disequilibrated systems transformation is the structural cause for the massive world wars of history. We now compare this explanation for world war with another "structural" explanation which also has received empirical support, namely, the transition between the dominant state and a rising challenger (Organski and Kugler 1980).[1]

Why is passage by a number of leading states through critical points on their power cycles in the same interval of history more unsettling to world politics than the transition of the leading state and a challenger at the top of the system?

First, with only two governments involved in a dispute, *uncertainty is kept to a minimum* through comparative ease of communication, intelligence gathering with respect to intentions and capability, and

---

[1] Transitions are dyadic and essentially non-systemic, since the time of a transition between two states is the same in absolute and relative terms. Conversely, a critical point, while nation-specific, is necessarily systemic, because critical points do not exist outside the context of a system and the relative shares of the states therein.

focused attention on the levers of bilateral policy. When a number of leading states pass through critical points contemporaneously, the "structural uncertainty" contributing to instability is compounded by "information uncertainty." When opponents become multiple, the amount of information needed to prosecute a dispute, and to prevail without serious damage to all, rises alarmingly. Information overload quickly overwhelms the decision maker. The important relationships between information, structure, and systemic stability, explored theoretically and empirically by Manus Midlarsky (1988), likewise have a bearing here.

Second, when only two actors fight, *the scope of the battle in terms of interests affected can be kept within limits* rather more easily than when many actors are potentially involved. When multiple critical points occur, the anxiety and belligerence associated with such a foreign policy experience spreads quickly and broadly the atmosphere of conflict. A bilateral dispute is not likely to raise the stakes as quickly as a dispute in which a number of leading actors all believe their vital interests are at risk.

Third, even assuming that information were perfectly exchanged, and that the perimeter of a dispute could be as easily circumscribed as in a two-actor situation, the matter of the *control of force use* is more difficult when many governments feel threatened. The history of force use shows that while the magnitude of force has grown, the bureaucratic and technical capacity to manage that force has also increased. But it has not demonstrated that the capacity for the control of force is a match for the proliferation of centers of power in a decentralized nation–state system *where a number of governments feel they are under siege*. That is why Kissinger initially deplored giving field commanders the authority to launch "battlefield nuclear weapons" if under fire themselves. With only two actors facing each other, and with control focused at the top, control is restricted to a very finite set of decisions, yielding some confidence that orders will be obeyed. With many potential participants in a conflict, the bureaucratic and technical instrumentalities of states potentially wear thin. War breaks out and escalates not so much through inadvertence as through inability to escape the hostilities, for reasons of loss of control.

An orderly international political universe is a peaceful universe no matter who are the leading actors nor what the degree of power concentration. Balance of power or its lack (whether between pairs of states or alliances) is not a *generative cause* of major war. Only when uncertainty and the stakes *suddenly* increase is force at the highest levels contemplated by governments that in normal times would never take such a magnitude of risks, risks that they feel called upon to assume at their own peril and that of the system at a critical point in the evolution of their foreign policy. Structural change must be examined in terms of its orderliness and predictability.

At most times in the systemic (relative power) dynamic, change is an orderly predictable process, proceeding according to the previous trend of linear projections for most states in the system. A system which proceeds in this orderly fashion – continuing existing trends in relative power – has a great deal of built-in predictability. This predictability of change on the vertical hierarchy, whether the system is multipolar, bipolar, or unipolar, is dependent solely on the absence of abrupt inversions in prior projections. Hence, since states make projections and plan ahead, both sides of a dyad or of an alliance can prepare for a transition in power levels, and develop less violent ways of dealing with it, *unless* the transition occurs in an environment of such unexpected yet definitive structural change that these past projections regarding future role and security become uncertain or wrong.

This distinction underlies an empirical comparison of critical points and transitions as cause of major war, using a single data set and a research design appropriate to each conception of war causation (Doran 1989c).

There are three possibilities. (1) In the presence of a critical point, a challenger passes a dominant state. (2) A transition occurs, but neither state undergoes a critical point on its power cycle. (3) A state traverses a critical point, but no transition between challenger and dominant state takes place. The null hypothesis also exists that war would occur with a high likelihood if neither the transition nor the critical point were present. The null hypothesis is safely rejected. But more relevant is the finding that (1) obtains strong statistical support; (2) receives no statistical support and is therefore rejected, and (3) obtains very strong statistical support.

A principal conclusion follows. When (1) occurs, both a transition and a critical point are present, and war is of a higher probability, but when (2) a transition alone occurs, war is not of a higher probability. Yet (3), in the absence of a transition but the presence of a critical point, a large increase in the probability of war is evident. What is driving war causation is clearly the presence of a critical point, not the transition, which only predicts to major war when in the presence of a critical point on the power cycle of one or both belligerents. A corollary, therefore, is that the transition notion, while not spurious, is misfocused, or in the language of behavioral science, is misspecified.

123

In international political reality, many transitions in fact have occurred with only a few impacts on major war, while the many fewer critical points have had a quite high impact on major war causation.

The transition notion was an important theoretical and empirical advance in that it focused on the vertical dynamic, hypothesized an identifiable, causal mechanism, and resurrected analysis of the balance of power (Houweling and Siccama 1988). Much less easily conceptualized, the "critical point" has frequently been equated with a transition point or with decline. But the "shift in relative power" which occurs at a critical point on a state's power cycle (inversion in the prior trend) is completely different from the "shift in relative power" involved in a power transition between two states. It is due to the bounds of the system and hence reflects the shifting "tides of history" that other concepts do not capture.

In theoretical terms, a problem with the transition notion lies in its dependence upon the First World War example, in particular on the "mastery of Europe assumption" that Germany's relative power trajectory was still rising prior to the war. That assumption has been shown to be wrong, based on an incomplete understanding of the relative power dynamic. Likewise, the speed and size of Germany's absolute growth are not matched by an equivalent rate of increase in relative power, which slowed down to virtually zero in the decade prior to the war. The structural dynamic of the pre-war period does not support the transition thesis, whereas it strongly supports the thesis of critical change.

Likewise, alliance equality or inequality is not a generative cause of major war. Balance-of-power calculations assume levels for each state that are fairly stable or at least fairly predictable, a situation which occurs at most times on a state's power cycle. Balance-of-power logic tends to assume greater uncertainty regarding outcome (win or lose in a war at that time) when power levels are about equal than when they are notably unequal (and the objectives valued equally). In this sense, power superiority by a defender has a better chance of deterring an aggressor than does power equality or inferiority. The important analyses by Bruce Russett and Paul Huth (1984) on deterrence outcomes demonstrate this effect on the aggressor's calculus empirically. But the converse is not the case. That is, power equality is not a cause for aggression simply because an aggressor has a better chance of winning than when its power is inferior. Balance-of-power calculations are insufficient explanation (misspecified cause) of the origins of major war. Moreover, balance-of-power logic may fail within a critical interval.

124

On the other hand, given a cause for hostilities, the situation of near power equality invites a competitive arms race because the temptation is so great for each side to play catch-up. Although fueled by external tensions, the arms race may not impact much upon overall stability (e.g., the Soviet–American post-1945 arms race). Arms control is another way of maintaining equality, and it likewise may or may not alter the overall stability. The underlying cause for instability is not power equality or inequality.

In sum, transitions predict to major war only in an environment where unexpected yet definitive structural change suddenly alters expectations regarding future role and security. The causes of massive systemic war must involve a perception of threat that is so great and so imminent, that is directed at a belief or goal so important, that hinges on uncertainties so uncontrollable and so pervasive, and that portends the need for action or adjustment so definitely, that the state and system decide that the costs of massive war are not excessive. Balance-of-power and transition are aspects of the relative power dynamic that in themselves do not meet these criteria and that therefore must be interpreted within a broader, more encompassing causal explanation of massive war. According to power cycle theory, that explanation is the occurrence of a critical disequilibrated systems transformation.

WHAT STATESMEN SAW, HOW THEY REACTED: THE TRAUMA OF CRITICAL CHANGE, 1905–1914

Historical example here will clarify elements of the power cycle theory of major war (chapter 4) while preparing for a fuller analysis of the causes of the First World War.

(1) Sudden realization that the world had changed

Germany had been accustomed to unparalleled growth and achievement in the last decades of the nineteenth century. Its dynamism was so great that contemporary historians have asserted the "mastery of Europe" thesis: had peace prevailed, Germany would have dominated all of Europe with its economic prowess. Looking at absolute growth in steel, iron ore, and coal production, these predictions seemed credible. It is not at all surprising that German strategists themselves expected the same thing, namely, continued ebullient growth and dynamism in international political (relative) terms.

125

But by 1905–07, something had happened in structural terms that changed entirely the German foreign policy outlook. Contemporary historians have been at a loss to explain this change in German foreign policy perceptions. They have found a fear, an anxiety, that seemingly had no justification in either the prior diplomatic behavior of Germany, or in the conventional foreign policy behavior of most other states at most times in history. It was epitomized by what Jonathan Steinberg (1966) dubbed "the Copenhagen Complex," a fear of sur- prise British naval attack, but it really was as much a fear of attack by Russia or France as well. Writes Steinberg, "To understand the Copenhagen complex, the historian must plunge into speculations which go beyond the events of traditional diplomatic or military history" (p. 39). Equally puzzled, Rudolf Stadelmann (1948) asserts, "What a strange and incomprehensible self-deception lay in this word *Gefahr!*" (p. 135, quoted by Steinberg, p. 40). What happened regarding foreign affairs at about 1905 inside the collective German psyche? Why was it so filled with anxiety, so bumptious and yet so pessimistic about the German future? This was the mentality of a government passing through a critical point on its power cycle, subliminally aware and increasingly strategically aware of the monumental reorientation of opportunity and status facing it.

What Germany had discovered was that the past set of foreign policy projections were no longer plausible. A new foreign policy *Weltanschauung* dawned. Jagow, the State Secretary of the German Foreign Ministry, saw the problem. So did Moltke, the German Chief of the Military Staff. The Kaiser understood the implications and struggled to escape them. Echoes sounded through the German press.

In relative terms, German power had peaked. German politicians, projecting forward, began to realize that "a policy of calculated risk could no longer be pursued" (Koch 1972, p. 17), and that German power like Austro-Hungarian power would be in relative decline. Keenly cognizant of the power dynamic in 1908, members of the military and diplomatic corps saw the future German power trajectory with increasing angst in July 1914. "In a few years," Jagow wrote, "Russia will be ready. By then it will overwhelm us with the number of its troops; its Baltic fleet and strategic railways will have been construc- ted. Our own group [Germany plus Austria–Hungary] will in the meantime have become much weaker" (Bestuzhev 1966, p. 91). At the much discussed so-called War Council meeting of December 1912, the Kaiser saw the German dilemma (Fischer 1967, discussed in Koch ed. 1972, pp. 12, 24). Increasingly the German policy elite and opinion leaders began to realize what the statistics on German relative capability demonstrate, namely that Germany had peaked even at a time when it was still suffering from the frustrations and irritations of a neglected and slighted foreign policy ego.

(2) Open acknowledgment of power-role gaps

Throughout the latter decades of the nineteenth century, Germany was in rapid relative ascendancy, while France, Britain and Austria–Hungary were in relative decline. Yet the other actors retained their colonies, status, and diplomatic perquisites while Germany was, in its own view, denied a "place in the sun." The special status of France and Britain was preserved through the Entente. Division of North African colonial responsibilities between them occurred not only to the exclusion of Germany but without consulting Germany, for many reasons discussed in a later section. "But what was it [the Germans] wanted," puzzles Steinberg. "They wanted *Geltung*, *Annerkennung*, *Gleichberechtigung*, a whole host of emotionally loaded and psychologically revealing objectives" (p. 42).

But why did Germany need these psychological reinforcements, these international political reassurances? And why did it need such at a time when it had never been more powerful? The answer is only found in the dynamic of the critical interval when a government is facing an entire reorientation of its future foreign policy outlook. Here is where the long-suppressed grievances over gaps between role and power come to the surface to befuddle both the government and its rivals who cannot understand the awkwardness and belligerence of the country's statecraft. Germany in the years between 1906 and 1914 had succeeded in alienating everyone in one crisis after another with no apparent recognition of what it had done or of why it was acting so abruptly.

(3) Structural uncertainty

For Germany, as for the other actors in this terrible interval of history, the problem was uncertainty, gross structural uncertainty. With familiar policy anchors gone, the likelihood of misperception of the nature of the foreign policy environment, and the intent of foreign policy initiatives, increased greatly. The foreign policy stakes were high. "A morally weakened Austria under the pressure of Russian pan-slavism," according to the German White Book that attempted to justify German war aims, "would be no longer an ally on whom we could count and in whom we could have confidence, as we must be

127

able to have, in view of the ever more menacing attitude of our easterly and westerly neighbors" (Great Britain Foreign Office 1915, p. 406). In contrast, as Sir George Buchanan, British Ambassador to Russia, telegraphed to Sir Edward Grey on July 15, 1914, Russia viewed Austria's action as "in reality directed against Russia. She aimed at overthrowing the present *status quo* in the Balkans, and establishing her own hegemony there" (p. 22). Structural uncertainty was so great that all were encompassed by it, not just Germany. "Examination of the facts shows that the policy of all the great powers, including Russia, objectively led to world war" (Bestuzhev, p. 107).

The likelihood of misperception of response to action likewise increases greatly. Buchanan's statement continued by saying that the Russian Minister of Foreign Affairs "did not believe that Germany really wanted war, but her attitude was decided by ours. If we took our stand firmly with France and Russia, there would be no war. If we failed them now, rivers of blood would flow, and we would in the end be dragged into war." A telegraph the prior day reported that France likewise believed war could be prevented by a firm commitment to "fulfil all the obligations entailed by her alliance with Russia, if necessity arose" (p. 14). Why was Germany so blind to this determined opposition to aggression, and to the fact that it would be viewed as the aggressor? Or, one might ask, why were the French, Russians, and British so blind to Germany's perspective and the depth of its anxieties?

(4) Increased inelasticity and paranoia

All are hostile; the war is inevitable. That is the prescription of a madman, or a paranoid. By 1914, Germany had succumbed to structurally induced paranoia. Contemporary historians describe the ravings of the Kaiser as delusions, but they were delusions clarified only by the rationality of hindsight. At the time, they were the inescapable fears and anxieties of international political paranoia in a critical interval on the power cycle. Force expectations all around had become inverted.

As early as the Russo-Japanese War, the Kaiser noted (his emphasis) that "the Russian military departments must be blind, if they failed to see that *England could begin the war at any moment, just as Japan had done*" (Steinberg, p. 30). "Behind all the glitter the Gorgon head of war grins at us," ruminated Moltke in August 1905. "We all live under a dull pressure which kills the joy of achievement, and almost never can we begin something without hearing the inner voice say: 'What for? It is all in vain!'" (p. 39). Structural uncertainty, a severe role disequilibrium that was being ignored, and the sudden realization that their peak of international political "might" had been reached, combined with one more element to create the paranoia and the heightened sense of threat.

(5) Encirclement: increased inelasticity of systemic response

Encirclement was the foremost thought in the German strategic consciousness of the time. Was there encirclement? High stakes were at issue. Britain's route to India, the "life-line of empire," was thought to be at risk in Austria–Hungary's advances in the Balkans (Fisher 1966, p. 16). Passage through their own second inflection point encouraged Britain and France to think in power terms rather than negotiation. A Russian statesman insisted in 1914: "As far as Russia is concerned extension into the Balkans is a political necessity and nothing short of the possession of the Bosphorus and the Dardanelles will end the intolerable situation" (Von Mach 1916, p. 24n). Whatever it is labeled and whatever prompted it, a conscious policy led to German encirclement, and this fact drove the German sense of paranoia as Germany passed through the upper turning point in its power cycle. Practicing the principles of the balance of power, Germany's rivals had no choice but to encircle and attempt to constrain it. A confluence of factors influenced the illusion that such a policy was appropriate.

(6) Austria–Hungary: excessive role surplus at the second inflection point

The second inflection point encourages delusions of grandeur since, even though that state continues to lose in terms of the level of relative power, the rate of that loss is decreasing. This provokes a sense of dread on the one hand, but of risk-taking propensity and some hope on the other. Austria–Hungary expressed all of these emotions in contemplating force use against Serbia. Germany encouraged Vienna in these thought patterns. Reminded Jagow, "Austria, whose prestige has suffered more and more from her failure to take resolute action, now scarcely counts any longer as a full-sized Great Power" (Albertini 1952, p. 157). A statement in the *Militarische Rundschau*, quoted in a letter of July 15, 1914 in the French Yellow Book, applies equally to both over-extended Austria–Hungary in severe

129

decline and severely status-disequilibrated Germany confronting its downward trajectory:

> The moment is still favourable to us. If we do not decide for war, that war in which we shall have to engage at the latest in two or three years will be begun in far less propitious circumstances. At this moment the initiative rests with us: Russia is not ready, moral factors and right are on our side, as well as might. Since we shall have to accept the contest some day, let us provoke it at once. Our prestige, our position as a Great Power, our honour, are in question; and yet more, for it would seem that our very existence is concerned – to be or not to be – which is in truth the great matter today. (Von Mach 1916, pp. 23–24)

Austria was goaded and enticed into action by other actors going through their own critical points of uncertainty, paranoia, and opportunity. But Austria, through its exaggerated concern for status and a restoration of its lost position in the power hierarchy, also dragged Germany into a war which Vienna could not possibly keep limited. Austria was too weak to maintain its position of leadership in the Balkans, but just strong enough to encourage Russia to take up arms against it.

(7) Decision to go to war: inverted force expectations

"In the last few days the whole situation had taken on another aspect and a *psychological situation* had been created which [from the German and Austrian points of view] unquestionably called for a settlement with Serbia by war" (Albertini 1953, vol. 2, p. 167). That psychological situation was the inversion of force expectations. War had moved from the merely feasible to the undeniably necessary. The linkage between the perceptual and the behavioral, between the preparatory and the actual, as far as Germany and Austria–Hungary were concerned, became explicit.

Force use that previously had been thought implausible now became acceptable as policy. On July 12, Austria–Hungary was informed that "once the decision to act has been taken, military considerations demand that it must be carried out in a single move . . ." (p. 173). The conditions for force escalation were already in place.

The lack of proper perspective in the critical interval led Germany totally to misjudge its rivals in a way that, at other times of less stress and less policy distortion, it would have been unlikely to have done. That same day Austria–Hungary's ambassador to Germany reported that, while Germany was convinced that Russia "is arming for war against her Western neighbors," it was "by no means certain that Russia ... would resort to arms" in support of Serbia since those war preparations were not complete. Moreover, "the German Government further believes it has sure indications that England would not join in a war over a Balkan country even should this lead to a passage of arms with Russia and eventually even with France" (pp. 156–57). Albertini concludes (p. 161) that "the World War sprang from this miscalculation of theirs." But what a miscalculation it was! It was the kind of miscalculation, not so much based on bad intelligence, as on a political judgment long under siege, with stress and anxiety causing distortions that in no other period of a state's foreign policy conduct would lead to so unwise a conclusion.

(8) Britain and France: the dilemma of peaceful change

Did Britain and France know of their impact upon the German collective political psyche? Why were they seemingly unable to alter their foreign policy conduct? In the early years, forced onto a declining trajectory by Germany's rapid growth, they were unwilling to "move over." The problem was not so much that they failed to understand their predicament, nor that they could not fathom the result of political inaction. The problem was that they started too late to make adjustments in terms of style and international political comportment. They redressed German grievances with too much hesitancy and even, in the view of some contemporary British and French observers, too much insincerity. How could diplomats have hoped for better relations, asked British MP Francis Neilson, "when we were in diplomatic agreement with Germany's ancient foes, France and Russia? Would the Foreign Secretary say the Franco-Russian relations helped in any way to bring about improved relations with Germany? Why talk about making new friendships by deserting old ones, when the policy of making the old ones was the cause of limiting the number of new ones?" (Neilson 1916, p. 160).

Throughout the period, in Germany as well as in Britain and France, the policy elite wrestled with the dilemma of peaceful change. How to adjust to the rising German capability, how to deal with the new structure of world politics. But there was too little domestic political backing for adjustment to a larger German role, either on the Continent or among the colonial possessions. As Germany's frustrations mounted and assumed an increasingly belligerent pose, and as Britain and France passed through their own second inflection points of improved relative growth rate, the problems acquired a new perspective. Interparty rivalry gave diplomats little room for longer-term concessions to an external foe. Leadership of the kind that would have grasped a slipping fate from foreseeable catastrophe was lacking. In the end, the dilemma of peaceful change was that, for complicated domestic political reasons, so little change of the sort necessary to sustain the peace ever was solemnly contemplated.

Lord Haldane himself made a trip to Germany in January 1912 to quiet anxieties that only an alteration of foreign policy, not an earnest speech, could silence. "We are told that there are masses of people in Germany who firmly believe that ... last year we were meditating and even preparing an aggressive attack upon their country, and that the movements of our fleets were carefully calculated with that object in view" (Neilson 1916, p. 164). The sense of the tragic is evident in this speech, uttered in a kind of political *naïveté* that conveys the depth of the dilemma of peaceful change. It is also evident in a note from Sir Edward Grey to the British Ambassador to Germany, on July 27, 1914: "Germany could not afford to see Austria crushed. Just so other issues might be raised that would supersede the dispute between Austria and Servia, and would bring other Powers in, and the war would be the biggest ever known" (Great Britain, Foreign Office 1915, p. 41). The greatest delusion was the belief that the war could be kept limited, and that it would be short.

EMPIRICAL EVIDENCE REGARDING STRUCTURAL CHANGE AND WORLD WAR: DISEQUILIBRATED SYSTEMS IN CRISIS

We here examine empirically whether multiple structural changes viewed as a systems-level phenomenon are to some extent collectively responsible for the inability of governments to manage conflict at seminal historical junctures. The hypothesis is that systemic war such as occurred during the hegemonic onslaughts of Habsburg Spain between 1585 and 1648, of Louis XIV between 1672 and 1713, of Napoleon from 1792 to 1815, and in the twentieth century's two world wars, resulted from the failure of the central system to cope with the rise and decline of states. In particular, we will test empirically the hypothesis that since 1815, this change in systemic structure was most severe prior to the world wars and was not equalled in its magnitude and scope at any other time in recent historical experience.

A direct and complete analysis of systems transformation would aggregate the various state cycles, specifying the type of critical point traversed, the level of relative power, and the nature and size of the

Table 5.1 *Temporal distribution of critical points by type*

1815	H	H	1814–17	Britain
1820				
1825				
1830				
1835	L	L	1832–37	Prussia/Germany
1840	H	H	1839–44	Austria–Hungary
1845				
1850	I_2	I_2	1851–56	Russia
1855				
1860	H	H	1858–63	Italy
1865	I_1	I_1	1864–69	Germany
1870				
1875				
1880				
1885	I_2, I_2	I_2	1882–87	Austria–Hungary
1890		I_2	1844–89	Italy
1895	L	L	1894–99	Russia
1900	H, I_2	I_2	1900–05	Britain
		H	1902–07	Germany
1905	L	L	1907–12	Italy
1910	L, I_1, I_2	L	1910–14	Austria–Hungary
		I_1	1910–15	U.S.
1915		I_2	1911–16	France
1920				
1925				
1930				
1935		I_2	1933–38	Germany
	I_2, I_1	I_1	1934–39	Italy
1940	I_1	I_1	1939–44	Japan
	L	L	1944–49	China
1945				
1950				
1955				
1960				
1965	I_1,H	H	1960–65	U.S.
		I_1	1960–65	Soviet Union
1970	$^*L_2$	$^*L_2$	1963–68	Germany
	$^*I_1$	$^*I_1$	1965–70	Japan
1975				
1980				
1985				

Legend
I_1 and I_2 = first and second inflection points
H = high point
L = low point
$^*I_1$ for Japan in 1965–70 is a recovery to its pre-WWII trajectory.
$^*L_2$ for Germany is the calculated *end* of the period of its decline.
Nevertheless, we include these two critical points in this statistical test because they only make the hypothesis all the more difficult to demonstrate.

133

power–interest gap for each state. Possible mathematical formulations (Doran and Ward 1977) are not easily operationalized and require data on role not yet available. But an indirect test of the two systemic implications of the theory is possible using a readily operational two-stage research design.

Stage 1: Periods of systems transformation and of massive war

Table 5.1 shows the temporal distribution of critical points between 1815 and 1985 (170 years). The 5-year interval that saw the greatest incidence of critical points was just prior to the First World War. The differences are equally striking when the interval is increased to 10 or 15 years. The Student t test (for comparison of means across small samples) yields high statistical significance. With 23 critical points, randomness predicts 1.35 per decade. But 7 occurred in the 15 years prior to the First World War, 3 in the 10 years prior to the Second World War. Far more structural change preceded the world wars than occurred at other times in the last two centuries.

Other empirical studies sought "snow-balling" of conflict which might tip off the analyst or policy maker that truly major war was in the making (Singer, Bremer, Stuckey 1972; Choucri and North 1974). But the trigger or precondition for systemic war lies not in the dynamics of conflict relationships *per se*, but in the governmental response to changing systemic structure. The reason analysts have repeatedly discovered *differing conflict models* to be applicable in the nineteenth and early twentieth centuries is that *different structural circumstances* did prevail in each century and ultimately would provide *different international political solutions* to the problem of world order. An important cause (precondition) of those total wars was the inability of governments to adapt to rapidly changing systems structure. This little empirical exercise supports the view that both the nineteenth-century balance of power system and the twentieth-century bipolar system were stable at maturity; the problem was getting from one system to the other.

Stage 2: Disequilibrium during systems transformation: the First World War[2]

Qualitative analysis of the historical record is the first step in acquiring "hard data" regarding role and perceptual uncertainty.

[2] A condensed version of this section appeared in Doran (1989c).

Analysis of the period 1885 to 1914 suggests how systemic order might be preserved even during a highly disequilibrated systems transformation.

The historical record is characterized by concerns about growing imbalances in power and role involving many states in the system. The First World War was a war over how to reconstitute the collapsing nineteenth-century balance of power system in a way that would (1) permit the balanced ascendancy of Russia and the United States on the outskirts of the old central system; (2) resolve the problems surrounding Austria–Hungary's inability to hold sway politically in Central Europe and the Balkans; and (3) in the process restore equilibrium in terms of power and interests among declining Britain and France and ascendant Germany. The war was a war to redress the excessive disequilibrium of power and role that vertical mobility created within the central system, a redress *requiring* either major adjustments of role by all the leading states or a redistribution of relative power. Equilibrium was the one problem most correctable by statecraft, but also the one problem which statecraft refused to address. War was felt to be "unavoidable" because this problem or "cause" was inescapable, and the states were not willing to make the necessary role adjustments.

Widespread uncertainty, perceptual variation, and diplomatic anxiety about the *long-term* power and security positions of all the leading states are historical clues to generative cause. These conditions are expected to occur when state and system are confronting critical change, especially when the system involves massive policy contradictions demanding adjustments of role or power. Contrast this situation with the high correlation between perceptions of power which occurs in an equilibrated and rather stable system (Doran et al. 1974). The fact of widely different, changing, and mistaken perceptions in the pre-war period is further historical validation that *at times of critical change* in relative power, decision makers recognize that the *existing trend will no longer hold* and that their future trajectory for both power and role is highly uncertain.

Key to the analysis are the type of critical point, the nature of the power-role disequilibrium, and whether or not the gap was being addressed (Table 5.2). The type of critical point involves a specific advantage or disadvantage over the prior trend of relative power growth. Whether the post-critical point trajectory is rise or decline also tells whether, without adjustment, the power–role disequilibrium is likely to worsen or improve, or appear to do so. The types of adjustments that were necessary, and the reasons for the failure of adjustments, then are unambiguous. The system, disequilibrated and

135

Table 5.2 *Critical points, power-role gaps, and adjustment delusions; disequilibrated system in crisis, 1885–1914*

Year of Crit. Pt.	Nation	Type of crit. pt.	Relative growth advantage	Post-crit.pt. trajectory	Nature of disequilibrium	Gap being redressed	
						Apparent	Real
1882–87	Austria–Hungary	I₂	Yes	Decline	Role surplus	Yes	No
1884–89	Italy	I₂	Yes	Decline	Power surplus	Yes	No
1894–99	Russia	L	Yes	Rise	Power surplus	Yes	Yes
1900–05	Britain	I₂	Yes	Decline	Role surplus	Yes	No
1902–07	Germany	H	No	Decline	Power surplus	No	No
1907–12	Italy	L	Yes	Rise	Power surplus	Yes	No
1910–14	Austria–Hungary	L	Yes	(Exit)	Role surplus	Yes	No
1910–15	U.S.	I₁	No	Rise	Power surplus	No	No
1911–16	France	I₂	Yes	Decline	Role surplus	Yes	No

in crisis from 1885 to 1914, finally collapsed in world war because of an injurious combination of critical changes which (1) obscured the need for vertical corrections of role while it (2) unduly increased confidence in short-term power balancing. This exercise reveals both the apparent rationality and the actual illusionary nature of many of these perceptions.

Devastating illusions at the critical points. The specific critical changes occurring during this crisis ironically deluded many states into believing that vertical changes in role were not needed (see Figure 2 in Doran 1989a). The three declining powers, Britain, France, and Austria–Hungary, had remained at the top of the system until 1870 when Germany surpassed all but Britain in power terms. All of these declining powers not only had a *surplus* of role over relative power, but all also experienced the second inflection point marking *improved* rate of growth of relative power. Efforts to speed economic renewal to offset the rapid rise of Germany had begun to pay off for Austria–Hungary in the 1880s, for Britain by 1905, and for France within the next decade. The effect of this sudden *comparative advantage in rate* was to make statesmen deny that any role adjustment was necessary on their part.

Three states, Russia, Italy, and Germany, had a *deficit* of role *vis-à-vis* relative power. Italy was highly assertive following its territorial consolidation, and Britain sought to increase Russia's role, but only at the expense of Germany. Germany, however, both *had a severe deficit of role* and *was denied an increase in its role*, even during the period of its most rapid rise. The final ingredient in this illusion was the differing critical points which occurred for Italy and Russia versus Germany. Whereas Italy traversed its second inflection point and Russia its lower turning point, each acquiring a comparative *advantage in rate* of relative power growth, Germany's rapid ascent in the European system was foreshortened by diminishing marginal returns affecting its own economic growth, the renewed growth of European contenders, and the constraint of the upper asymptote. Furthermore, whereas the other European countries tended to ignore rising U.S. power as peripheral to the European system, Germany was well aware that the United States had taken over its own trajectory of rapid growth after 1900, and that the United States was indeed a further contender for those very interests Germany was being denied.

Finally, Germany's sudden comparative *disadvantage in rate* of relative growth also portended actual *decline in level* in the future. It thus appeared that Germany would never again be able to demand the role

137

adjustments it had so long been denied. Traversing this disadvantageous critical point with such an enormous role gap appeared so threatening to Germany's future role security that the costs of war seemed acceptable. The concurrent situation of power symmetry and transitions, descriptive of the entire period, acquired causal significance secondarily to this sudden discovery (1) that the peak in its relative power position may have already occurred while (2) the other state projections denied it its long-overdue role adjustments.

The uncertainties of multiple critical changes could not have led to a more devastating combination of new projections and, indeed, illusions. Confidence that horizontal balancing meanwhile could mitigate the gaps fueled an inversion of force expectations for the other states as well.

Failure of horizontal balancing. Originally horizontal balance worked because for the most part Bismarck used it in a way that did not deny the vertical changes. Indeed, the very success of balance in these early years fed Germany's illusion that others too would understand how to make it work. Austria–Hungary and Italy both crossed critical points early in this period, and it was only the proper use of the balance of power that prevented major war from occurring at that time.

Austria–Hungary, in crossing its second inflection point of improvement in rate of growth, entertained visions of an enhanced role in the Balkans, at the cost of Russia, for example in the Bulgarian situation. But through the *Dreikaiserbund*, and later outside it, both Bismarck and the Russian Tsar exercised constraint on Austro-Hungarian activity that in any case could not have been justified by its relative decline in power (Kennan 1979). Similarly, the ambitions of youthful Italy as it passed through its second inflection point did not immediately lead to war because the other members of the system integrated Italy into the fabric of the alliance schematic. For example, Bismarck negotiated the Triple Alliance among Germany, Austria–Hungary, and Italy, and he promoted *entente* between Britain on the one hand and the Italians and the Austrians on the other (p. 249). Italian ambitions were neutralized *vis-à-vis* the European continent as Italy was offered the perquisites of alliance equality, and it turned its ambitions toward Africa where it engaged in war with Ethiopia within the decade after its critical point. The very success of accommodation and balance in this period fed the illusion that the balance of power alone was sufficient for stability.

Conversely, in the post-Bismarckian period, a failure to effect a stable balance of power reinforced the sense that war was inevitable; indeed that attempt made war inevitable. As the capacity of governments to project their power and place in the central system grew increasingly suspect, the immediate response was a flurry of alliance activity (Walt 1987; Siverson and Duncan 1976). Statesmen sought to offset the uncertainty and the suddenly discovered misperception in their foreign policy futures initially by forming highly flexible alliance coalitions, but these shortly gave way to more rigid alliance arrangements (Job 1976). The logic was balance of power: to control the uncertainty regarding role by establishing a new uncertainty regarding the *results* of a war: "a rough *equilibrium* ... between the two alliance blocks ... [would make] the results of a Great Power conflict more *incalculable*, and [hence] *less likely*, than before" (Kennedy 1988a, p. 250, emphasis added). But once the power–interest gaps became unmanageably large and visible, the rigidity of the alliance system was tantamount to admission that the central system could not adjust. Only force, it was concluded, could adjust disequilibrium that diplomacy and inflexibility of alliance relations had forsaken.

The problem was that all these estimates of balance, and of the likely costs of war, were based on short-term actualized potential and assumptions that the war would be short. However, the horizontal adjustments via alliances so exacerbated the vertical gaps that by 1905–13, when Germany, Britain, and France were undergoing their critical changes, the system was excessively disequilibrated. No short war could resolve this disequilibrium. The rigid alliance structures that polarized the system ensured that the war would be long and of large magnitude (Sabrosky 1975). Alliances, the substitute for systemic adjustments in role, spread the war and brought enormous resources to its pursuit, ensuring that it would be major.

In sum, disequilibrated systems transformation is a tumultuous interval for state and system, a period characterized by extremes of uncertainty, misperception, and a pervasive sense of threat. For many states, prior expectations regarding its trend are proven wrong, and the likely response to state initiative is not so easily fathomable. The horizontal chessboard of balancing that works so successfully when vertical changes are less prominent has less chance of succeeding. In addition, it cannot provide the role adjustments which are necessary when the system becomes disequilibrated. Historically, excessive perceptual uncertainty, together with the mistaken belief that horizontal balancing was sufficient to offset massive systemic disequilibrium resulted in an inversion of force expectations by decision makers seeking to preserve and protect their power and role. The consequence was world war. Statesmen must seek a generalized equilibrium, incorporating both strategic power balancing and equilibration of power and role for states in the central system, to increase the likelihood that systems transformation will be peaceful and secure.

Part 3

DYNAMICS OF GENERAL EQUILIBRIUM AND WORLD ORDER

6 PREREQUISITES OF WORLD ORDER: INTERNATIONAL POLITICAL EQUILIBRIUM

International politics has its own understanding of general equilibrium that is *sui generis* to the field, and while not incompatible with the notion of Pareto optimality, is not dependent upon it.[1] A distinctive characteristic of the determination of general equilibrium among a few leading governments in the central system in terms of the distribution of power and foreign policy role is not knowledge of what equilibrium is, or even where it obtains (see theoretical discussion in chapter 1). The distinctive problem for world politics is that (1) because of short-term tendencies toward power maximization, and (2) because of rigidities in the capacity of government elites to adjust to new international political circumstances, governments often are unable to move toward a generally acceptable equilibrium point. Thus, in world politics, the focus must be on strategy and motivation necessary to get governments, in their own long-term collective self-interest, to move to such positions of international political equilibrium.

BALANCE AS SYSTEM VERSUS BALANCE AS FUNCTION

In the nineteenth century, the European diplomatic system came to be considered as synonymous with the *balance of power* (Gulick 1955; Wolf 1970; Zinnes 1967). The assumptions of the balance-of-power system were quite simple. Only five actors composed the central system: Britain, France, Russia, Austria-Hungary, and Prussia.

---

[1] The Pareto notion is that a distributional point is found where no one in a system can be made better off at the cost of someone else. All factors of production are being used most efficiently, so no possible mix could yield a greater output. In the abstract, all systems of general equilibrium must manifest these characteristics. Problems of application to actual systems include: (1) interpersonal utilities are not additive; (2) imperfections of knowledge and factor flow impede both its calculation and realization. In international political systems, the problem is both more difficult (less precision in the calculation of equilibrium) and easier (utilities are much more easily aggregated across a few nation–states, and the "ultimate authority" for foreign policy decisions is more easily identified).

This number was neither too many to facilitate information flow and accountability nor too few to allow for stable movement of governments between coalitions. Despite a growing disparity between the absolutism of the central European powers and the democratic preferences of France and Britain, ideology for the most part was absent, thus easing the task of judgment based on power considerations rather than affinity. Relative equality of power existed only after mid-century, for in the brief interval immediately following 1815 Britain towered over everyone else (Braudel 1979). Yet movement of a government from one coalition to another had enough of an impact on the perceptions of a potentially expansionist actor to discourage that behavior. Each actor's weight was a significant component of the overall balance and could not be dismissed as inconsequential by the other members of the central system. Finally, Britain, because of its island status, its colonial and maritime orientation, its relatively large navy and small army, and its consequent lack of interest in territorial aggrandizement on the European Continent, performed a special role helpful to the balance-of-power system. Because of its geopolitical situation and interests, Britain could act as the quintessential balancer of coalitions in opposition to aggression on the Continent. Disputes in the colonial world, however, could feed back on the central system.

Balance as *function* is possible in any international system regardless of type, provided that some flexibility is permitted by the structure of the system for coalition formation and shifts of actor allegiance.

THE BALANCE-OF-POWER NOTION AS INSUFFICIENT EXPLANATION

A number of brilliant critiques of the balance of power in the 1950s set the tone for much of the debate about international politics for the next three decades. Haas (1953) noted the confusing and even contradictory ways in which analysts have used the balance idea: (a) as a statement of the existing distribution of power among states, and as a defense of a particular condition of equality; (b) as an equality of power, and as a situation in which a state has a comfortable margin of power in its favor; (c) as a "universal law of history" in which the balancing process is inevitable and virtually automatic, and as a prescriptive guide to policy making in which decision makers must opt for conscious choices; and (d) as a technique designed to maintain peace but which may require the use of armed force to be implemented. Note that these criticisms challenge not the use of coalitions and shifts of alliance *per se*. At issue are the *rationale* for undertaking these external and internal actions and the *nature* of the "balance" such actions are designed to achieve.

It is possible either to emphasize the contradictions or disparateness of these meanings and thereby to undermine the validity of the concept of balance, or to show how the legitimate differences of viewpoint about the balance notion can be further examined and perhaps reconciled.

Goals of equilibration reassessed

As the arms race literature employing the Richardson-type equations stresses, an "equilibrium" in the generic sense as a "condition of equality" can either be stable, that is permanently at peace (in the physical science sense, "at rest") or only temporarily at peace because of a "saddle-back" or other locus of points that is always potentially subject to disjuncture and collapse (Zinnes 1967). Britain, Canada, and the United States are "permanently" at peace in that the equilibrium is stable; Israel and Egypt may be at peace only so long as the Camp David Accords prevail. But regardless of whether a particular condition of balance is comparatively permanent since all the political forces seem to converge in favor of that stability, or whether that condition is quite transient, each such balance in international political terms also accounts for a distribution of power among countries. There is no contradiction between balance as "condition of equality" and balance as "distribution" so long as it is recognized that a "condition of equality" is able to occur with a variety of different "distributions of power." A problem also emerges if an analyst asserts that *any* distribution of power, regardless of its composition, corresponds to "equilibration" or balance. Thus, all international equilibrations or balances of power among states, whether "stable" or not, are distributions of power nonetheless (Jones 1980).

The problem with balance used as "equality of power" and balance used as "a margin in one's favor" is more troublesome. At heart here is the profound issue of what conduces to stable equilibrium, not mere conceptual ambiguity. At issue is *explanation* about how the international system operates and individual governments respond to threats to security and attempt to provide for security. Is the individual government willing to settle for an equality of power with rivals, or is it likely to be comfortable only with a margin of power in its favor, that is, with a superiority of power? *Vis-à-vis* U.S.–Soviet relations today, does balance in the arms race mean equality of power, or is balance likely to be interpreted by each as superiority on its side?

145

What a government wants in the abstract and what it must in reality accept are often at odds, just as they are for the individual. In the absence of a capacity for optimization, the decision maker must settle for even more unpleasant choices. Both the United States and the Soviet Union would prefer superiority on their own side as a seemingly better guarantor of stable balance from their own partial perspective. But if that superiority is impossible to obtain (or, if obtained, to preserve), each government may opt instead for an equality of power that neither will upset. In fact, as long as each government has a substantial capacity to transform a stable balance into an unbridled arms race, each government is better off if it settles for power equality. Power equality is presumably less threatening to opponents than the quest for or the actuality of superiority.

This would not be the case only in a situation where an opponent has through slow aggregation obtained predominant power. This is what has come to be known as "hegemony." Each government must then simply accept the facts of superiority and attempt to adapt foreign policy behavior to these facts. But in situations where an actor believes it can offset superiority, it will tend to try, introducing a virtually perpetual dynamism (instability in the vernacular of arms control) into the power acquisition process and therefore into the notion of balance itself. The outcome of this logic is that superiority may ensure unstable balance in the power acquisition process just as it may deter expansionism, whereas equality of power has a chance of converting an unstable balance into a stable one.

Although power equality may be regarded by each actor as the second-best choice, it is surely the first choice of the system as a whole. Power equality will likely be less irritating to the respective rivals, creating a systemic situation in which each is best able to preserve its own security without endangering the security of its opponents. This latter condition, the provision of one's own security while providing security for others, is at the heart of the balance-of-power notion. Only by certain self-limitation is the dynamism of power acquisition constrained on each side, and self-limitation is only thinkable as a minimum condition when a state possesses a rough equality of power with its rivals (Aristotle 1961, p. 76). Since superiority *below that of actual hegemony* only invites efforts to match or exceed those levels possessed by a rival, a rough equality of power is a systemic ideal.

Hence, in the absence of clear cut dominance by a single actor, the balance of power involves rough equality of power between or among the leading actors of the system. An attempt by one actor to gain a marginal superiority of power for itself is incompatible with the

146

balance-of-power ideal and will tend to lead to situations where two or more other actors form a coalition against the increasingly superior rival. Marginal superiority is thus not a reciprocal condition. It has no hope of creating a stable balance.

The third question is the matter of automaticity and inevitability in the operation of balance. The most plausible answer is that there is room for automaticity and for conscious decision making in matters of balance. But the comparative mix of each can make a difference in statecraft. *In extremis* the members of the system will respond to serious acts of aggression to prevent military conquest. This response is the basis of the notion of collective defense. Once aggression is massive, governments normally require little urging to defend their own interests. The matter at issue is timing and manner of response.

A remarkable aspect of the first Napoleonic campaigns, for example, was how Napoleon was welcomed as liberator by the societies he overran (Fournier 1911). Not until most of the Germanies and much of Italy were under Napoleon's domination was there much of a *collective* response to French expansionism and then only after the nationalist energies of the dominated states began to seep into the consciousness of the military leadership in the disparate opposition. The same criticism has been made of League of Nations' behavior regarding Italian expansionism in Ethiopia.

Whether the operation of balance is automatic depends on the rapidity and the correctness of the response. When it arrives, balance is automatic; but the response may be so belated that much damage has already been done. On the other hand, if governments overreact to a threat that is not real or that has been misjudged, the response itself can become a source of instability rather than an appropriately measured antidote to limited aggression. A government must decide whether aggression has occurred and with what consequence to itself and the system. It must determine whether that aggression is likely to continue. It must evaluate its own resources for response and whether alliance abroad would aid in deterring the possible expansionist state (Dupuy 1979). None of these decisions is likely to be automatic unless expansionism is so far advanced that a response is a *fait accompli* (Weede 1976).

The final question is perhaps the most akin to antinomy. Proponents of the balance notion have long argued that the operation of balance promotes peace. Yet the century which saw the flowering of the balance-of-power notion ended in the tumult of world war. More precisely, critics note, balance fails to deter the actual use of force. Promotion of balance is supposed to assist in the maintenance of peace, yet promotion of balance may require opposition to expansionism through the readiness to use armed force. If readiness leads to actual use, hostilities may break out. The effort to use balance to prevent war may lead to war. In what sense has equilibration thus contributed to the maintenance of order?

This dilemma associated with the concept of balance – that the coalition forming against an expansionist threat must be prepared to use force if necessary but not necessarily to use force – is a dilemma at the heart of all order-maintenance, not just that associated with balance. But it is a problem that critics of the balance idea have become so troubled by that some have been willing to dismiss the concept of balance itself, since it seems so imperfect, in pursuit of a more radical plan to achieve peace. Yet, short of world government, all other such plans suffer from the same predicament. Peace is dependent upon the capability to use armed force which, if used, reflects the failure of the balance strategy and results in war.

Resolution of this antinomy is found in the prefix, not the antecedent, to balance. The one failure of balance may be more impressive than the dozen successful applications. Perfection is hard to come by in human affairs. As the costs of failure mount, the price of perfection seems more bearable as refinements to the doctrine of deterrence attest. But the chief analytic task is to figure out ways to improve the success ratio of the balance notion in world affairs, not to discard an idea that if refined might serve more effectively than other less familiar proposals.

Returning to the essence of the antinomy as originally expounded, the balance of power achieved these things. It preserved the integrity of a pluralist and decentralized international system. It preserved the sovereignty and territorial boundaries of most if not all of the states in the system, and it did maintain the peace on numerous occasions when war might otherwise have broken out. If avoidance of war is the only criterion of utility, the notion of balance is quite faulty. If, however, preservation of the international system and security of the nation–state are higher goals than peace alone, because peace alone could deprive the state of interests including its identity, then the notion of balance looks better. Closer scrutiny shows how its record in preventing war might be improved.

Limits of equilibration in new perspective

(a) *The static, chessboard image.* Balance-of-power politics readily lends itself to the chessboard image. The number of players is assumed known; rough equality of power exists among the players in the central system; strategic moves involve balancing the power of a potentially expansionist state, internally through actualization of the capability base, externally through coalition formation; the players concentrate on the power shifts and understand the implications and rules of the balance game. The chessboard image is appropriate because it summarizes so much that is useful in the calculations of statesmen, but it also epitomizes an important shortcoming of the classical balance-of-power paradigm. It is static.

(b) *Dynamic impact of the power cycle.* Not only *process* is changing in world politics, but *structure* as well, more slowly but ineluctably (Nitze 1976; Waltz 1967; Bobrow and Cutter 1967). Problems emerge here not because of any difficulties within the process of short-term balance or equilibration. Problems emerge because *long-term structural changes in the system* prevent the actors from making the kind of calculations they have become accustomed to make to preserve the balance.

Massive structural change is debilitating of balance because it creates substantial inequalities of power among the principal members of the system that may have nothing to do with whether a government will pursue a benign or a malevolent foreign policy. But these slow, incremental inequalities in relative power become confused with the short-term actualizations of military and economic capability that have always been taken in balance-of-power terms as indicators or omens of bad intent. Long-term changes in relative power and short-term mobilization of resources for possibly expansionist purposes may look alike to the decision maker, but their respective origins and purposes are likely to be quite different. Long-term changes are far less conscious and within the capacity of decision-makers to shape. They for the main part tend to happen as the unintended result of internal economic and commercial behavior, even though the result depends upon the behavior of other states as well. But the architects of balance must cope with all forms of structural change, long-term as well as short, contrived as well as unintended. Adapting to long-term structural change appears to be particularly difficult, for the classical balance of power tended to react in the wrong way to such incremental yet profound alterations in structure.

The architects of the classical balance tried to offset the internal actualization of resources of the possibly expansionist state by forming a coalition against the government in ascendance. The inclination was always to bolster weakness. But long-term changes in relative capa-

149

bility created situations in which the *ascendance* of major states need not be offset because the ascendance was essentially benign and in practice could not be offset through coalition formation in any case. With the advent of bipolarity, the perverse result occurred (perverse according to the classical rules of balance) that the smaller members of the system rushed to the side of the ascendant actor so as to protect themselves from the similarly ascendant actor on the other side. No coalitions formed against the ascendancy of the United States or the Soviet Union after 1945. In fact, the marginal character of the non-aligned movement was tantamount to the futility of this type of balance in attempting to cope with long-term structural change (Cline 1979; Krasner 1985). Coalitions instead tended to form around each ascendant actor in a fashion that had no analogue in classical balance-of-power terms.

Likewise, by attempting to balance or halt incipient structural *decline*, the balance of power worsens the eventual outcome of structural change by creating a false atmosphere of apparent power equality and apparent equilibration. The architects of the classical balance, confused by the type of power change occurring in the system, overlooked an even more fundamental rule of international politics: *rising power (of a long-term incremental sort) cannot be offset*, and *such declining power cannot be bolstered*. To try either of these futile exercises is to worsen the condition of international politics when the fiction is eventually laid bare. An analogy is the trader who with limited resources attempts to continue to buy when the market moves against him. He may feel better in the short term than if he had sold out and taken an immediate loss, but in the longer term the buy strategy may cause him to go bankrupt. So with the international system, the architects of balance who attempt to halt structural ascendancy, or to camouflage structural decline, may simply have to face more serious collapse of the system later when the artificiality of the balance effort has been revealed.

(c) Neglected function of state interest. The balance of power also had the limitation that state interest and role responsibility were not effectively incorporated. Balance in the balance-of-power framework was therefore forever incomplete. What for the most part was left out of these deliberations was a well-formulated idea of how legitimate state interests – long-standing and traditional state interests – fit into the balancing equation when the relative power of one or more leading state changes extensively. All governments were assumed to be equally capable of threatening the system since, at least

in the early nineteenth century, the liberal notion of "good" and "bad" governments had not made much headway. There seemed to be no room on the chessboard for any further and more complicated elaboration of state interest and role perception as they affected foreign policy decision making and therefore how balance ought to take place.

In sum, a valid notion of international political equilibrium that goes beyond the shortcomings of classical balance-of-power thought must include: (1) awareness that states move up and down long-term cycles of power, and that this movement will have a distorting impact on balance calculations (such as on the number, identity, and resilience of the members of the system); (2) acknowledgment that in certain intervals on these cycles, the state's foreign policy will experience above average tendencies toward instability and even bellicosity; and (3) willingness to bring interests and power together for each state in an overall format of general equilibrium. Equilibrium must encompass both the disruptive effect which the long-term rise and decline of states has on the balancing process, and the complications of balancing the ends of foreign policy with the means of statecraft. In the absence of fuller elaboration of balance, equilibrium is bound to fail.

WORLD WAR: THE FAILURE OF EQUILIBRATION DURING SYSTEMS TRANSFORMATION

Comparison of the twentieth-century world wars lends historical support to these assessments regarding maintenance of world order during systems transformation.

Incongruities in balancing a state "so powerful and yet so restless"

From 1910 to 1913, Germany was perhaps the most bellicose state in the central system, although not the most heavily armed; it was also the most frustrated. The ill-will that preceded the war flowed directly out of two problems which the balance of power as classically conceived was unable to alter: German power had grown rapidly to match that of France and Britain, but their state interests and global role still vastly outdistanced that of Germany. The problem of equilibrium in 1900 was not just that German power was in imbalance with that of France and Britain, as depicted by some classical balance-of-power theorists. The crux of the order-maintenance problem was that there was a disparity in the ratio of ends to means for each state.

151

Because of the rapidity and unanticipated nature of structural change in the system, the governments were unable and unwilling to eliminate this disparity so as to preserve equilibrium. Power and state interest were as much out of line in 1900 as they were ever likely to become in modern statecraft.

Austria–Hungary was at the heart of the structural incongruities that precipitated the war. Habsburg pretensions lived longer than its relative power position, apparently convincing other members of the system that equilibrium was still feasible in old terms. Instead of recognizing that Austria–Hungary had become a liability and that it could not preserve the peace between Germany and Russia, France and Britain attempted to bolster its place in the central system through offers of alliance association, and they counted on it performing its traditional role of balancer in a fashion that it could not.

Austria–Hungary's pretensions, backed by extended guarantees from other actors rather than by unilateral capability for action as in the era of Metternich, accordingly invited challenge and experimentation from even the smaller polities in the Balkans. When the challenge became more than Vienna could handle, it turned to one of the actors that it had traditionally sought to balance, Germany, as the way to escape from its foreign policy imprudence. Austria–Hungary thought not in terms of sustaining the European balance (Germany was considered perhaps the strongest member of the central system), but in terms of saving the last vestiges of its own prestige. Lamentably, neither France nor Britain, let alone Russia, saw the tragedy in this course. They never anticipated that it would become vassal to the government that was most likely to harbor expansionist feelings and capability. Europe sought to *buttress structural weakness* rather than seek a new equilibrium less dependent on the contributions of the enfeebled member of the central system.

By the 1890s, enough structural change had occurred to require adjustments between means and ends for Britain and France as well. They could no longer sustain their colonial empires either economically or militarily; their role in the European balance was excessive. Britain attempted to reverse its policy of quasi-Continental isolation while controlling the seas. Germany demonstrated that the seas were as vital a German interest, and were as much subject to the German naval presence, as they were vital to Britain. France could no longer coordinate policies with Austria–Hungary or Russia in the interest of European stability in the Balkans in part because of the military vulnerability revealed in the Franco-Prussian War.

In contrast, Germany had *earned* greater prominence than it *received* in world affairs. Because of its relative ascendancy, Germany had a right to expect more visibility and a larger role in European affairs as well as on the periphery of Europe. Warning signals of the deep frustration building within the post-Bismarckian governing elite of Germany should have been clear in the awkward struggles going on for European dominance in Africa and in Persia, where for the most part Britain and France outflanked and out-maneuvered the less experienced, less adroit, but more powerful Germans. The great colonial actors could continue to exclude Germany from a larger place in the peripheral areas because they were already there and Germany was not. They could attempt to rely on the old balance of power in Europe to keep Germany in check on the Continent. But they ran the risk of further antagonizing an increasingly hostile and frustrated German polity. They could not block or halt the rise of German power, but they likewise refused to adapt to it.

The implicit policy of encirclement was demeaning and unworkable. It was a bit like the norm of international law regarding blockade, conditional upon whether it is enforceable. Germany appeared "*so powerful and yet so restless* that her neighbors on each side had no choice but either to *become her vassals* or to *stand together* for protection" (Trevelyan 1922, p. 443, emphasis added). It marked the failure of the balance-of-power strategy to constrain the rise of new states. To Germany, the policy of encirclement seemed a kind of taunt flung by a declining actor in the system unable to maintain its place either alone or in combination with European allies.

Germany for its part allowed its pretensions and emotions to guide its policy. Yet rationality does not easily prevail in a critical interval. How immense must have been the shock of Germany's sudden realization that even its rapidly growing economy was not able to further increase its share of relative power. What would become of its heretofore denied greater role, its "place in the sun" so long awaited? Like many a state in history, Germany thought it could force Europe to allow it to increase its world role, its systemic perquisites, and responsibilities. It thought the disparity between German power and interest would be self-correcting if it simply used enough muscle.

But the cause of war is broader, and the responsibility lies with all the states in the system. Our conclusion bears repeating. The breakdown of equilibrium resulted from the excessive disparities in ends and means of the respective governments and the unwillingness of the members of the central system to eliminate disparities gradually and peacefully in advance of shocking critical change. The First World War could have been prevented.

"The malice of the wicked ... the weakness of the virtuous"

The need for a more encompassing equilibrium is also exemplified by the failures of diplomacy leading to the Second World War.

What caused the Second World War? We have a three-part answer. First, in the three decades between 1916 and 1945, structural change was again disturbingly rapid. Some five states passed through critical points on their power curves, three during the ten years prior to the war. So much abrupt alteration in the contours of the central system was only exceeded in the decade prior to 1914. When one considers that all this change in foreign policy expectations was set against the background of a monumental ideological revolution in one of the principal states, and the worst world economic depression in more than a century, the true impact of this structural change, not only on the outlooks of statesmen but also on the psychologies of the masses, is properly felt.

Upheaval in the leadership ranks of the international system was ongoing in the interwar period. All of this change, coming on the heels of exhausting war, greatly unsettled the diplomacy of the period. In the aftermath of Versailles, the United States not only turned its back on its president, the chief architect of the treaty; it turned its back on its allies. France was left with indefensible frontiers and unenforceable strictures against German rearmament in the Rhineland. Britain could not repay the debts that would strangle its economic recovery because Germany could not repay its debts to Britain. Austria–Hungary was dismantled in the name of the self-determination of peoples, but no alliance structure was built to constrain a revanchist Germany to the East. Stalinist Russia, in the throes of its own self-inflicted annihilation of the peasantry and its military elite, was unprepared to cooperate with the democracies to head off disaster. France thought Britain had benefited from Versailles at the cost of the French; Britain thought France was intent upon restoring itself as the leading military power on the Continent and therefore ignored the German threat. Thus the hierarchy of leadership had been destroyed in the central system, and each state vied with the others for a greater role, even as the legitimacy and stability of the system continued to crumble.

Second, *all three of the belligerents, Germany, Italy, and Japan, passed through critical points in the interval between 1933 and 1940.* Each of the governments that contemporary history holds responsible for brutal premeditated attacks on docile neighbors was undergoing wrenching change in its own foreign policy role and security position. This is the structural cause underlying their sudden increase in demands and bellicosity.

Germany had entered relative decline just after the turn of the century and continued on a deteriorating trajectory for two reasons. First, even within the European subsystem, it was beginning to feel the constraints of the upper asymptote on its relative power growth, even though its absolute growth far exceeded that of any other European nation. Second, it was unable to match the rapid industrial and population growth elsewhere in the system, most notably in the Soviet Union and the United States. Certainly, the effort to repay reparations, the wild inflation, and the effect of depression all hurt Germany, but many of these economic problems were also felt by other states. But as early as 1933, Germany, although continuing to decline in relative level, began to enjoy a reduction in the rate of decline.

Thus Germany had passed its second inflection point by the time Hitler embarked upon rearmament. All of the contradictions associated with this point on the power cycle were evident in Hitler's foreign policy: headiness that the rate of decline was falling off and could be turned around; fear that the level of relative decline nonetheless was continuing; bravado mixed with anxiety that could easily become paranoia. At the second inflection point, governments tend to overreach themselves. "[Hitler] overreached and exceeded his capabilities; his will overreached and exceeded his actual power" (Baumont 1978, p. 180). Hitler wanted to play for the highest stakes, Continental supremacy, driven onward by the contradictory push and pull of power signals at the second inflection point. Implicit in the comparative improvement in rate of growth at the second inflection point is the belief, or hope, that this improvement is permanent and of immediate impact in inverting the trend regarding level as well. Hence, a state which both fears further decline and desires increased interests may adopt the posture of a newly ascendant state.

Italy, albeit at a much lower level of capability than the other major players, passed through its first inflection point somewhere in the interval 1934–39. Mussolini captured the mood of the country – that Italy had a place in the central system which it had to advance before the "wolves" of that system stripped Italy of the opportunity. Fascism was just the ideology in which to make the appeal to foreign policy adventurism. It built on the aspirations of the Italian leadership to count for something in the central system while playing upon their anxieties about a sudden decline in the rate of power aggregation. The rapid improvement in the Italian power position since the beginning

155

of the twentieth century was beginning to slow. Fear of what this meant for the Italian foreign policy role, and for Italian security, was what Mussolini skillfully manipulated to keep himself in office and to plunge Italy into war at the side of Germany.

Japan on the eve of the war had crossed its first inflection point. Anxiety over the meaning of a slow-down in the rate of Japanese industrial advance was felt in its search for oil, iron ore, and other natural resources. In 1940, the United States chose exactly the wrong strategy to deal with a country undergoing the self-doubt and tumult of the first inflection. Instead of maintaining vigilance while acting nonmenacingly, it dropped its military defense while taking policy actions that were guaranteed to send shock waves through Tokyo. By cutting off sales of raw materials and recycled metals, the United States threatened Japan with future constraints on economic growth. At precisely the time that Japan discovered its own sudden decline in growth rate, with all of the ominous significance for its future foreign policy projections, it was confronted with external resource shortages that seemed to confirm its worst fears about decline.

Perhaps the denial to Japan of access to scrap metal and resources in the United States, combined with an apparently indifferent American defense, were the trip-wires that actually led to the bombing at Pearl Harbor. But Japanese anxiety over its capacity to continue its industrial development at the same pace, brought to the surface of official consciousness by the crossing of the inflection point, led Japan to risk massive force use to acquire oil fields in Indonesia and elsewhere in Asia. Like Germany, Japan also suddenly became preoccupied with the expansion of its *Lebensraum*, outside Manchuria and China, and throughout South-East Asia. Passage through a critical point simply heightened awareness of the limits on Japan's physical and territorial space in ways that were more pressing than before. If the rate of power growth was slipping, Japan had to strike out even faster and harder to assure that the "sun" would not set prematurely upon its fortunes.

Thus, at the systems level, aggregate structural change was exceeding the capacity of statecraft to assimilate such change. And at the level of the individual government, each of the belligerents crossed a critical point on its power curve that eased the step toward conquest. In addition, none of the power–interest gaps that plagued the system in 1914 had been satisfactorily resolved. Marshal Foch of the French General Staff, upon seeing the Versailles settlement, exclaimed, "This is not a Treaty, it is an Armistice for 20 years!" (Baumont 1978, p. 180). The power vacuum created by Austria–Hungary was not filled by dismantling the country into smaller, isolated units with no alliance cohesion to withstand revanche. Neither the United States nor the Soviet Union were prepared to assume the responsibilities that first France and then Britain after 1936 could no longer be expected to shoulder. Yet notwithstanding power–interest gaps, the international political landscape in a dynamic sense was very different in 1936 than in 1906. When a nation is in decline, its very demand for increased interests is questionable. What level of increase in interests for Germany would have been commensurate with its relative power position? Certainly not the seemingly unlimited increase envisioned by Hitler. Certainly not the illegitimate territorial claims on other sovereign states. The allies in the 1930s failed to learn the lessons of the First World War, or rather they failed to reach further back into history and to *unlearn* the mistakes and narrow response to those mistakes of 1914; and that failure greatly harmed their management of world order.

This is the third component of our explanation of what caused the war. The system responded to the gathering storm clouds in a fashion that the allies hoped would counter the mistakes of 1914. In fact, by so attempting to offset, in unimaginative and short-sighted ways, the mistakes that led to the First World War, they ended up repeating history. They precipitated the war instead of preventing it.

The appropriate solution to the "German problem" at the beginning of the century would have been to give Germany a larger place in the system commensurate with its larger share of power. An enhanced foreign policy role for Germany would have satisfied hurt German pride at being excluded from most of the colonial world and consigned to non-maritime status. A more self-confident Germany could have acted with more assurance in matters of Continental order-maintenance, restraining the weakened Austria–Hungary, as had Bismarck in 1886, but not doing its bidding unchecked. This larger diplomatic role would to some extent have come at the expense of the visibility and influence of France, Britain, and especially of Austria. But the resulting adjustment in status distribution and international political responsibility would have more than compensated them for their concessions.

Following this logic of the need for systemic adjustment, the future alliance partners proceeded to adopt independently and in opposition a very belated and inappropriate policy of appeasement toward Germany in the 1930s. Chamberlain tried to appease Hitler in Munich. France tried to ignore his aggression in Eastern Europe and Czecho-slovakia's pleas for assistance. The Soviet Union attempted to go a step further, ignoring all the dialectical opposites of fascist and

157

communist ideology, forging an actual military pact with Germany at Rapollo in 1922 (admittedly prior to the Nazi emergence), and again in 1939. Each government was attempting to undo the mistakes of 1914 with policies that ignored structural change and changed diplomatic circumstance. The resolution of the problems of 1914 could not fit the conditions of 1938 even with the best of diplomatic intention.

First, Hitler's Germany was not Wilhelmine Germany. Starting from virtually zero, Hitler had built a new and ominously powerful war machine by 1938. Wilhelm's war machine was offset by the equally large war machines of other members of the European system, so that each military arsenal at least could be interpreted as defensive. But Hitler's intentions regarding territorial aggression were not well-concealed. Furthermore, this type of mobilization of resources was precisely the type that the nineteenth-century balance of power was designed to offset. Mad though Hitler was, he was a careful observer of the balance of power; and, had it operated properly in 1936–38, he may not have taken the risks that he otherwise was able to convince the German people once again to shoulder. Evidence for this was the sudden caution expressed in his Reichstag speech of May 21, 1935 when challenged by the ill-conceived, yet coordinated challenge of the Stresa front (Baumont, p. 136). This was also the *post hoc* conclusion of Churchill:

> Up till the year 1934, the power of the conquerors remained unchall-enged in Europe and indeed throughout the world . . . [The] strict enforcement at any time till 1934 of the disarmament clauses of the Peace Treaty would have guarded indefinitely, without violence or bloodshed, the peace and safety of mankind. But this was neglected while the infringements remained petty, and shunned as they assumed serious proportions. Thus the final safeguard of a long peace was cast away. The crimes of the vanquished find their background and their explanation, though not, of course, their pardon, in the follies of the victors. Without these follies crime would have found neither temptation nor opportunity . . . [With hindsight, we see] how easily the tragedy of the Second World War could have been prevented; how the malice of the wicked was reinforced by the weakness of the virtuous . . . (Churchill 1948, pp. 14–16)

On the grounds of short-term mobilization of resources and aggressive intent, Hitler's government ought to have been opposed collectively by the same governments that instead chose to appease him.

Second, the allies misread the collective structural changes in the system. However well they understood their own positions of relative power, they were unable to put this information together in a more comprehensive sense and then collectively to act upon it. Their foreign policies did not reflect the fact that Germany by the mid-1930s was in substantial diplomatic decline relative to other major actors in the system and relative to Germany's position on its power cycle three decades earlier.

Hitler himself understood this dynamic. He used this understanding of imminent German decline in relative power to chastise the German people and goad them into military activity by belittling their past efforts and warning them that they would never again have a chance to predominate in world politics. Hitler used knowledge of the dynamic for a perverse and lamentable purpose – military onslaught against tired and piously hopeful neighbors (chapter 4). Germany was no longer a match for the principal members of the system, the United States and the Soviet Union. The system had grown up around Germany and dwarfed it.

It is tragic that the allies learned the lessons of the First World War only too well and were unwilling or unable to draw conclusions about the situation in 1938 that were much more in keeping with classical balance-of-power thought. German power and interest were not disparate, at least not on the side of a too-small German role in the international system. If anything, so much had changed in *structural* terms in three decades that German pretensions in 1938 were far greater than its actual capacity to assume enlarged diplomatic, economic, and even peace-keeping responsibilities. The shadow of the United States, of the Soviet Union, and in a complicated fashion, Japan (a country that was treated by the other allies in the 1930s much like Europe treated Germany in 1914), in each case was longer than that cast by Germany. Yet with the exception of Japan, none of these governments was clamoring for a larger world role. In fact, if the Soviet Union and the United States had been a bit less inward-looking and more self-confident regarding world responsibilities, Hitler would surely have had second thoughts about embarking on world conquest. Deterrence and only deterrence was a valid policy for the allies to have practiced in 1938. An equilibrium taking fully into account power and interest, and not treating one or other in isolation, would have led to this not-very-striking conclusion. But instead the allies ignored the imperatives of stable equilibrium and sought partial solutions based on partial lessons from history strongly influenced by their diplomatic errors in 1914.

A complete concept of stable equilibrium must take into account both ends and means. Disparities in either direction for any of the major actors in the system are dangerous and provocative of systemic

159

collapse, especially during rapid structural change when the nature of the system is being transformed.

In sum, the First World War might have been prevented if the declining states had been persuaded to yield to ascendant but interest-poor Germany a larger role in both the central system and in the colonial regions. This did not mean toleration of German aggression, against which defenses had to be maintained. On the contrary, transference of status and perquisites is an act of accommodation which is designed precisely to avoid military calamity in a period when systems transformation is advancing.

The Second World War might have been averted if the allies had *not* tried to correct their failures toward Germany prior to 1914 (and in the Versailles Treaty) by employing appeasement policies toward Hitler. That the appropriate strategy for dealing with Hitler was *collective military opposition* was not only evident because Hitler psychologically responded cautiously to strength, and because territorial and other claims threatening the security of another state are illegitimate and must not be condoned. A strategy of collective military opposition was also appropriate because Germany was in substantial decline and could no longer claim a large role in the international system. Its claims were illegitimate as well in the sense that they were excessive given the level and direction on its relative power curve.

Thus, order maintenance in one case required accommodating a belligerent state on the rise (Wilhelmine Germany), especially given a system in which the other states were no longer capable of maintaining existing interests. In the other case, order maintenance required balancing with military coordination a belligerent state in decline (Nazi Germany) making excessive and illegitimate demands for increased interests. In each instance, for equilibrium to have prevailed, the ascendant United States and Soviet Union ought to have taken a larger share of order-maintenance responsibilities appropriate to their power.

POSTSCRIPT TO HISTORIANS AND STATESMEN

Historians have recently shown a welcome sensitivity to the structural characteristics of world politics, confronting thereby the need for strategic judgments in the context of overall international relations theory.

In a penetrating critique of the origins of the two world wars, Donald Kagan (1987) draws the important insight "that today's discontented power [the Soviet Union] is in some respects more like the Kaiser's Germany than Hitler's." On the other hand, he establishes a single analogy between the two world wars and the present system which obscures the full implications of that insight: neither of the Germanys "could be appeased by reasonable concession. Both could be stopped only by effective deterrence or by war" (p. 39). This assessment implies that Germany was in the same structural situation *vis-à-vis* both capability and intentions (notwithstanding the greater "volatility" of Hitler) and had to be dealt with by means of the same strategy and tactics. According to this logic, if in each case Germany had been opposed by timely and active means, each war could have been averted.

Our preceding analysis shows there was a fundamental difference between these two periods in German history. In structural terms, the Kaiser's Germany was an ascendant power facing a number of states in advanced decline that nonetheless expected to hang on to all of their perquisites, status, and role responsibility. In contrast, Nazi Germany was in relative decline and thus was in no position to make legitimate further major claims for influence upon the system. Moreover, given the different structural circumstances, the Kaiser's Germany had a right to assert a more visible role for itself, accommodated by the declining powers, whereas Hitler's Germany required a strong military response and concerted military opposition. In each case, active defense of allied interests was essential, but only in the latter was the German intent unambiguously illegitimate, aimed at vital security interests of the other powers. The generative cause of the First World War was deeper, and without its resolution, would opposition have been *sufficient* to prevent the war?

This implication of structural change for order maintenance – the obligation of the European powers to accommodate Germany's rising relative power via commensurate increase in its foreign policy role in the system – runs counter to Paul Kennedy's (1980, 1988b) assessment of Britain's "grand strategy" in the late nineteenth century. Britain's so-called "graceful retreat" from world affairs (1988b) is laudable for its efforts to balance means with ends and its concern for Continental stability, but to focus its military strength on *opposition to Germany* was neither correct nor laudable grand strategy. As strategy, it was both misguided (based on illusions about the trends of relative power) and misdirected (designed precisely *not* to accommodate rising German power through a reordering of roles within the European system). The older powers had an obligation, which Nicholson, Churchill, and others at the time pointed out but Kennedy dismissed (1980, p. 467), to accommodate the rapidly rising power of Germany on the world

161

and European stages. The problem with the strategic component of the graceful retreat thesis is two world wars.

The argument that the First World War was a tactical "mistake" since Germany could have risen to European preeminence within a couple of decades otherwise captures balance-of-power logic but confuses absolute and relative power trends and the realities of statecraft at the time. Analysis must not dismiss the fuller range of strategic options, based on the differential power changes, actually considered by statesmen of the period. Of course Wilhelmine Germany's resort to force is totally unacceptable as a means to correct its perceived inequities. But if the purpose of analysis is to explain behavior rather than merely to provide moral judgment, the explanation is not difficult to ascertain. If the task of the analyst is to try to learn from past error, and to provide policy prescription, the causes of force use must be understood and, if possible, avoided or eliminated before that use occurs. Otherwise, all the burden for stability will fall on a military response, a response that may come too late to deter aggression.

Eric Hobsbawm (1989) is right, even if "imperialist rivalry" is taken to mean broader German claims for status and role, when he argues: "On the eve of 1914 colonial conflicts no longer appeared to raise insoluble problems for the various competing powers – a fact which has, quite illegitimately, been used to argue that imperialist rivalries were irrelevant to the outbreak of the First World War" (p. 311). Such rivalries and economic interests tend to be more important for rising states with a perceived interest deficit than for declining states. Pierre Renouvin (1969) shows that they had little to do with Hitler's war aims, but figured early in the calculations of rising Japan (p. 25).

As both Hobsbawm and A. J. P. Taylor warned, historical interpretation involves arguments that can be wrong. After the Second World War, the obvious causes of that war influenced interpretation of the First World War in such a way as to distort how statesmen actually wrestled with the dilemma of peaceful change, and why they failed.

Our own interpretation of the causes of the First World War established three errors of strategy on the part of the European powers which helped create excessive systemic disequilibrium. (1) In the 1860s, Britain agreed not to come to the aid of France in the event of war with Germany, rationalizing this decision on the grounds that Germany did have some basis for its claims on Alsace-Lorraine. Britain was still more concerned about the possibility of French revanche than about any threat from the new German state. It was still thinking in terms of the assimilative strategy worked out at the Congress of

162

Vienna so successfully in 1815, yet the structure of the system was changing one-half century later (Doran 1971). The new equilibrium strategy required a mix of firmness against territorial aggression, combined with acceptance of the new status to be accorded vibrant Prussia. (2) The continuing rise in German power after 1870 seemed to require no adjustment because of Bismarck's diplomatic adroitness in counterbalancing coalitions in favor of stability, albeit a rather static stability. Even Bismarck eventually succumbed to the rapidity of structural change, and to the new rigidities that emerged in response. (3) At the same time that Germany experienced an "inversion of force expectations" upon reaching its high point in about 1905, Britain fell prey to a similar response to its own comparative improvement in rate of growth, participating in a naval "arms race" rather than finally yielding some legitimate role and status to Germany to help it adjust to its critical point.

Further strategic errors at Versailles and in the 1930s exacerbated the earlier errors and again foreclosed the possibility of peaceful change. The latter error underscores the thesis that the timing of a policy is at least as important as its substantive content.

Robert Gilpin (1981) highlights E. H. Carr's argument that the strategy of appeasement in 1933 failed because Germany's high actualized power and new-found ambitions meant that any concession would only whet its appetite for more. This was precisely Churchill's argument. Power cycle theory asserts that there was no structural reason, no interest deficit, that legitimized the need for interest adjustments at that time; furthermore, Hitler's demands were not legitimate. The theory also acknowledges as partially correct Carr's statement that some "concessions to appease Germany's *legitimate* demands" were necessary but should have been made *much earlier*. But by arguing that concessions (not merely less punitive measures) should have been made to Germany *after the First World War at Versailles* rather than earlier, Carr revealed an essentially static understanding of this fundamental dilemma of order maintenance – a static view that implied policy recommendations that could have worsened rather than improved the chances of peaceful change.

Concessions to Germany's legitimate demands for increased role should have been made far in advance of Versailles in the period of rapid rise in German power: the First World War could have been prevented by a dynamic concept of general equilibrium. By Versailles, most of the legitimate demands were no longer valid because Germany had already entered relative decline. Such interest adjustments at Versailles may have served only to further frustrate Germany regarding its lost opportunity, for it certainly would not have been able to manage those additional interests to the same degree as it had anticipated during its years of rapid ascendance – as late as 1900 projecting a high point well into the third decade. But the greater danger of the static view of order maintenance – in particular, of the argument (expressed by many during the inter-war period) that actual concessions should have been made *at Versailles* – is that an error in timing of a policy feeds the fuel of aggression as much as does a mistake in substance. The Nazis used that very argument as an indicator of the softness of the allies' will and of their difficulties of balancing their interests and capabilities. To argue that mistakes were made at Versailles regarding supposed legitimate interests (rather than merely regarding the harshness of some of the punitive measures) was only to whet the German appetite for another attempt to obtain by force what even its opponents seemed to be asserting was "legitimately" theirs.

Therein lies the danger of Carr's partially correct conclusion. A policy of order maintenance depends essentially upon the dynamics of structural change: the legitimacy or justice of demands can only be defined in terms of the context of the power cycle dynamic. Had Carr been able to attain such a dynamic conception of order-maintenance and justice, he would have been less skeptical that a "harmony of interests" between states – a notion from the prior century – could ever again be invoked. He tried to replace this notion with that of a self-imposed state morality, responding to the break-down in public morality so glaring in that era of Stalin and Hitler. But deleting the *concept* of harmony, in international politics and economics, leaves a conceptual void. With such a void, international political order cannot be explained, nor can principles for its maintenance be adequately prescribed. Power cycle theory, in effect, fills this void by rescuing the notion of "harmony," but in the fuller context of an equilibrium of interests with power, an equilibrium sensitive to the dynamic of the state power cycles.

According to power cycle analysis, statesmen must seek a strategy that is both *appropriate and acceptable (satisfying)* regarding the *legitimate* demands of another state. The way to increase the likelihood of its being acceptable is for the strategy to aim at *preventing* the dissatisfactions and sense of threat associated with disequilibrium of power and interests. The "moral obligation" of a declining state to yield role and status need not conflict with its "moral right" to protect vital interests. As argued in chapter 7, justice involves much more than whether a state is "satisfied" with its power and interests in the system.

Our own analysis of the two world wars, through a dual analogy, becomes the prelude to the last section of this book in which we examine possible problems which structural changes may create for U.S.–Soviet relations and Soviet–Chinese relations in the coming decades. If the Soviet Union is more like the Kaiser's Germany than Hitler's, as Kagan says and as our own analysis indicates, then certain strategic responses ought to follow. But, for that very reason, it is essential that (1) that the correct structural dynamic for the Soviet Union be determined; (2) that the legitimacy of Soviet intentions be correctly and honestly assessed; and (3) that strategic responses appropriate to different structural dynamics be ascertained. Where is the Soviet Union on its power cycle, and where is it likely to be in the near future? What will the nature and scope of Soviet interests be at those respective times? These questions must be answered in the context of other power and interest changes occurring throughout the system. Adaptation to the timing of change is an imperative, and in the coming decades statesmen must determine how this timing of relative power change will affect Soviet foreign policy outlook, Japanese, Chinese, and European international political interests and roles, and the strategies and instruments available to the United States and its allies.

What combination and sequence of strategies is most likely to maintain world order during advanced systems transformation? Power cycle analysis has shown why the policies chosen failed historically. We now turn to the more challenging task of asking whether certain combinations and sequences of strategies, taking the structural dynamic and legitimacy of claims into consideration, can be a more reliable guide to peaceful resolution of the trauma of systems transformation. World order is neither fortuitously achieved nor automatically sustained. Statesmen must nurse a genuine equilibrium into existence, and the lessons of history revealed by power cycle analysis may assist diagnosis and prescription.

7 WORLD ORDER AND SYSTEMS TRANSFORMATION: GUIDELINES FOR STATECRAFT

IN SEARCH OF A DURABLE CONCEPT OF WORLD ORDER

A central proposition of this study is that major war can be dissociated from systems transformation. We have demonstrated that failure to manage systems transformation properly has led to extensive war. But while systems transformation cannot be avoided, it can and must be made more responsive to administrative control.

To use an analogy, systems transformation is a period in history which is like the traffic situation at a busy intersection. Along normal stretches of the road, drivers are allowed to pass each other and do so without catastrophe according to well-developed "rules of the road" that are akin to the "norms" of the balance of power. But when drivers attempt anything unusual in a busy intersection (e.g., acceleration, deceleration, change of lanes, passing, or taking their eyes off the road), they are inviting accident, major accident. Too much traffic activity is taking place to make clear judgments.

Hence we come to the crux of the problem of maintaining international political order and of coping with structural change. Statesmen must have sufficient vision as well as diplomatic skill so as to constitute a new world order even as the old equilibrium is being undermined by change which cannot be halted.

From the power cycle perspective, world order is a set of variable relations among states that is reasonably compatible with their values and goals and that is constructed on a stable equilibration of power and interests. This definition starts from values and goals (interests) and then encompasses means (power). It begins with the actor and moves toward the system. The very definition of world order is shaped around the notion of a general international political equilibrium encompassing changing interests and power. For world order to prevail, this equilibrium must be stable, that is, capable of being sustained in the face of competitive disagreement and uncertainty.

166

The set of relations constituting world order suggests some patterned or norm-like behavior on the part of the leading states. In a decentralized international system, world order is what distinguishes that system from one in which anarchy prevails. In anarchy, the normal mix of competition and cooperation in human affairs shifts toward a monopoly of the former, and the anticipated consequence is increased tension, political uncertainty, and violent conflict. Pure competition is undesirable in a system in which law is weak and the means of violence are quite accessible. Perfect cooperation is impossible in such a system because no actor has sufficient confidence in the operation of such a system to trust the commitments of the other actors. World order is a measure of the extent to which competitive relations are replaced by more cooperative relations in a more relaxed and productive international political atmosphere still marked by the struggle over the distribution and management of scarce resources.

World order at a minimum means absence of major war, measured by a high score on three indices: intensity (casualties), duration (nation-months at war), and magnitude (number of participants times power rank). In the nuclear age, duration may shrink and the number of combatants may be few, but the destructiveness of nuclear weapons and the sophistication of transport capacity may be sufficient to cause enormous casualties. Or, nuclear war could be protracted, especially if governments opt for isolated tactical uses of nuclear weaponry that do not escalate. But unless two or more major participants in the system become involved in such a war, it is still not likely to be regarded, as were the wars of France's Louis XIV, for example, as altering the general equilibrium of the world system. Truly major war, however indexed, signifies a collapse of world order.

The essence of the management of systems transformation is that rapid structural change must be allowed to proceed without an increase in the likelihood of major war. Major war cannot, by default, be the arbiter of future systems.

GENERAL INTERNATIONAL POLITICAL EQUILIBRIUM AND WORLD ORDER

The balance-of-power idea as classically regarded, either as a full-blown system of international relations, or merely as the functional attribute of some other type of system, was flawed. The conception of equilibrium that it conveyed was very partial and incomplete. It focused on one aspect of balance only, namely, how power itself was to be equilibrated among states.

Other alternatives to balance of power – formalized collective security, the League of Nations, the United Nations, deterrence in its various forms – all experienced shortcomings as well and possess no track record of superior peace-keeping accomplishment (Bleicher 1971; Claude 1962). Yet the deficiencies of the balance of power cannot be excused by shortcomings of other techniques of order-maintenance.

Ultimately, successful statesmanship on the balance-of-power chessboard requires an understanding of the power cycle of the nation–state. The statics of power balancing on the horizontal plane of analysis have to be informed by the dynamics of upward and downward movement of nation–states in power terms, and in terms of what this movement means for interests. By combining the horizontal and vertical perspectives of analysis, and including the relation between power and interests, the logic of partial equilibrium expressed in the balance-of-power notion makes way for a more encompassing concept of general international political equilibrium as a basis for world order.

(1) Power balancing

Power balancing, or balance, is a term we will use for short-term strategic power considerations, our so-called horizontal plane of analysis. Power is balanced in this short-term sense in essentially two ways, internally via a mobilization of forces and other capability, or externally via the formation of coalitions and formal alliances. The key in each case is to aggregate power in the short run to offset potential aggression facilitated by sudden, high actualization of the power base of a belligerent. In the *long run*, however, power can be neither artificially augmented nor satisfactorily constrained by these internal and external efforts to bolster it.

Aggregation of power by State A to offset growing aggressiveness on the part of a recently more powerful State B is not appropriate as a long-term strategy. If State A has merely actualized a larger part of its resource base, it very likely could successfully handle this kind of threat from a rising power in the short run. But if such a balance-of-power mode is pursued over long time periods, the only consequence is the ever more strained attempt by State A to augment a smaller and smaller relative base of national capability while attempting to hold on to the same role and responsibilities in the international system.

The glaring gap between power and interest for the declining state cannot be artificially bolstered through alliance arrangements either. Other more powerful actors must take over the leadership roles in the system, or the responsibilities of leadership must be adequately redistributed among several actors. Otherwise, the danger of an attempt at radical restructuring by an ascendant but dissatisfied state is quite likely.

The flexibility needed to make balance-of-power strategies more successful in both the short and long term is a different kind of balancing that is at once internal to a state and external.

(2) Equilibrating interests *vis-à-vis* power

In a system composed of two states, a decline in State A's interests may lag behind a decline in its relative power. This lag results perhaps because governing elites in State A are reluctant to "move over" and to allow State B to adopt a larger systemic role, or perhaps because of initial hesitancy on the part of domestic elites in State B to assume larger systemic responsibilities. But, eventually, as the power of State A declines and that of B increases, the interests of State A will begin to contract and those of State B will begin to expand.

None of this adjustment suggests that the universe of power or interests in the system is static; indeed, it is expanding in the sense that growth is likely in the absolute levels of capability and in the nature of interests. Note that adjustment involves changes in both power and interests.

General international political equilibrium involves dual adjustment – adjustment internal to the state and adjustment external to it between states – in a two or three stage process. External pressure for adjustment may occur first. The state sees that its power is slipping, or other states in the system by various initiatives may remind it of that fact. They may challenge it and probe for tactical weakness, and it may find that it is no longer able to live up to its obligations. The view that South Korea was such a probe by the Soviet Union is supported by theory (George and Smoke 1974).

Domestic foreign policy elites inside the state must then invoke the next stage of adjustment. They must either decide to seek accommodation through a contraction in the scope and magnitude of state interests abroad or attempt to deal with the consequences of inaction for their own security. When the state brings its interests into alignment with its power, the second stage of the adjustment process has been completed.

State B and other states are then free to make adjustments accordingly in the scope and magnitude of their own interests to make them consonant with their own relatively larger capability – the third

169

adjustment stage. Power and interests are now balanced *internal* to each state and *externally*, and general equilibrium once again prevails throughout the system.

The adjustments required for maintaining such equilibrium, however, are not so easily effected. First, either the declining state or the rising state may not want to yield to necessity. The declining state may refuse to acknowledge the disparity between its surplus of ends and paucity of means. It may instead attempt to hang on to vestiges of past prestige and systemic responsibility until other countries on the ascendant attempt to wrench part of that process away, perhaps by armed force. On the other hand, the rising state may not want to assume the burdens and costs of increased leadership. If both of these situations occur, the disequilibrium will become even greater, and the adjustment will become even more difficult to effect.

This situation ultimately reverts to a second situation in which a rising power demands adjustment on the part of one in decline, or a declining power tries to use force to retain those interests it can no longer legitimately claim based on its power trajectory. The difficulty of adjustment depends in part upon when that demand occurs – upon how great is the disequilibrium, how capable is the declining power of protecting those disputed interests, and upon whether the state is experiencing the trauma of sudden alteration in foreign policy projection at a critical point.

Suppose in our example that State A declines incrementally for several decades but attempts to conceal this decline from its citizens and from State B through a combination of foreign policy pomp and contrived activity. It cedes no interests or responsibility and claims the same foreign policy role that it had earned decades earlier. This is the position taken by the Ottoman Empire in the first half of the nineteenth century (Kinross 1977; Shaw 1976). Such disparity between means and ends in foreign policy is not likely to go unnoticed even if it is partially concealed through a veil of formal alliances and lofty statecraft. State B may become restive under the circumstances of this situation and frustrated because of a perception that the system is artificially constraining its power and foreclosing a larger foreign policy role in world affairs that is rightfully its own. Both Russia and Prussia asserted this prerogative at various times in the early nineteenth century *vis-à-vis* the Ottoman (Jelavich 1964). Such rifts in the fabric of international political equilibrium are most likely to become evident at critical points on a nation's power cycle when the government is *forced* to come to terms with its sense of historical destiny. The heightened sense of tension during those periods introduces further rigidities toward change and increases the probability of major war.

In an *n*-actor system, individual sources of disequilibrium may stand out as starkly as in the two-actor version of the system. But a reequilibration of interests *vis-à-vis* changes in relative power has so many pathways that disagreement over the preferable pathway may overshadow the benefits of the redistribution. This third dilemma for adjustment is tied to a fourth.

Redistribution of interests may not go smoothly or evenly since there is no arbitrator or other authority to so manage the process, and since rules are ambiguous as to who should assume what. In practice, states clamor for what they can get. Indeed, regarding *vital interests* such as territorial sovereignty, no massive *peaceful* adjustment has ever occurred historically except *after* the wars fought over them, through the peace conferences at the end of major wars. Important incremental redistribution of non-vital foreign policy interests, however, can and must occur at other times so as to prevent disequilibrium from building up and to prevent these other interests from becoming confused with true vital interests. Not to do so is to guarantee that warfare will become the arbiter.

Equilibrium deals with the *responsibilities* of states, individually and collectively, to prevent disequilibrium and tensions conducive of instability. But it also deals with the *rights* of states, individually and collectively, as members of the global political community to possess a role commensurate with their power. When the power of a state increases substantially over time, the state has a *right* to expect greater leadership and order-maintenance functions. On the other hand, it has the *responsibility*, given its increased capability in the system, to assume this greater leadership function and the financial and political costs associated with it.

Conversely, if power is in decline, the declining state has an *obligation* to acknowledge this relative decline by ceding some of its interests to other states in the system and by yielding some of its status and salience. When the declining state no longer has the same capabilities to enforce order maintenance, it has the *right* to expect that other states better endowed should assume such tasks.

(3) Preventing systemic disequilibrium and the inversion of force expectations

Analysis in this book has argued that passage through a critical point activates the "anticipatory mode" of transformation: new

171

projections of future power and role suddenly increase the salience of existing disequilibria between power and interest. New projections of future role and security outlook rapidly set off change in the productive, interventionary, and strategic modes as well. Regarding the latter, a so-called "counterintuitive mechanism" (which does not apply under normal circumstances) of inverted force expectations rapidly moves these processes of systems change into a situation of greater tension with an increased likelihood of major war. How structural disequilibrium stimulates a "disequilibrium of behavioral response" leading to massive war is the issue we return to here.

The view that systems transformation predicts to massive war when there is such a power–interest disequilibrium at the systemic level emerged from historical study of hegemony and assimilation and was subsequently applied to the rank disequilibrium paradigm. A similar interpretation of international political reality has been gleaned by a number of analysts from a variety of perspectives. For instance, George Liska (1957, p. 15) argued from history and theory that equilibrium occurs "when individual states feel that the existing distribution of security, welfare, and prestige is the best possible one relative to their power positions, and could not be substantially improved by unilateral efforts at redistribution." More recently, Robert Gilpin (1981), linking the status disequilibrium paradigm, the dilemma of peaceful change, and hegemonic stability theory, argued that massive war results from "disequilibrium in the international system [which] is due to increasing disjuncture between the existing governance of the system and the redistribution of power in the system." Gilpin also recognized the limits of the hegemonic stability conception of order maintenance in not being able to resolve that dilemma. Although those analysts do not utilize the notion of a power cycle, and do not further develop the dynamics of equilibrium and disequilibrium, the interpretations are complementary and the explanations for forces underlying equilibrium and disequilibrium are reinforcing.

Equilibrium occurs when there are no gross inconsistencies between the claims a government makes upon the system in terms of role and asserted responsibility and the capability it possesses to make these claims legitimate in the eyes of its own constituents, or policy elite, and the other governments in the system. Systems transformation from one condition of structural equilibrium to another will occur regardless of the purposeful actions of statesmen. Hence, the time to do something about disequilibrium is when the first structural flaws appear, not when the structure of the system is nearing collapse under

172

the additional weight of fear and divergent understanding accompanying critical change.

How can the architect of foreign policy prevent an inversion of force expectations from occurring? Since it is this abnormal set of expectations about force which leads to massive war, this is the principal question facing statesmen during systems transformation. Once a crisis involving inverted force expectations begins, very little in all probability can be done to stop it. Hence the frustration and horror expressed by some of the diplomats and observers at their own inability to halt the conflict process as the events of the First World War, for example, sadly unfolded. The time to manage world order, to prevent a situation where statesmen are virtually trapped into inverted force expectations, is when gross disparities between interest and capability come to be evident for some of the leading states in the system.

In our application of the inversion-of-expectations syndrome to the arms race setting (Doran 1980a), we showed how the nature of the "game" can be altered during crisis periods from a stable to a non-stable situation where fear and uncertainty preclude a return to the rules of normal behavior. But must the "game" be so altered? Must the line regarding role ascription become more inelastic? Here we will analyze a similar phenomenon in the realm of energy economics to show (1) how a disparity of interests and capability gives rise to inverse force expectations, and (2) how early management of this disparity might have precluded the rise of such inverted expectations. Such analogies, while certainly not perfect and while involving different assumptions about competition and strategy, are nonetheless quite instructive.

An inversion of energy expectations. When energy prices shot up fourfold in November of 1973, the dynamic that drove them there was an inversion of the normal expectations about supply and demand (Doran 1980a; Conant 1982; Shwadran 1985). Normally, when price goes up, two kinds of behavior follow. Buyers drop out of the market until price comes down again; sellers enter the market to take advantage of the improvement in prices. A new price/quantity equilibrium emerges where price declines and the quantity offered of a good increases. But, under the circumstances of the oil embargo of October 1973, the opposite set of market expectations occurred.

As the price of crude oil increased, buyers bought more oil, not less, under the abnormal (inverted) expectation that the future price of oil would go even higher; producers of oil sold less oil, not more, under

173

the similarly abnormal market expectation that despite the initial price increase, the price would go much higher, thus enabling them to get even a better return in the future. Expectations about price were exactly inverted from those that normally clear the market.

The conditions that underlay the inversion of energy price expectations in 1973 are likewise instructive regarding how to manage systems transformation. Prior to 1973, the "management" of the world oil market occurred through the collaboration of the Texas Railroad Commission, an administrative body with authority over the large East Texas oil fields, and the major oil companies. But, as far back as 1971, the East Texas production of crude oil was at "100 percent allowable" (that is, it was producing at a maximum level), the price of oil had not been raised to equilibrate the market in accordance with this level of production, and the world demand for oil was pushing consumption further upwards everywhere. Under these conditions, no one in actuality was in control of oil price, and this price was up for grabs by any producer with excess production capacity. Saudi Arabia more than anyone else possessed such excess capacity, and the events of the October War precipitating the oil embargo enabled Saudi Arabia and a few other OPEC members to discover the leverage that they in fact had possessed for at least two years but that had gone unused.

In short, what led to the inversion of energy price expectations in 1973 was a *world-wide disparity* between *burgeoning demand* and *recalcitrant supply* that was ignored and unmanaged. If the United States and the other oil consumers could have allowed the oil price to rise more rapidly in the late 1960s, some of the demand would have disappeared and more non-OPEC supply would have come on line; hence no disparity between supply and demand would have occurred, and the power over energy pricing would not have shifted from the Texas Gulf Coast to the Persian/Arab Gulf. But the oil price revolution of 1973 was set into motion by a wild inversion of price expectations in November caused by this *unmanaged widening gap* between world demand for petroleum and world supply. The only way to have prevented the abrupt and excessive climb in oil prices in 1973 was for the consumer nations and oil companies to have addressed the gap in world oil supply and demand sooner, and the gap was indeed evident at least as early as 1971.

PREVENTING INVERSION OF FORCE EXPECTATIONS

The analogy to international political equilibrium is clear. The way to manage world order so as to prevent the conditions emerging where force expectations are inverted is the timely elimination of aggravated disparities between state interests and capabilities among the leading actors.

Where such disparities do not occur, the situation of normal force expectations conducive of security and equilibrium prevails. A potential aggressor is discouraged from using force because to do so would unleash overwhelming force against itself and against the interests it has secured. A potential defender or deterrer is discouraged from using force because its expectation is that its security is guaranteed without having to actually employ force. It therefore is able to hold force prudently in reserve but not actually to use that force. Attitude and action are highly elastic.

Conversely, in the situation where an aggravated disparity of interests and means exists within the international system, a quite different set of force expectations may begin to emerge. A rising nation, for example, may see that its means exceed the interests acknowledged by the other members of the system and yet that its rate of growth has suddenly slackened, threatening the interests it already legitimately claims but has not yet obtained as well as lessening the rate at which it might be able to obtain more interests in the future. Frustrated and possibly even belligerent, this potential aggressor feels justified in using force to obtain what negotiation and the normal rules of international politics have denied it.

Likewise, in this example, a leading nation now in relative decline becomes conscious of a growing disparity between its own interests and its means, and hence, in the absence of the creation of a new more acceptable equilibrium, feels compelled to use force as a defense or deterrent to protect its interests since in the future it will have even less relative capability at its disposal. Thus, out of this inversion of force expectations on each side comes the climactic deployments of massive force from which neither actor or set of actors feels able or inclined to back down. Force, instead of acting as the arbiter of peace, becomes the fulcrum of all-out war. Attitudes rigidify.

Only by eliminating or curbing the emergent disparity of means and ends within the international system can this catastrophic breakdown of the norms of world order be averted. It does little good to lament the "hardening of the international atmosphere" or the "spiraling of hostility" once the inversion of force expectations on each side of the dispute is unleashed. Management of the crisis must predate the last minute rush into war. By identifying disparities of interest and capability early, and by employing the proper mix of adaptation and power balancing, the true crisis often associated in the past with

175

systems transformation can be averted. Normal expectations about force use and security can once again be restored and international political equilibrium will prevail.

Jervis' deterrence model and the power cycle

It is instructive to see how this general equilibrium notion resolves some of the questions raised by other studies probing mechanisms for peaceful resolution of conflicts. Jervis (1976) contrasts the "spiral model" of decision interaction where one threat leads to another in a series of counterpoised escalations, with the "deterrence model" in which the use of threatened action halts a hostile response. He asks what circumstances account for the difference in the two models of foreign policy behavior and the basis of the difference in the two sets of actor responses. His hypotheses are drawn from the short-term decision environment and include the costs of "standing firm," risk-aversion, the prospect of retreating without breaking important commitments, and whether the deterrer refrains from humiliating the other actor.

Power cycle theory offers an additional explanation for why deterrence may succeed or fail depending upon the position of the challenger (deterred state) on the power curve. *Other things being equal* (e.g., clearly defined rules of arbitration, certainty regarding appropriate adjustment requirements, and the like), the deterrent model is more likely to prevail over the spiral model when the deterred state is outside a critical interval on its power cycle, rather than inside. Furthermore, the likelihood of its success increases as well when the deterred state is in decline rather than in ascendancy. The first hypothesis is explained by the abruptness of adjustment and the psychological tumult experienced by decision makers attempting to traverse a critical interval and hence the greater likelihood there of irrational, unconstrained action such as aggression and the inversion of force expectations which escalate resulting conflicts. The second hypothesis is explained by the lack of legitimacy associated with claims made by the state in decline since it is already likely to possess a surplus of interests over capability and is therefore on very weak ground to convince the deterrer to yield. Conversely, a state in the ascendancy, possessing because of lag effects a deficit of interests over capability, will be a much tougher actor to oppose because of the legitimacy of its claims on the system. Thus the long-term dynamics of the power cycle will contribute to an understanding of when and where the spiral versus the deterrence model will better apply.

In sum. International political equilibrium seeks to achieve adjustment through the transfer of legitimate interests and obligations in the international system from the declining polity to the ascending polity. *The essential territorial sovereignty of the declining state is not affected by the transfer.* What is affected is its foreign policy role, its prestige, and its place in the international political hierarchy. World order is preserved, not by an accretion of power and a confrontational approach as in the balance of power, but through an adaptational approach involving an accommodation of interests to reflect the diminished power base of the declining actor (Mansbach and Vasquez 1981).

A disparity between means and ends in the foreign policy of individual states inevitably creates disequilibrium. Where means/ends disparities are multiple and highly visible, because a number of states are passing through a critical point on their respective power curve in about the same historical period, the system itself is undergoing metamorphosis, and general international political equilibrium is most strained. The transformation *will* occur, but the disequilibrium need not become so excessive that an inversion of force expectations throughout the system escalates the anxieties into all-out systemic warfare. This most difficult test of statecraft is to help nurse the system gently back into equilibrium and to facilitate the orderly transformation of systems.

We turn to the main task of this chapter: to determine adjustment procedures that are appropriate to the structural dynamics existing at any given time.

POLICY RECOMMENDATIONS FOR EQUILIBRIUM AND WORLD ORDER DURING SYSTEMS TRANSFORMATION

The process of systems transformation encounters an initial cause or set of conditions responsible for the onset of major war, an efficient or immediate cause of war occurring most probably in a critical interval on the power cycle of an aggressor, and efforts by the defender states to manage it.

The relationship between the prevailing authority structure of the system and the disposition of potential challengers is a key consideration with respect to whether the system remains stable during transformation (Figure 7.1). Fundamentally, two types of actor disposition exist and two types of systemic response to challenge are possible. Either challengers are rising powers whose interests lag behind the increase in capability because the competitive international

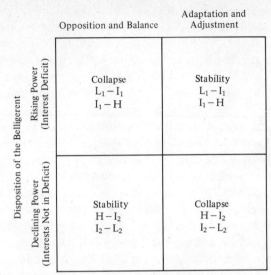

Figure 7.1 Conditions of equilibrium

system refuses to make room for these actors at the top of its hierarchy. Or the challengers are declining powers and there is no interest deficit (since the role of the state in the system ought to diminish as its capability diminishes) yet the state uses force to try to restore its fallen status and position within the hierarchy of states.

In each case, the challenger may be regarded as a source of disruption and as a threat to the continuity of world order. But the two situations in reality are very different. Not only does one involve rising power, the other declining power; in the former situation a legitimate grievance may exist if the state has been denied an appropriate role in the creation and management of world order and in the functions that yield status and visibility to foreign policy conduct despite an increase in its capability to carry out such responsibilities. In the latter situation, there has been no denial of role by the other members of the system and hence no justification for a challenge to the authority arrangements and international regimes that characterize the system. Responses to each of these separate threats to world order must therefore be very different.

In general, the members of the central system, threatened by a challenger, have two choices. (1) They can oppose the challenger by force, and can seek to balance the challenger by forming a coalition against it. (2) They can seek to adjust their own foreign policy behavior

178

so as to appease the challenger and to make greater room for it in the councils of the central system through adaptation. The basic thrust of these choices is very different. One is to constrain the actions of the challenger by opposition; the other is to yield place for the challenger so as to create a larger role for it in regime and order maintenance. The determination of which choice is the correct choice in a particular circumstance is central to the preservation of peace during systems transformation.

The decision to oppose is the correct decision when the challenger, despite its declining power base, threatens to use force to expand territorially. There is no plausible international political justification for this attempt to restore historical stature, either real or assumed, by this confrontation with the other principal actors. The use of force by the challenger is provocative and belligerent. To respond in any other way than through balance and opposition is likely to be interpreted by the challenger as a sign of weakness and will be exploited.

Conversely, if an ascendant state, experiencing resistance to an expanding role for itself because of the reluctance of others to cede interests and responsibilities, challenges the prevailing international regime and is met with forceful opposition, the triggering condition for major war is at hand. Legitimate demand for a larger role commensurate with growing power is met by illegitimate but forceful opposition. War is likely to follow.

On the other hand, if the frustrated, interest-deficit ascendant state is dealt with fairly and reasonably, there is some chance of diffusing a conflict before it becomes serious. Those older members of the system in decline must cede some of their status and responsibilities to the newly ascendant state. Adjustment within the composition and status-ordering of the central system will tend to reduce tensions between the new and old members. Interests and responsibilities can shift without sacrificing the security of individual members and without endangering the pluralism and decentralized nature of the global system.

Whether systems transformation is peaceful is a direct result of how it is managed by the leading states (Doran 1971; Rosecrance, Alexandroff, Healy, and Stein 1974; Zartman and Berman 1982, pp. 47–49). When a balance-of-power approach to challenge is worked out and attuned to the disposition of the declining actor, keeping it within proper territorial limits, peace is likely to prevail despite tension and turbulence. When a response employing judicious adjustment and compromise of state interest becomes necessary in the face of rising power and a new interest deficit on the part of a government that is a potential challenger to the other members of the system, stability once again is feasible, despite background conditions of structural change that are not optimal. But to confuse these responses is to jeopardize the long-term stability of world politics. In sum, to understand the utility of each response in the appropriate circumstance is to begin to manage systems transformation successfully.

Strategies to cope with order-maintenance

The international political dilemma for a principal actor is two-fold. It must continue to preserve its own security and that of governments dependent upon it, and it must attempt to promote stability during systems transformation. The dilemma is particularly acute if the state is in decline. Hence, our discussion of techniques of order maintenance will focus on the types of problems which weaker states or states in decline must deal with when confronted by a challenger state. If the challenger is itself in decline, we have argued, opposition and balance are the correct strategies. How then can states themselves in decline confront the challenge of systemic unrest from a belligerent declining power?

Opposition and balance. When the challenger is in decline and this general response is called for, a state – especially a declining state – has a limited number of strategies available to it.

(1) Actualization of the capability base is a plausible first consideration. But for reasons earlier discussed, actualization may be very difficult because other commitments of resources for social or political purpose may be compelling, the economy may be at or near full employment, fear of inflation may discourage initiative, actualization that is misinterpreted may trigger an arms race, or bureaucratic and market flexibility and mere political will may be lacking. But actualization of capability is a first recourse because all control of decision-making lies within the state undertaking the effort.

(2) New coalition formation, another common strategy, is facilitated by the sense of threat felt by the other governments in the face of belligerence from a challenger. New coalition formation may also create difficulties for a major state with many other alliance commitments since the commitments required of the state may begin to outweigh the defense contribution of the new member (Deibel 1988; Weinstein 1969). Many small members add little to the deterrent effect of new coalition formation, since it is difficult to aggregate or make congruent their contributions.

The principal advantage of coalition formation as a means of opposing belligerency is that it is cheap. It makes use of someone else's resources. Its shortcoming is that it may not be credible because of the unreliability of commitments.

(3) Redistribution of alliance burdens is a way for a declining state to offset the military advance of a belligerent without forcing a restructuring of the alliance (Myers ed. 1980; Krauss 1986). The new strength of the alliance is not lessened if, although the leading member faces cutbacks because of relative decline, the other members pick up the slack in the collective interest of preserving order. The problem is that reallocation of alliance burdens is unlikely, as the experience in NATO reveals, unless the threat of a shake-up of commitments or a restructuring takes place. As long as the members' sense of threat does not increase, complacency sets in.

Redistribution of alliance burdens may become easier, as the Canadian experience shows, if two considerations are met (Kirton 1972; Jockel and Sokolsky 1986). A defense-sharing arrangement can be worked out with the alliance leader so that the economic costs of purchases by the smaller member can at least partially be offset by purchases of goods and services in that state. Second, and with less evident success in the Canadian case, a sense of specific mission clearly identified with the defense contribution of each state is helpful in obtaining domestic political support for a redistribution of defense burdens proportionate to the state's size and wealth.

(4) The state in relative decline, in the effort to offset a belligerent that is also in decline but is attempting to alter the status quo by force, may also find advantage in adopting an opposition strategy that employs lower-cost tactics. The first such tactic is to address more fully one's comparative advantage in military preparedness (Huntington 1983). If one's advantage favors capital over labor or territory over capital, one's defensive effort ought to reflect this advantage so as to augment defensive activity per unit of resources expended. This logic may lead to greater reliance on technology, for example, and less upon personnel. There are clear limits to this kind of reliance upon comparative advantage, as the retreat from the doctrine of massive retaliation implied in the 1960s for the United States.

A second way to employ lower cost tactics may be to place the belligerent state in the opposite military posture from that which it traditionally has assumed. If the belligerent has traditionally employed guerilla warfare to advance its interests, because these tactics are inexpensive, the declining state seeking to defend its interests and those of its allies may have to shift to support for

181

subconventional warfare against the interests of the advancing belligerent. Accustomed always to being on the offensive, the expansionist state will then discover that it must also defend its past gains at considerably higher cost than it had previously been accustomed to pay.

(5) Transference of responsibilities to a trusted client-successor state having similar interests and outlook on international politics may be a timely kind of last resort for the polity that must contend with expansionism on the part of a belligerent. Finding the client-successor is tougher than merely identifying a government with a potential for increased regional or global visibility. The client-successor must have internal political stability and a capacity for prudent foreign policy conduct. More than this, the client-successor must in general share the values and foreign policy outlook of the state seeking to transfer responsibilities.

Adaptation and adjustment.   In general, adaptation and adjustment is the correct response when the potential belligerent is a rising state showing signs of anxiety, perhaps over its recently discovered falling rate of power growth but in particular harboring frustration and bitterness over its exclusion from systemic leadership (interest deficit). The challenger will in the future have more power, not less, and it is likely to become more aggressive, not less so, since the disparity between its perceived interests and its actual capability will have widened. Under these circumstances of power–interest disparity, opposition will only incite the state to contemplate aggression to force a new arrangement of role and status on the system. Prudent adjustment of interests and responsibilities among the leading powers is necessary to forestall collapse during systems transformation.

(1) For the state that feels discriminated against by a system that seems unresponsive to its growing capability, symbolic enhancement of role is very important. Symbolic role enhancement can take many forms. Historically, cooptation of a state into formal diplomatic proceedings signified a new role. Formal diplomatic recognition and exchange of ambassadors carries symbolic importance. Acknowledgment by the United States that the People's Republic of China ought to sit on the UN Security Council was an excellent example of symbolic role enhancement (Pollack 1978).

Symbolic role enhancement does not seem costly. It confers prestige and at no monetary cost. But behind the conferral of prestige is a genuine transfer of privilege, place, and opportunity. Awareness of this transmittal is what causes governments to begrudge the use of symbolic role enhancement. It is what follows role enhancement that worries the transmitter.

Yet there is in actuality little to fear from symbolic role enhancement. It is a way of diffusing hostility by inclusion rather than by exclusion and opposition. Whatever additional influence symbolic role enhancement provides would be obtained in any case, perhaps by far less attractive means. Instead of inviting through recalcitrance a potential recipient to take by force a new role, the symbols and perquisites of that role are advanced with grace and magnanimity. The role is not hollow. Political substance is also conveyed. But the sting of denial has been eliminated from the political equation at the top of the system at a crucial time of its transformation.

(2) Altered participation in multilateral activity is another benign method of diffusing build-ups of hostility over a deficit of state interest relative to growing power. Many organizations such as the United Nations and the International Labor Organization are virtually universal. But many important organizations are exclusive, that is, by invitation only. Even though the substantive criteria for membership have been met, membership in the International Monetary Fund, in the General Agreement on Tariffs and Trade, or in other economic forums is often by invitation. It has been said, for example, that the invitation to Canada to join the Club of Seven noncommunist industrial states for their annual meetings was the single most important event affecting Canadian foreign policy in more than a decade (Putnam and Bayne 1984).

Decisions to invite or not to invite a state to participate in multilateral activity are contested among the participants. Out of pride, a government will often feign reluctance to show interest in an invitation but indirectly will let friendly governments know of its availability. Germany, for example, envied the colonial empires of Great Britain and France. The tensions in Northern Africa and in Persia led in no small way to the sense of ostracization felt by Germany in 1914 in a way that was never understood in Paris or London.

Participation in multilateral activity, even if a direct benefit ensues such as access to aid or technology, will normally not be sufficient to dissuade a government bent upon force to acquire territory from doing so. The key is to coopt a state early enough into the "family of nations" or an "economic club" or an "educational and cultural exchange" such that pent-up frustration and aggression is allowed to vent itself *before* plans for military expansion are already in place. Increased visibility and functional activity place obligations on a government. These obligations, plus the added status associated with collective involvement, can have a positive impact on the sense of role and place felt by a society and its government. Even more tellingly, poignant exclusion can act as an irritating stimulus to aggression at a time when background structural factors are likewise conducive.

(3) Opportunity for increased mediation and peacekeeping activity at the local or regional level can usefully occupy the energies of an ascendant actor, although such activity can very easily be abused. France, regarded as a candidate for revanche after the Congress of Vienna in 1815, used involvement in the Spanish Civil War as a way of breaking out of the "pillars" erected around it. Peacekeeping activity, when not multilateral, can become an excuse for military intervention and occupation. Multilateral peace-keeping activity composed of rival and uncooperative governments can become more a problem than a solution. But, properly administered and safeguarded, increased mediation and peace-keeping activity can become a method of diverting a potentially aggressive government dissatisfied with its role in the system from undertaking more adventurous designs.

(4) Challenged by a rising actor, the declining state cannot afford to conduct an untidy foreign policy. Insofar as possible, the declining state must leave unattended no opportunity for aggression that could be exploited into something larger. Provided that the terms of settlement are minimally acceptable, the hard-pressed government ought to try to settle all marginal quarrels with the ascendant state. By settling marginal disputes with a potential challenger in the ascendancy, the hard-pressed state removes the opportunity for exaggerated future demands and subsequent extortion.

(5) A major strategy of adaptation and adjustment is the redefinition of alliance parameters and perimeters. By parameters we mean the terms and conditions of alliance formation. By perimeters we mean the number of states receiving commitments and the territorial extent of those commitments.

The delicacy of the issue of the definition of perimeters and the dangers of delineating "vital" interests is well illustrated by the prelude to the Austro-Prussian War of 1866 (Taylor 1967, pp. 101–10). Austria's declaration of vital interests were used by Prussia, a third party, despite a precautionary denial of threat, against the peaceful aims of Austrian foreign policy.

From the perspective of adjustment and adaptation, coalition change is a useful strategy in facing the ascendant actor where, as far as the alliance relationship is concerned, the burden of commitments exceeds the benefits of contribution; or as far as the alliance membership is concerned, the converse is true, namely that the costs of contribution exceed the value of security. Coalition change is most effective as a strategy of maintaining equilibrium when nuances are employed: *rapproachment*, detente, entente, bilateral agreement, formal alliance ties. The declining state is obliged by weight of responsibility to constrict its alliance perimeter and to rethink alliance parameters.

If the alliance perimeter is redefined precipitously, it is an invitation to aggression. If the parameters of alliance are shuffled too vigorously, the security of small states can be placed in jeopardy and the credibility of alliance commitments overall may be undermined. But parameters can be altered so that only certain levels of commitment are guaranteed or conditions are placed upon guarantees. Parameters can be modified so that the junior members of an alliance, despite the free-rider tendency, are expected to increase contributions in proportion to their capacity to pay or in proportion to the severity of the threat that they may be expected to face (Olson and Zeckhauser 1966; Greenwood 1984; Cohen 1979). Alliance perimeters can be adjusted so as to treat straits and passages for example differently where a blue-water naval presence is necessary, or to alter responsibilities to meet a manned bomber threat or a sub-conventional capability.

For adjustments to effect the equilibrium between ascendant and declining state, the ascendant state must obtain a larger set of responsibilities and interests without upsetting the peace and security of the system.

(6) The ascendant state whose power in the future will be even greater than at present can afford to look at its obligations to client states, and to any entanglements that may result, in a different light than the declining state. The great danger for the declining state, especially after the second inflection point on its power curve, is to expect a revival of its fortunes as the rate of decline lessens, encouraging the state to view itself in its former glory and to take foreign policy risks that may overwhelm it. Relations with client states in this condition of contradictory foreign policy impulse are especially problematic.

On the one hand, the client state, seeing its patron weakened and yet somewhat strident, is likely to probe the outer boundaries of the relationship with the declining patron, by reopening old quarrels with neighbors and by attempting to drag the patron into these quarrels as an equalizer. The danger for the principal actor is that it will begin to believe in its old capability to manage international relations, to keep third parties out of a dispute, to discipline its client, and at the same time to extend security to that state.

185

Since in hierarchic settings patron–client relationships are common, the frequency of this type of problem at the second inflection point on a power curve is pronounced, historically. This dynamic explains how the Crimean War of 1853 started (Russell 1966). The declining great power must put client states on warning not to exceed the limits of prudent foreign policy lest they precipitate far more serious confrontation by their actions than their initial grievances would intimate.

Global and regional interaction

An equilibrium at the top of the system cannot guarantee stability throughout the system concerning all outbreaks of violence. An equilibrium at the top of the system preserves world order from the worst catastrophe, world war. Equilibrium in the central system may do a great deal to reduce tensions at the regional level especially regarding the tendency for competitive intervention. It may, however, also exacerbate the tendency on the part of some states in the central system to invoke sphere of influence arrangements. Sphere of influence arrangements may promote external stability among the members of the sphere because of the capacity of the external power to dissuade the various client members from using force against each other. But a sphere of influence may also encourage member states to adopt unduly repressive policies internally. A better approach is to achieve regional stability through regional equilibrium (Hansen 1979).

Ideally, the international system will enjoy an equilibrium among the members of the central system that is compatible and congruent with various regional equilibria throughout the system. One level of equilibrium does not come at the expense of another. Rather, equilibrium at each level tends to reinforce and make more durable equilibria elsewhere in the system at all international political levels.

A JUST WORLD ORDER AND THE POWER CYCLE DYNAMIC

Beware the logic of Thrasymachus. Thrasymachus in Plato's *Republic* advocates a definition of justice that equates justice with the will of the stronger. Socrates, like most critics of authoritarian rule, rejects "the will of the stronger" as an acceptable definition of justice because such a definition offers no safeguards for the preferences of the weak (Plato 1961). Internal to the well-ordered state, some more effective political mechanism, operating inside a framework of law, must ensure that justice emerges out of adequate consideration for the preferences of all of the members of society.

So, in international society, the "will of the stronger" is no more adequate a doctrine for the establishment of order with justice than was the Thrasymachus notion internal to the state. Yet in the decentralized nation–state system, where law is weak, law-making and adjudication are marginal processes, and anarchy often leads to outbreaks of war, the power of dominant states is an evident aspect of world politics. What can the power cycle notion of equilibrium contribute to the search for a more just world order? How does power cycle theory reconcile power, public morality, and other core values of politics?

According to power cycle theory, the most grievous miscarriage of international political justice involving the nation–state, apart from direct territorial aggression, occurs when a *serious disparity between the capability and interests of one or more of the leading states is allowed to upset the international political equilibrium of the system*. Responsibility for this very structural notion of injustice depends upon the particular circumstances. Responsibility lies with the declining state when it refuses to curtail the scope of its interests in the face of declining relative capability. Responsibility lies with all the powerful members of the system, rising or declining, when they refuse to yield place and position to a state that has rapidly ascended its cycle of relative power. Responsibility lies with a rising state when it refuses to assume a role commensurate with its increased relative capability.

Governments unwilling to adjust their role and interests to match the changing position on their relative power curves on grounds that "the will of the stronger" shall prevail, have not even attained the level of moral legitimacy of a Thrasymachus, *because they are no longer "stronger," yet they seek to hang onto the perquisites of prior superior position*. Translated to world politics, the Thrasymachus problem is not so much that the strong shall lead, but that the weak may be denied legitimate security and rights, including the right of succession. Unwillingness to make timely adjustments and accommodations is likely to yield precipitous demands in critical intervals when both state and system are least prepared to respond in a manner that upholds international political order.

A quick reading of the argument might lead to the concern that there is a conflict between core values. On the one hand, if a serious disparity between power and interest is considered a monumental injustice, is aggression justified to resolve it? Is this argument an

187

argument justifying aggression and war? Conversely, if a state uses force against a second state to try to attain interests to which it feels justified because of its increased power, is the second to give way rather than face a major war, which is also a monumental injustice? Is this argument an argument for accommodation and pacifism in the face of such "justified" aggression and a threat of war?

Nothing could be more distortive of the intent of the argument. Territorial aggression by force is never considered acceptable behavior in a just world order. Territorial aggression by force, leading to major war, is the principal object to be avoided at all times in a nation's history. Moreover, sufficient territorial aggression always leads to major war, so aggression and war are essentially synonymous. Power cycle theory asks what, in broad structural terms, underlies aggression and major war. It answers that the structural condition underlying aggression and major war is a disparity of power and interest for the aggressive state, and perhaps also for the defensive state, that is serious and unassuaged. Thus a serious disparity between the relative power of a state and its international political role, what is frequently labeled a "rank" or "status" disequilibrium, is the condition to be equated with injustice. Because of its cataclysmic consequences and costs, such a disparity between power and attained interests, in the context of the decentralized nation-state system, equates with the most damaging types of injustices that mankind faces.

But this injustice is not to be remedied by another injustice – neither war nor the loss of vital interests. Accommodation must not involve the transfer to the rising state of interests and responsibilities that are territorial or involve unnegotiated losses of sovereignty for another state. Power cycle theory does not imply pacifism in the face of a threat to vital interests, certainly not in the face of aggressive behavior threatening those interests. As has been repeatedly emphasized, defensive force must be retained throughout the nation's history. The implications of power cycle analysis are not that a world free of weapons would be a peaceful world, since as long as interest–power disparities remain, nations will find a way to fight, and all such disparities are unlikely to be erased. Moreover, passage through critical points will continue to demand dangerous and difficult adjustments. Essential to the argument here is that a rising state must be allowed more visibility but not at the expense of the vital interests of other states. To try to deny the rising state such a place, to exclude it, or to encircle it, without accommodation and transfer of interests and responsibilities, is to condemn it to frustration. Ultimately, especially if it is a major actor, it is likely to unleash its fury onto the system.

Accommodation in this context of rising power is a key to *avoidance of aggression*, not a strategy that facilitates aggression. The so-called "dilemma of peaceful change," examined in the prior chapter with respect to nineteenth and twentieth-century Germany, has a just solution in the context of the power cycle.

Handing over one's territory, or that of one's ally, is scarcely what is meant by a transfer of interests and responsibilities. Accommodation can take many subtle pathways, as we have seen above. Britain transferred to China rights to Hong Kong so as not to have to confront China militarily over this sensitive issue. Seen from the perspective of a weaker but rising power, this was a very important action, conducive of stability.

But does the notion of equilibrium articulated here imply "equality of power," a condition that is hardly to be achieved, it would seem, given the disparity in size and condition of nation-states? Power cycle theory asserts just the opposite, namely, that the distribution of power is always changing.

Finally, a quick reading of the argument so far advanced might also lead to the judgment that there is no room for *morality* in the principal thesis, which might be viewed as too "positivist" or "scientific." Not only would this judgment be wrong, but such a judgment stands the book's thesis on its head. On the contrary, the argument herein advanced is that, unless a minimum public morality consonant with long-term systemic interest is present, future systems transformation cannot be disengaged from the occurrence of major war. Indeed, there is no argument involving public morality that is stronger than the one expected to confront *unearned privilege*.

Since a state does not yield easily the role and status that it has long held – even in the face of vanishing capability to sustain that position unchallenged – public morality must insist that the state acknowledge the higher value of international political equilibrium and forego its excessive claims on another member of the international system.

Public morality also must confront the privilege of free-riderism by a rising state. When a rising state enjoys the personal benefits of systemic membership but refuses to assume its share of the costs of order-maintenance, strains are put on other members, now less able, to protect systemic stability. Like the declining state reluctant to yield role and influence, the rising state reluctant to assume the costs of greater participation must acknowledge the higher value of international political equilibrium. If it does not do so, the system will be strained into a disequilibrium that will be much more costly to all the

189

states in the system. Public morality speaks to both rising and declining states.

An imperative, so as to avoid future systemic crisis, is the necessity of a higher morality consistent with the long-term interest of each nation-state. Neither the security of the individual nation-state, nor the peace of the global system can be maintained without a commitment to this minimal but all-important concept of public morality. In the late twentieth century, this concept of public morality transcends cultural, institutional, and ideological preferences other than those which preserve the integrity and security of the individual nation-state (Hoffmann 1984).

These lessons of the power cycle are not in conflict with other core values which contribute to a greater sense of justice, such as social opportunity, the elimination of global poverty, environmental betterment, and human rights (Beitz 1979; Ruggie 1983a). A truly just world order must give great attention to all of these core values. But, according to the power cycle notion, *structural adjustment at the international level* is perhaps a prerequisite to attaining these other values because of its implications for global political stability. Massive territorial infringement involving another world war would imperil all of the other core values as well as peace, and can only effectively be prevented through the twin imperatives, power–interest equilibration and power balance. A third imperative is that the leading actors in the system have a sense of justice that encompasses all of the core values. The imperatives of general international equilibrium, necessary for the establishment and maintenance of that order, are indeed the foundation on which any other concept of more viable world order must rest.

If the foundation of a viable world order is so simple to determine, then why have statesmen failed in the past to establish and maintain it? Consider the following paradox. The reason adjustment is so difficult, and by default often ends in war, is that when adjustment is possible in advance of conflict it is not seen to be necessary and is often depreciated, or postponed, or ignored. When the necessity for adjustment becomes obvious and overwhelmingly acknowledged (as it was in the summer of 1914), that adjustment is too late because by this time the rigidities and resistance to change have so hardened that all accommodation among conflicting governments becomes impossible.

Timing strategic response to the dynamics of the power cycle is the key.

Part 4
SYSTEMS TRANSFORMATION AND WORLD ORDER AT CENTURY'S END

8 SYSTEMS CHANGE SINCE 1945: INSTABILITY AT CRITICAL POINTS AND AWARENESS OF THE POWER CYCLE

The post-1945 period of bipolarity has been remarkably stable, at least when measured by the standards of the first half of the century. But it has not been a period without tensions and major war stemming from passage through critical points on the power cycles of the major states. Yet, management of crisis internationally, combined with internal constraints on force use, has dampened the instability that followed these abrupt changes in power and role projections. Particularly since the 1960s, the system has found the capacity to assimilate the degree of structural change that has so far occurred.

Before assessing the individual cases of rapid structural change and their consequences for security and stability, three general observations regarding the application of power cycle theory are appropriate. First, the impact of rapid structural change on war is a *probability*: every instance of a crossing of a critical point will not necessarily lead to major war. Only the *likelihood* of major war increases.

Second, many manifestations of tension and strain short of war may reveal the onset of trouble for the system nonetheless. These manifestations may be contained, or they may break into confrontations which are violent and major. In either case, they reveal strains in the system that, if not resolved, may accumulate and lead to a more violent and systems-wide confrontation later. But even systems transformation does not have to end in warfare.

Third, the probability of major war increases when a sizeable gap develops between a state's foreign policy role and its power to effect that role. That gap is likely to become most visible when the state is suddenly forced at a critical point to confront a new projection of future foreign policy outlook. Conversely, absence of such a gap can help mitigate these tensions of critical change.

CRITICAL POINTS SINCE 1945

At first glance (Table 5.1 of chapter 5, p. 133), it appears that quite a bit of significant structural change has occurred in the five or so decades after the Second World War. But the analyst must exercise caution in this judgment. Everything is not quite what it first may seem.

Old, new, and renewed states

While Britain and Germany appear to have crossed a lower turning point, the calculated critical point in each case is an end point of decline that does not threaten to eliminate the state from the major power subsystem. Whether the power cycle is generally reversible, or whether for the individual actor the cycle is unlikely to repeat itself, is an issue to which we turn in chapter 9. To date, only Germany, augmented by unification, shows signs of an upturn of the cycle. Whether either society is able or desires once again to concentrate its national energies in terms of accelerated growth of the type witnessed in Taiwan or South Korea, for example, is not fully evident. Under circumstances of continued steady growth and acceptance of an essentially *regional* role within the European sphere, no gap between power and role would emerge. Although the German trajectory could again turn abruptly upwards, whether it does so is not a direct function of the addition of some 17 million East Germans to its population base, but depends much more on what happens to the overall German economy and to the society's political outlook. The process need not send shock waves through the international system (chapter 10).

Japanese passage through its first inflection point, following an interval of recovery that witnessed torrid economic growth between 1945 and 1960, is actually just a restoration of the status quo ante. But the difference in terms of Japanese domestic and foreign policy behavior is extraordinary. Instead of translating the shock of a passage through a critical point into military activity, the anxiety was trans-lated into renewed foreign *economic* expansion, both regarding trade and finance and regarding foreign investment. The Japanese response to a slowing of domestic economic growth was an invigorated search for raw material imports and for markets abroad. The post-1970 "trading state" mentality in reality reflects Japan's effort to offset perceived relative decline (in rate of growth) through external economic rather than military means (Rosecrance 1986; Waldmann 1986). For Japan, adjustment to diminishing marginal returns in power then took the comparatively more benign route of the quest for greater trade and commerce abroad. This route chosen by latter-day Japan demanded great adjustments from other states in terms of role, but these adjustments were far easier to make than those the system faced in 1939.

Note that the presence of these critical points for Britain, Germany, and Japan, no matter how qualified in theoretical and historical terms, was fully represented in the empirical test concerning the impact of critical points on major war. It is customary in empirical studies of major war to exclude both Germany and Japan after 1945 because they were disarmed. Since they are non-war instances, the inclusion of those two critical points, despite legitimate doubts about their significance for military instability, had the effect of making the empirical results about war causation even more conservative, and therefore credible. Their inclusion is justified, on the other hand, because they do represent an important part of the *structural change* in the system, change that may have military impact via another state.

China was born in the turbulence of Japanese occupation in the interwar period and in the aftermath of communist revolution (Fairbank 1986). It was as much a creation of the turbulent interwar period as it was a precursor of the type of system yet to come. China thus is estimated to have crossed its lower turning point in 1946, the year of its formal emergence into the system.

China under Mao had at least as much impact upon the thinking of North Korea prior to the Korean War, and upon the outcome of that war, as any other state. The paranoia mixed with belligerence of the Mao government certainly did not contribute to constraint on the part of the Kim il Sung government and perhaps contributed to its opposite. China under Mao sought to express its sphere of influence in Asia, and while it did not do so in terms of outright expansionism, it did so in terms of the encouragement of ideological subversion by forcible means that ultimately led to violent external confrontation.

Although this fact was difficult for other governments at the time to acknowledge, Mao's China was a prima facie example of status disequilibration. Almost immediately because of its great size, and because of the policies Mao pursued that led to ostracization first by the Western community and then by the Soviet Union, China expressed a gap between the power that it had achieved and the power others ascribed to it. The lower turning point on the Chinese power cycle bared this gap between power and role in a way that led to the Korean War. When the U.N. forces led by the United States crossed the 38th parallel into North Korean territory and bombed north of the Yalu River, the gap between how China regarded itself and how others were treating it precipitated a flood of Chinese troops onto the battlefield.

With the death of Mao, the internal Chinese renaissance, the shift of the world balance of power, and various foreign policy adjustments, the status gap for China fortunately was breached by diplomatic recognition, acceptance into the United Nations, a shelving of the two-China problem, and integration into the world trading community. Thus, a more serious impact upon the global international system of China's role gap and rapid ascension was averted.

United States high point, 1960-1965

A sensitive matter for Americans is the question of whether the United States is subject to the same norms of the power cycle as other states, or, as in many other issues of politics, whether the United States is exempt. The painful answer is that although democratic institutions may have warded off the most damaging consequences of radical structural change for the United States (and for the system *vis-à-vis* the United States), the United States is not exempt from the dynamics of the power cycle.

According to our empirical findings, the United States crossed its upper turning point early in the decade of the 1960s. It was the best of times and yet the worst of times for the United States and for those who had to guide its policies. Its harried Secretary of State said the United States did not want to be the "policeman for the world," yet that was exactly what it was, or thought that it had to become, to be sure what many countries in the world had come to expect it to be. Its young President, who was only spared by an assassin's bullet the mistakes of his brutally criticized successor, declared that "there cannot be an American solution to every world problem" and yet promised, "We shall bear every burden ..." (Schlesinger, Jr. 1986, p. 412). The United States was experiencing the uncertainties and conflicting expectations and demands that accompany the "inversion in the prior trend" of projections regarding future role characteristic of passage through a critical point on the power cycle; contrast the interpretations in Liska (1967) and Hoffman (1978).

Behind all the rhetoric was a profound fear, and a dawning awareness, that the United States was on the brink of a new era in which it was no longer paramount. It was still the most powerful state in the system but it was at its apex. It was about to enter decline. The "missile gap" was proven wrong. Yet a more serious gap was beginning to open up. American prestige was no longer sufficient to accomplish order-maintenance responsibilities alone. A gap between ends and means was beginning to become evident not just because, relentlessly, within a decade, the Russians were catching up in nuclear strategic terms, but because the cost of global commitments was increasingly difficult and increasingly expensive for the American polity to bear, or at least to bear in the fashion it had a decade earlier. The decision to aid South Vietnam in its struggle against communist aggression from the North was the result of the American effort to grapple with its own trepidation over a new trajectory of relative decline.

One of the great puzzles for historians of this period, if the threat of communism was the leitmotif of U.S. foreign policy conduct and apart from the more trivial issue of tactics, was why the United States would expend such a pitiful effort at the Bay of Pigs in ridding the Hemisphere of communist dictatorship sixty miles off American shores, while it would fight a ten-year war thousands of miles away in Vietnam for the same purpose. The answer is only found in the irrationality of foreign policy decision making in the critical interval on the power cycle. In neither the case of Cuba, nor the case of Vietnam, was the territorial security of the United States *per se* at risk. In each case, however, the political freedom of a people was being mercilessly denied. But so before, and so since, in places as diverse as Cambodia, Ethiopia, and Afghanistan, the political freedom of peoples was subverted, yet the United States would not send troops to save them. In fact, the corruptness and ineptness of the Diem regime and its successors made South Vietnam a questionable choice for the high-minded pursuit of the defense of free people. What was special about Vietnam? Nothing. It was the very ordinariness of the place, and of the situation, that revealed the American frame of mind in the interval of radical change in foreign policy projections and future role.

The image of the "domino theory" was very apt. The United States government did believe, for the most part, that a failure in Vietnam would mean a failure elsewhere in South-East Asia (in part true) and an unraveling of alliances everywhere. Like Korea, Vietnam was thought to be a probe, a test. But unlike Korea, the United States bitterly miscalculated the odds of success. Even more sadly, it was its own rhetoric and "figures" that made it miscalculate, a typical instance of the irrationality of decision making in the critical interval on the power curve. Invariably, Washington believed that "there was much more at stake" than just the outcome of the war itself. In fact, what was regarded as at stake was the whole foreign policy role and security position of the United States, in the eyes of its allies, and in the eyes of its enemies. U.S. foreign policy was thought to be on trial

197

in Vietnam. It was this "larger than life" character of Vietnam for the United States that induced it to overreach itself.

What happened in Vietnam to U.S foreign policy is not atypical of states that suddenly find themselves in relative decline. What perhaps *is* atypical is that the United States stopped itself short from making an even more serious blunder. To that credit one may attribute the impact on foreign policy of democratic institutions, notwithstanding the Lippmann view that such institutions only act as a shackle upon foreign policy conduct. They do act as a shackle where the issue of means in concerned, because that level of knowledge and specificity a mass public cannot have. They do act as a wise policy guide where broad policy ends are concerned, in this case in a way that ultimately saved American foreign policy.

The reason the United States did not prevail was not that North Vietnam was more powerful militarily than the United States, even though North Vietnam used all of its power and much of that of its allies and even though the United States used only a fraction of its military capability. The reason the United States did not prevail was that the American people did not value the utility of the objective of "winning" to the same extent as did the North Vietnamese (Gelb and Betts 1979; Berman 1982). That does not mean that the sacrifices of American soldiers were slight, nor that American ethical objectives regarding a defense of liberty were less worthy. This result only means that North Vietnam, fighting on its own territory, as well as in the South, felt the war objective more intensely.

But, by the same token, the reason the United States did not undertake actions that could have expanded this conflict into a truly major war of the sort that filled the first half of the twentieth century (in the way that might have occurred had the United States invaded Hanoi, and thus threatened the territorial security of both China and the Soviet Union), was that enough sense remained, in this tortuous interval of American history, to pull back. When Senator Goldwater said either enter a war to win it, or do not enter it at all, he was in many respects reinterpreting history, but doing so in a way that went to the American heart. The doctrine of limited war is not one easily understood. But, even with limited war the object is not to lose, but to prevail at a limited cost. Most Americans were saying to Goldwater that this was not a war to win on U.S. and South Vietnamese terms, limited or otherwise, just as the U.S. military had warned in 1959–60. Conversely, if the United States had tried to escalate the war to very high force levels, that is, to the level of full-scale invasion or of nuclear weapons use, does anyone today doubt that President Johnson and the American people were right not to ? A third world war would have been at hand.

The Soviet Union and the shock of slow growth, 1960–1965

Through a combination of extreme austerity (high savings rate) and forced draft industrialization in heavy manufacturing, the Soviet Union managed to squeeze out of its awkward economy a respectable growth rate through the middle decades of the twentieth century (Bergson and Levine, eds. 1983; Cracraft, ed. 1983). Its growth in military capability was even more impressive especially in its specialities of heavy artillery, tanks, large missiles, and advanced submarines. Moscow had come to expect that this growth would continue, allowing the country an ever larger international political role and a status congruent with the annual displays in Red Square on May Day.

Our empirical evidence indicates that the Soviet Union crossed its first inflection point approximately in the 1960–65 interval, perhaps a few years earlier or later, after a long steady ascent in power. Discovery of this reality – that its rate of growth in relative capability suddenly was beginning to decline – was to have a profound consequence on thinking about foreign policy in the Kremlin (Doran 1986).

The two most serious crises facing the international system in terms of potential for escalation stemmed from what the Soviets were later to describe as "adventurism" (Ulam 1974). Both were so serious, more serious than any wars occurring in this period, because the crisis involved threats of vital interests to the extent that nuclear weapons use might have been triggered.

The first crisis was the Cuban Missile Crisis of 1960 in which Khrushchev attempted to change the nuclear balance abruptly by locating offensive missiles on Cuban soil. Interesting for power cycle interpretation was that Khrushchev apparently was attempting to use foreign policy to cover up for the weaknesses of Soviet economic achievement, especially in agriculture. Khrushchev was trying to demonstrate to the Politburo that the Soviet Union was not facing a slow-down in its accretion of power and that Soviet foreign policy was even more dynamic than in the past.

A second crisis of similar dimensions occurred during the October War in 1973 when the Soviets threatened to intervene militarily on behalf of the Egyptian Third Army in a way that might have profoundly altered the regional balance of power in the Middle East. The

Nixon Administration, according to its Secretary of State, Kissinger, responded by calling a nuclear alert as a signal to the Soviets that they had threatened vital interests. That the Soviet Union reversed its plans for a military landing on the west bank of the Suez Canal, accompanied by American willingness to halt the Israeli advance, contributed to a resolution of the crisis. The Soviets said afterwards that never would the United States interfere with their foreign policy again, but the Soviet action had been prompted by this very sense of disparity between what they thought they had achieved in power terms and how they were viewed. Passage through the first inflection point onto a trajectory of slower relative power growth made them anxious to eliminate this disparity.

At the 24th Congress of the Communist Party of the Soviet Union in 1971, Foreign Minister Andrei Gromyko said, "Today there is no question of any significance which can be decided without the Soviet Union or in opposition to it" (Aspaturian 1980, p. 1). In this statement, the Soviet Union was claiming that not only was it to be treated as a coequal with the United States in nuclear strategic terms as in enshrined in the SALT I Agreement, but that it had a right to be recognized as a global actor coequal with the United States in its exercise of general foreign policy. Such a claim to equality presumably meant that the Soviet Union had a right to be involved in and consulted on all foreign policy issues, not just military issues, everywhere in the system. Echoed in 1980 by the statements of the Soviet Ambassador to France, S. V. Chervonenko, this expanded Brezhnev doctrine was used to defend the Soviet invasion of Afghanistan: the Soviet Union "has the full right to choose its friends and allies, and if it becomes necessary, to repel with them the threat of counter-revolution or a foreign intervention" (p. 17). In the same speech, he rejected claims by the United States of vital interests in the Persian Gulf or elsewhere.

In Soviet parlance, the "correlation of forces" in the 1970s were moving in favor of the Soviet Union and against the West. This convenient phrase is to be distinguished both from the notion of national capability and from the balance of power, and, as used here, from equilibrium. The "correlation of forces" was a catch-all term that included not only military power and the other elements of national capability, and the subjective factors such as national will and cohesion, but also the elements of ideology and class which were to determine receptivity to Soviet ideas and affiliation (Simes 1983; Garthoff 1985; Parrott 1987).

Under Gorbachev's foreign policy, the notion of a "balance of forces" was replaced in part by a new notion of the "balance of interests." A balance of interests entailed the reciprocal definition of interests. The Soviet Union acknowledged its failure in Afghanistan since its intervention threatened the interests of Iran and particularly of Pakistan.

THE SUPERPOWER CYCLES AND SYSTEMS TRANSFORMATION

From the static systems perspective, bipolarity and multipolarity are regarded as responsible for varying degrees of international political stability: the structure of each system determines the degree of stability, and the literature is divided as to which system is the more stable. From the perspective of power cycle theory, it is not the structure of the system as such that is responsible for stability, or its absence, major war. Rather, it is the process of systems transformation – namely, the movement from one system at maturity to another system – that is associated with major war. Of course, systems transformation from bipolarity to multipolarity involves preeminently two states, the Soviet Union and the United States. The movement of these two states on their respective power cycles therefore impacts greatly (but not exclusively) on the stability of the global system.

Absolute levels of power. In brief, the Soviet Union, through austerity and concentration of effort, was able to catch up with the United States in many areas of military capability during the 1960s and 1970s. In terms of nuclear throw-weight, heavy missiles, artillery, numbers of tanks, size of the manned army and of the submarine force, and number of surface ships, the Soviet Union was at least the equivalent of the United States, if not in some other military areas. But, to accomplish this, the Soviet Union had to spend at least twice, perhaps more, the fraction of its GNP devoted to military considerations as the United States, which had an economy that was at least twice as large as that of the Soviet Union. Indeed, except in the European theater, the United States still projects far greater clout in global naval and conventional military terms than the Soviet Union. Furthermore, the United States still accounts for one-fifth of the GNP of the entire system. Thus, in overall power terms, the United States was more powerful than the Soviet Union in the immediate post-1945 period and remains so today.

Relative power trajectories. On the one hand, the United States appears to be slightly beyond the apex of its relative power curve. Empirical evidence suggests that the United States reached this high point on its power cycle in the 1960–65 interval and that incremental decline has set in, indexed by a host of indicators both financial and commercially related (chapter 9). Military strength has been less affected but in the face of nascent economic decline must eventually be impacted as well.

On the other hand, the Soviet Union – with its huge natural base, talented scientific establishment, commitment to high military expenditure, and somewhat younger labor force – still has the opportunity to continue its ascendancy. The importance of *perestroika*, and by derivation *glasnost*, is that they are the vehicles whereby the Soviet Union is going to try to stave off relative decline on the Soviet power cycle, despite question whether the economy can be revived.

Soviet attempts to stave off relative decline.　Gorbachev believes in the Soviet "political system." Defined here in Soviet terms, "political system" means the future of Soviet power. Others in the present Soviet Communist Party do not share this belief. But for those who do accept Gorbachev's program of reform, the Soviet Union is believed to be able to stave off relative decline.

The route the Party elite has chosen is to reform politics and political structures first, then subsequently to attack economic problems via the support gained from the intelligentsia through their sympathy for liberalization. To have described past Soviet society as "the evil empire" was far too generous, as most educated Soviet citizens know. Gorbachev has attempted to reform a "gangster society" created by Stalin and his successors and to transmute it into what Soviets today term a "normal society." The Gorbachev government has attempted to reduce the extreme centralization of decision making in foreign policy, to relax censorship and all forms of control over expression (modified by the prohibition on extreme criticism of Gorbachev himself), to undercut economic authoritarianism, and to begin to allow market forces to operate. But the government needs time, both internally and externally, free of pressure. Yet time is exactly what it is running out of.

The Soviet Union is in chaos. Reforms are not working. Anarchy is present. Nasty ethnic discrimination bounds and sometimes turns violent. Crime is organized and devastating. Shops are more empty than before. The sense of mission and political purpose has gone. Transmutation of socialism is arduous and daunting.

Faster reform, especially of the economic base, is necesssary, but people already reject the pace of reform as too fast. Politics gets out of kilter with economic change (relaxation of production targets, for example, without introduction of full price competition and incentives.) Expectations exceed the capability to meet those expectations. The consequence is a society driven to the edge of survival and stability as the government tries to rescue itself from imminent relative decline. Notwithstanding the good things it has brought to Soviet society, and the relaxation of East–West tensions, *perestroika* has led to stagnation and to paralysis.

Superpowers out of sync. Thus, the main problem in the 1970s was the fact that the Soviet Union and the United States found themselves out of sync in terms of their understanding of what politics held in store for themselves and for each other (Doran 1986). The trajectories of their power differed. Each country's perception of its future role in the system also was at variance with that of the other. The Soviet Union emphasized its "favorable correlation of forces" whereas the United States stressed its greater absolute level of power. Each country saw the flaws in the power position of the other, yet neither was prepared to acknowledge the shortcomings of its position on its own power cycle. Hence, the Soviet Union and the United States had much upon which to disagree in structural terms.

But, by the 1980s, an even greater peril awaited the Soviet Union and the system as a whole. The Soviet Union's economic and political crisis demands not only internal reforms but also serious reassessments and adjustments in foreign policy. The peril is that a crisis of Soviet foreign policy could become a crisis of systems transformation.

AWARENESS OF THE CYCLE: CAN THE SOVIET UNION ADJUST?

Adjustment to new foreign policy projections under Gorbachev

It took nearly a generation after the Soviet Union passed its first inflection point for new younger leadership under Gorbachev to accept the implications for Soviet foreign policy of more constrained power growth rates. That the interval of adjustment was so protracted speaks to the difficulty with which the Soviet Union wrestled its foreign policy expectations into line with its slowing rate of growth in relative national capability. Soviet historian, Stephen Cohen (1985), observed that "whatever else may be characteristic of Soviet leaders, they are intensely proud of their country's great-power status, achieved only in their lifetime and at enormous cost, and thus they are profoundly resentful of any perceived challenge to its international prestige" (p. 142). To be sure, Gorbachev had not given up the central aims of Soviet foreign policy, nor the goal of enhancing Soviet power. Indeed, the premise of *glasnost* and *perestroika* was that the next generation of Soviet policy makers would have more to work with than the last.

A reinvigorated Soviet economy could push military spending to new heights while at the same time better meeting the consumer needs of a larger population (Gelman 1986; Goldman 1983). The trick was to get the Soviet military to postpone some of their demands to the future when the economy would be comparatively much stronger (Weitzman 1983; Bergson 1978). To accomplish this reinvigoration, some of the military investment foregone would have to be placed in the civilian economy rather than be consumed directly. Unlike China which had sought to attack the problems created by an overly communalized and centralized agriculture directly, and to reduce the costs of a bloated army and bureaucracy by disbanding sections of it, but without relaxing the controls of the central party machinery, Gorbachev sought to minimize the actual changes in agriculture, the army, and the bureaucracy while "opening up" the society to new ideas, exchange of information, and individual rights removed from Party control. Thus, the Chinese and the Soviet routes to post-Marxist–Leninist modernization were quite different.

In terms of authority, the Chinese market reform did not challenge the essence of Marxist–Leninism, that is, the "dictatorship of the proletariate," and the dominant role of the Communist Party, whereas Soviet party reform eventually did challenge these areas. Yet Soviet reform only very belatedly addressed the market place in a fundamental way while that is where Chinese reform began. Neither Deng nor Gorbachev intentionally did anything to undermine their own power. Indeed, they sacrificed much of the reform objective ultimately to aggregate their own personal power so as to remain in office. Each leader sought to strengthen the party against the bureaucracy on the one hand, and against the nationalities or regional communal groupings on the other. Deng tried to let reforms concerning income, incentives, managerial autonomy, and indoctrination earn the support of the elites and masses directly. Gorbachev sought to use greater artistic and intellectual freedom to achieve the same kind of allegiance. In the end, the same question could be asked of each government. How compatible was the feudalism of contemporary Communist hierarchy with a modern, responsive, flexible market economy, once the first bursts of creativity had been released by the most sorely needed reforms?

For Gorbachev, domestic economic reform was essential to an activist foreign policy. But a pull-back from the most far-reaching and vulnerable of Soviet foreign policy efforts was also necessary so as to give the economy a respite and the polity an opportunity to concentrate upon domestic reform. Accelerating its foreign policy initiatives as though it had an interest deficit in the 1960–65 interval, the Soviet Union created an interest burden that by the late 1980s it had difficulty maintaining. The foreign policy role to which Brezhnev and others had aspired perhaps could have been maintained if the Soviet slowdown beginning at that inflection point had not proceeded so rapidly. Indeed, the extremely high cost of maintaining such objectives in the present age was not foreseen by either the United States (e.g., Vietnam) or the Soviet Union. Adjustment to the new set of foreign policy projections of role (which was foreseen at the first inflection point) took more than two decades, testifying to the inertia in the original pre-1960 set of Soviet goals, prior even to the doctrine of "peaceful coexistence," tailored to the nuclear age. But this is not to say that the new set of projections for role has been fully accepted.

An index of how difficult the revised Soviet foreign policy outlook was to accomplish is the restatement of Soviet military doctrine (Meyer 1984; George 1984). Former chief of the Soviet general staff, Marshal Akhromeyev, said that the Soviet Union gave up its offensive strategic doctrine for a more defensive posture. For a year or so, after its promulgation, no impact on deployment patterns or military procurement was yet evident. But, by the beginning of the 1990s, both the withdrawal of Soviet military divisions from East Germany and elsewhere and a genuine reduction in the level of Soviet military spending were discernible.

Perhaps the first impact of military retrenchment was to confirm that the Soviet Union is a great Continental land power, not a sea power. Naval units were pulled back to less demanding strategic locations where logistics were easier. Reductions in the number and duration of deployments, and in the dimension of the surface ship program, led the way in the Soviet effort to redefine its military and naval roles in terms of a more realistic assessment of its security objectives.

Gorbachev's foreign policy was new in terms of its *intermediate goals*, contrasting sharply with the initial reaction to the Soviet discovery of slow growth at the first inflection point. The initial reaction under Khrushchev and Brezhnev was a pompous contempt ("We will bury you!") for the limits imposed by a declining rate of growth. Crises that followed, and a far-flung attempt to expand the Soviet presence abroad, were only checked by eventual recognition under Gorbachev of the need to temper goals to match the stalled rate of increase in capabilities.

Soviet decline: an optimistic scenario of Soviet response

But suppose the Soviet Union is unable to extract from *perestroika* a sufficient bonus to continue the Soviet economy on an upward growth track. Suppose that the Soviet Union cannot perpetuate its slow ascendancy, albeit at a lower level of power than that of the United States. Under these circumstances, Soviet relative power will have peaked and will confront decline. What are the implications for the defense policy of the Western alliance?

Much depends upon whether the Soviet Union appears to accept relative decline, or attempts to deny it, perhaps through saber-rattling or a more expansionist foreign policy. If the Soviet Union accepts decline, and adjusts smoothly to its new projection of foreign policy role and status, however arduous the process of internal adjustment may have been in the party apparatus and ruling Politburo, benign adjustment may lead to a more general relaxation of tensions and broader foreign policy dividends to all concerned.

Such benign Soviet adjustment to decline could take pressure off U.S. forward defenses. If matched by lasting unilateral and negotiated defense budget cuts and a genuine restructuring of the Soviet armed forces to a defensive posture, it could facilitate not just a single reduction but a series of reductions in American defense spending. Debt reduction, increased investment in the civilian economy, combined with renewed technological research and development in non-military areas, could have very substantial long-term payoffs for the future robustness of the economy and the capacity of the United States to postpone decline on its power cycle.

This scenario may also have a downside as America's allies also rush to reduce their military spending. Canada's 1989 cut-back in its already disproportionately small military budget may be taken as a forerunner of this disposition. Cohesion within NATO and in bilateral alliance terms will be more difficult to sustain as the perception of a common external threat wanes. But the benefits from an overall relaxation of tensions may well be seen to offset any future risk that might attend the common defense.

A pessimistic scenario: dealing with decline according to the Grand Master's strategy

The nature of the structural crisis still facing Soviet foreign policy is quite clear. This structural crisis results from the perceived disparity in the trajectories of the two power cycles and the implications for leadership roles in the international system. In the 1970s and the 1980s the Soviet Union regarded itself as on the ascendancy in the international system and the United States as in decline. It therefore expected a larger role in systemic affairs (which, we argue, it was entitled to receive commensurate with its level and its trajectory but only *vis-à-vis* legitimate interests). It demanded equality with the United States, or "parity," the term used in strategic nuclear circles. What the Soviet Union was unprepared to admit was that with respect to absolute levels of national capability, the United States still predominated. Thus, the Soviet Union was very frustrated with its current position in the system. The problem for the system is how the Soviet Union will deal with its frustration if it faces actual relative decline but is unprepared to forgo parity and an increasing role in the system.

From the Soviet perspective, a gap exists regarding the Soviet sense of its achievement in power terms and the way the United States ascribes power to it. This sense of a role gap continues to persist despite the recognition under Gorbachev that actual Soviet means required some realignment of Soviet foreign policy objectives. In the U.S. view, Soviet foreign policy pretension remained inflated, despite the reality that the level of U.S. relative power was itself past its peak.

Suppose now that the Soviet Union discovers that its relative power is in decline and that an entire reorientation of its foreign policy is necessary, not as a tactic to sustain ascendancy, but as an irreversible necessity because of the reality of decline. Will the Politburo accept such a permanent diminution of the Soviet role?

Now if reform proves inadequate, what is the likely consequence of all of this internal political struggle, struggle to maintain the rate of Soviet power increase? Two consequences compete with each other as alternatives. The first is fragmentation of the internal Soviet empire. External fragmentation has already occurred in the withdrawal from Afghanistan and Eastern Europe, no matter how cost-effective and tactically successful, or reversible. But neither the proclamation of independence by the Georgian Communist Party, and the party organs of other nationalities, nor the serious anti-Russian attitudes of the Republics, suggest that amity will be easy to achieve or is even feasible. As the pull of communist ideology disappears, the attractiveness of nativist and traditional nationalist ethics acts as a substitute. Outright break-up of the Soviet Union is a prospect. Or, conversely, the use of force to avert such a break-up becomes even more of a prospect.

The other outcome, similarly devastating for the Soviet polity and for the West, is the emergence of a Napoleonic replacement for Gorbachev, a new Stalin perhaps, who, through brutal repression and recentralization, forces the Soviet Union into submission, and erases the reforms so painfully and precariously augmented on a too-narrow market base.

Some analysts will object that the reforms have "already gone too far" to be reversed, just as they will claim that the Soviet Union could never again assert its hegemony in Eastern Europe. Lamentably, such criticism is founded only on the circumstances of a reform government in Moscow, not on the circumstances of Bonapartism which rallies the tattered energies of the lumpen-proletariat against the well-intentioned but weak leadership of the intelligentsia, the modern equivalent of an aristocracy of conscience. Under such a scenario, the Soviet Union will not unseat the immobile, emotionally drained peasantry or unseat the exploitative and indifferent bureaucracy that constrains the possibility for true reform. Rather the country will slip back into orthodox Marxism–Leninism.

What makes the problem more serious, and therefore a subject of systems transformation, is that rapid structural change is occurring for both of the superpowers as well as a number of other leading states.

What are the possible consequences of each of these trends for foreign policy? At least four worrisome outcomes are possible; under such circumstances of cyclical downturn, each is more likely than a benign alternative.

First, a restoration of a conservative Marxist–Leninist alliance between the Soviet Union and China, each burned by its experiment with market capitalism and democracy, each determined to save its "system" along traditional lines, each isolationist and hostile to a West that it sees determined to upset its priorities and its place in the global system. Less ideological conviction, or the success of centrist economic and political policies, and greater determination of traditional elites to retain what power they have while projecting a foreign policy role of a self-reinforcing place in world politics, would drive this restoration of the international political status quo back to the Cold War.

Second, and not necessarily alternatively, a hard-pressed Soviet regime in this critical interval of adjustment could use foreign policy to try to cover up its domestic shortcomings. It could try to distract public opinion in the Soviet Union with an adventurist foreign policy that would enable its citizens to forget about the torments of their everyday lives with the visions of a great Soviet Union on the world stage. For this diversion to work, visible achievement, not another Afghanistan of constraint and defeat, in the form of military domination and rule abroad would seem a prerequisite, and that would come at the cost of global stability.

Third, fragmentation of the Soviet internal empire could spill over on neighboring countries. Azerbaizhan is only one possibility with implications for Iran and the Persian Gulf. But Turkey and Greece are no less possible trouble spots than Manchuria or the Polish border region. The difference here is that instability could emerge not because of expansionist desire but because of inadvertent entanglement in what might at least start as a Soviet civil war. An effort would be made to contain the dispute. But individual republics might seek outside assistance and such contact would spread the violence and broaden the war.

Fourth, the Soviet Union could, with a restored conservative government, merely revert to traditional imperial wars. Traditional desires for buffers and for access to coastal areas, reducing its land-locked containment, would once again threaten its neighbors.

None of these scenarios is probable under the leadership of Gorbachev since the assumptions conform to neither the premises of his foreign policy conduct nor the priorities of domestic political and economic objective. They necessitate expenditure of capital rather than management and acquisition. They involve a larger foreign policy role rather than the "balance of interests" against capability. But, nevertheless, the rigors of passage through a critical point in the power cycle cannot guarantee the longevity of the Gorbachev government nor its salutary vision of an entry into the circle of civilized nations.

Russia has long favored sphere of influence politics, notwithstanding the contemporary desire for ideological and territorial buffers in Eastern Europe, now foregone. Spheres of influence are cheap to create and, because they are exclusive, safe to maintain. Russia sought spheres of influence in Poland in the 1790s, in Persia at the turn of the twentieth century, and with Hitler in 1939. So also the Soviet Union under Brezhnev sought a sphere of influence in the contemporary Middle East frustrated only by the Carter Administration's idealism about such matters (Katz 1985; Marantz and Steinberg eds. 1985).

The Brezhnev scheme for sphere of inflence demarcation revealed

209

the unity of Soviet thought regarding geopolitical aims in the region (Coffey 1987; Luttwak 1983; Miyoshi 1987). As Zbigniew Brzezinski (1986) showed in a compelling geostrategic analysis, from Syria to Afghanistan, the Soviet Union had sought to create a buffer of friendly states much like it had in Eastern Europe and Manchuria, states dependent upon the Soviet Union for direction and foreign policy initiative.

More pointedly, although history and religious fanaticism had conspired to conceal the reality from the eyes of the affected statesmen, the Soviet Union had a single target for expanded influence in the region that surpassed all others. Iran was the richest prize on the Soviet border (Ajami 1981; Limbert 1986; Quandt 1986). From the Soviet view, Iran alone would have made a carefully prepared strategy of regional domination worth implementation.

One object of Soviet expansion into the Middle East and Africa was to squeeze Saudi Arabia and the oil-rich countries of the Arab world in a vice built of ideologically compatible and strategically dependent regimes on the outskirts of the core area. For this reason the set-back in Egypt was a large Soviet liability (Freedman 1984; Kamel 1986). Egypt was the key to entry both to North and East Africa and to the Middle East proper. Egypt was the continental bridge. He who controlled Egypt controlled movement of commerce and the establishment of an air and naval presence in the region. Loss of Egypt meant not only that the Soviet Union sacrificed an important entry point into Arab politics. Regardless of Egypt's differences from the rest of the Arab-speaking world, without Egypt the Arab world could not coalesce around a single strategy or policy.

Soviet withdrawal from Afghanistan, and willingness to negotiate with respect to Angola and Cambodia, indicate how hard-pressed Moscow was by the late 1980s in terms of foreign policy over-extension and in terms of commitment to domestic reform. The Soviets are literally testing the power cycle notion by attempting to show through *perestroika* that the Soviet Union is able to continue its slow but resolute ascendancy. If the reforms fail, so will the Soviet claim to parity with the United States. Both states will have entered relative decline in power levels, but the Soviet level will remain inferior to that of the United States. This will amount to bitter reality for a Kremlin long bent on a world role of equality with Washington.

Whether the Soviet Union, past the apex of its power curve, frustrated and belligerent, would accelerate a strategy of penetration and encirclement in the Middle East is difficult to determine. But a Soviet Union facing foreign policy crisis, the crisis of gradual with-

210

drawal and constraint, is very likely to take a long look at the chances of prolonging its world role, and such a strategy is high among its options. This is not a preferred strategy under Gorbachev. It is a strategy of the Grand Master, Gromyko, or of like-minded geostrategists. A Soviet leader is "like a driver on a slippery road," said French Foreign Minister, Roland Dumas, echoing the analogy we used to explain the dynamic of the power cycle: "He can't take the turns as if he were on a dry highway" (Markham 1989).

The analyst of international politics can only note that a world in which several states are passing through critical points at the same time that the Soviet Union is passing through the apex of its power curve is a world of much additional uncertainty (Goodpaster, Stoessel, and Kennedy 1986; Liska 1982; Hoffmann 1984). History has shown that such periods of rapid structural change are dangerous periods for statecraft, prone to over-reaction and to massive upheaval. Regarding the present system, consider the statement of Dr. Yurii Afanasev of the Moscow Historical Institute: "There is no alternative to *perestroika* other than descending into an abyss, and if that occurs, it will not be our internal, national abyss. We will necessarily drag many others behind us" (Meyer 1989). While the temptation in the West may be to discount such a statement as morbidly introspective or politically self-serving, such an interpretation may be correct without grasping the essential gravity of the situation as seen by the Soviet leadership. In Washington, this gravity was acknowledged by the Commission on Integrated Long-Term Strategy in its report, *Discriminate Deterrence*, published in January 1988. Noting that the Soviet share of world power may shrink during the next twenty years, they warned that this perceived "failure" may "drive the regime to seek legitimacy in military successes abroad" (p. 8).

The failure of *perestroika* is a passage through the upper turning point on the Soviet power cycle, the beginning of full-fledged systems transformation, and, as this statement advises, the possibility that the Soviet Union will drag the system into "an abyss" of instability. Such a period would require a most sophisticated response from the international system, a response led by the United States but not limited to the United States. Whether stability or systemic war results will depend in considerable degree on the ability of the system to guide the Soviet Union through this difficult period of adjustment on its power cycle.

9   IS DECLINE INEVITABLE? U.S. LEADERSHIP AND THE SYSTEMIC SECURITY DILEMMA

Whether decline on the power cycle is inevitable for a state at some advanced stage of its international political development is a central historical and theoretical question. Must a state succumb to fatalism regarding its decline, or is decline perhaps a function of policy choice as much as some inexorable process or law? How great is the inertia of change on the power cycle, or conversely, how large is the realm of policy choice for society and decision maker in consciously directing structural change?

As long as decline is thought to be inevitable, neither theorists nor policy makers will seek alternatives to decline. Such acceptance of "inevitability" ironically introduces additional "uncertainty" into strategic policy planning, increasing the chances for a wrong decision. Conversely, if decline is not inevitable, policy makers will have a threefold task: to manage and try to control movement along the power cycle, to bring interests into line with new power relations, and to develop a strategic policy within these constraints that confronts security issues directly.

The question of U.S. decline is not simple, in terms of either the cause and extent of decline, the implications for U.S. security policy, or the choice of policy instruments. Nor is the question of Japan's rise so simple. The relationship between the U.S. and Japanese power cycles requires careful assessment. An error of grand strategy is more than a mistake for a single government. Bad strategic thinking can worsen both the economic situation and the security dilemma throughout the system.

ASSESSING DECLINE ON THE POWER CYCLE

"Decline" on the power cycle can have three different meanings, each bound up with the dynamics of the cycle itself.

First, decline can mean the matter of advanced decline. Here the amount of relative decline from the state's peak is already great, and

212

the state tries to thwart or mitigate further decline in level of relative power. If such an attempt is successful, it can lead to the second inflection point where the rate of decline slows down. In theory, it can even lead to the low point where the state will remain at a fixed level of relative power or perhaps even begin a new ascendancy in relative power some time in the future.

Second, "decline" may mean crossing the high point on the cycle, or peaking. The object here is to *avoid* an actual reduction in the level of relative power. The object is either to extend the peak upwards or to flatten it so that the apex extends over a long interval of history. The high point therefore would be not a "peak" but a period of "peaking." The onset of decline would thereby be postponed.

Third, efforts to reverse "decline" may constitute the attempt to slow the decline in *rate* of relative growth that begins after the first inflection point. The object here is to reverse the pattern of "diminishing marginal returns" regarding *relative* capability so as to allow a long interval *before* the peak is reached. For *"decline" on the power cycle begins at the first inflection point* at which, for the first time, the state experiences a reversal of its previous trend of ever increasing rate of growth in relative power. Hence, although the first inflection point may occur long before diminishing marginal returns set in regarding *absolute* capability growth, it is the beginning of the state's diminishing rate of growth *relative* to other states – its diminishing *competitiveness*.

Causes of rise and decline: a first look

An explanation for the growth of state power in the system is not very hard to come by. Later industrializers have had advantages over early industrializers (Lewis 1978; Rostow 1978). Those states that adopted technology more recently have been more competitive than those who attempt to rely on older, now obsolete technology. The principal military powers today perfected a type of weaponry previously inconceivable. Some of the recent entrants to the central system have had larger territorial bases and more available resources than their predecessors. For all of these reasons and more, nation–states have risen to (varying) heights of relative capability in the system.

Reasons for the decline of the nation–state from the apex of the power curve are not so transparent.

The decline of "empire" is often attributed to military over-extension, but the reasons for and nature of over-extension are seldom made clear. For Rome, over-extension involved the difficulty of both

213

policing the frontier of a territory that encompassed 1.6 million square miles, stretching from the Rhine to the Black Sea, and of putting down domestic insurrection. In the later empire, the Roman legions spent more time maintaining order within the Empire than in defending it against incursions from external tribes (Bernardi 1970). Over-extension occurred for two reasons. Rome suffered a crushing short-age of manpower, magnified by the refusal of Roman citizens to join the armies, and leading to the less effectual incorporation of the "barbarians" into the fighting ranks (Finley 1970). Second, sources of capital dried up as output declined and as the nobles balkanized the economy while avoiding taxes.

Over-extension for Holland in the eighteenth century was a matter of naval deficiency leading to the collapse of the Dutch East India Company in the face of competition from the English. In the Nine Years War (1689–97), the Dutch launched 100 ships and 24,000 men annually, but could only muster 17 ships and a mere 3,000 men by 1781 in the battle of Dogger Bank (Boxer 1970). The depopulation of the seacoast towns resulted from failure to compete successfully either in the maritime carrying trade they once dominated or in deep-sea fishing and whaling.

Over-extension was obvious in seventeenth-century Spain where the population base in Catalonia, the province that provided most of the tax income and peasant soldiers, faltered agriculturally in a downward cycle of excessive governmental demands and diminished productivity (Vives 1970; Trevor Davies 1965). Over-extension in the sense of government expenditure in seventeenth-century Italy from Florence to Genoa to Milan had more to do with excess consumption than military defense. Combined with deteriorating economic compe-titiveness were manpower shortages created in part by the devastating plague that killed a third of Italy's population.

Causes of decline are undoubtedly multiple and highly intertwined. Primary causes are difficult to disentangle from secondary and tertiary causes. A common characteristic was the increasing alienation of the wealthy classes from the poor and the shocking disappearance of the productive middle strata. Put dramatically by the Dutch newspaper *De Borger* (October 19, 1778), it seemed as if "the body of the Common-wealth would shortly consist of little more than rentiers and beggars – the two kinds of people who are the least useful to the country" (Boxer 1970, p. 238). While these societal cleavages may have resulted from bad public policy (despite efforts to correct these trends) since the rich were allowed to escape taxation, and to further impoverish the peasantry and the urban poor, the cleavages also probably resulted from economic failure to compete with goods and commodities from abroad. The small rural freeholder disappeared because of this economic failure as often as the industrialist or merchant exporter.

This pattern of societal cleavage accompanied by the disappearance of middle strata during decline was apparent in the late Roman Empire, sixteenth-century Catalonia (Spain), seventeenth-century Northern Italy, and eighteenth-century Holland. Its presence is probably both cause and effect of decline.

A temptation is to believe that small size is detrimental to economic competitiveness, and it probably is in industries where economies of scale are important. But the decline of the Chinese and Byzantine empires, which stretched across trade routes and broad territorial areas, belies the efficacy of size as a means of rescuing competitiveness (Diehl 1970). Indeed, the fact that Chinese merchants could count on internal trade in such goods and commodities as textiles and salt suggests that profits could be made without facing the challenges of external trade. But without these challenges, internal industries sank deeper into inefficiency and backwardness.

Two other factors are present in the prominent examples of decline. They were visible within the textile industries of the ancient Arab world, China, Italy, and Holland perhaps because this industry was so important to the early preindustrial and industrial economies and because the industry so reflected the sensitivity of comparative advantage. First is the heavy burden caused by a failure to innovate and apply new ideas and technologies to manufacture. Confidence in the "old way" is perhaps the single most debilitating source of economic decline. The second factor is the society's increasing fear and inability to assume economic risk. Success breeds conservatism in economic outlook, and such conservatism eventually undermines economic success.

Decline stems from the greater rigidity of states bureaucratically as well. According to Louis Galambos (1982) and Mancur Olson (1982), special interest groups are able to bring about regulations that halt competition and invite paralysis of administration. Also, certain interest groups arise that tend to stress equity over efficiency, thus creating greater government regulatory burdens and reduced productivity. These rigidities and inflexibilities are more a function of age than size, Olson contends. Most governments are unable to reverse these trends through reform because such reform measures are not sufficiently popular. Younger states thus retain bureaucratic advantages over older states.

In addition, economies of scale reach their peak and cost curves

215

begin to turn upwards. The rate of economic growth slows down as optimal plant size and spatial relationships are exceeded. That is, economic growth begins to falter when huge size inhibits the flow of information and the efficient distribution of goods and services. Neither small markets nor huge markets, it is argued, are as efficient as optimal-sized markets. Similarly, government size must be optimal because it must be responsive as well as powerful. Huge governments – governments that also tend to be older – may be less capable of providing services and meeting the needs of constituents, despite efforts to decentralize administration.

Other quite different yet complementary reasons for decline are examined by Robert Gilpin (1981): (1) increased costs of protection reflecting external burdens of leadership; (2) rising consumption reflecting internal desire for more public and private goods and services; (3) declining productive investment because of low savings and scarcity of available capital; and (4) external diffusion of technology. Kenneth Oye (1983) notes that Britain and the United States top country rankings regarding proportion of national product devoted to consumption. Declining productive investment should result from the combined effects of increased leadership costs and rising consumption, and the first three causes make replenishment of technology to offset diffusion of technology extremely difficult. But why declining productive investment coincides with the other factors can only be explained by the lag in perceptions of the society about its changing international wealth status and by the well-known "ratchet effect" concerning resistance to down-side reductions of living standards during contractions of national income. Diffusion of technology alone would not contribute much to decline if capital were available to supplant old technology with new.

Causes of rise and decline: a second look

For purposes of analyzing the causes of rise and decline, several conceptual distinctions are essential (Table 9.1).

First is the complex relationship between absolute and relative change. Clearly, causes of decline include any and all factors which differentially favor *absolute* growth in other states. As we have seen, many factors internal and external to a state – problems of productivity, excessive private and public consumption, foreign borrowing, military over-extension, resource or manpower shortages, among others – can adversely affect its absolute (and thus relative) growth rate. In addition, a state's relative growth rate can be affected by new

216

Table 9.1 *Some causes of decline and their locus*

Factors affecting both absolute and relative growth rates directly

a, b	Excessive private consumption (opulence; low savings ratio)
a, b	Excessive public consumption (government over-spending)
a, b, c	Military over-extension
a, b, c	Foreign borrowing that leads to unfavorable exchange rate
a, b	Loss of technological innovativeness
a, b	Dimunition of risk-taking propensity
a, b	Regulatory rigidities that impede efficiency
a, b, c	Capital outflows that are not recovered
a, b, c	Manpower shortages: military, civilian labor
a, b, d	Lower literacy
a, b, c, d	Built-in limits to growth: environment, resource, physical space
a, b, d	Declining net new investment
a, b, d	Reduced competitiveness regarding market share

Additional factors affecting only relative growth rates directly

d	Past industrializers overtaken by more recent industrializers with larger territorial and population bases
d	Impact of entry and exit of states from central system
*	Impact of upper asymptote on rate of growth in relative power (based on finiteness of systemic shares)

Legend *a* internal to state in decline
     b absent or present to lesser degree for other states in system
     c external environment, including existing economic and political regimes
     d historical epoch
     * the dynamic of logistic growth

actors recently industrializing, or recently entering or exiting the "central system" of economic and political competition for leadership, if their absolute growth rates alter the "systemic norm." Finally, the very finiteness of systemic shares constrains the rate of growth in relative share even as absolute growth rates remain unchanged.

Second, causes of decline are not merely the inverse of the causes of rise. Although the causes of rise are akin to those explaining economic growth and development such as technological innovation and the creation of capital, the evolution of military capability, population growth, and the consolidation of territory are more important to power cycle analysis than they may be to theories of economic growth. However complex and multiple the causes of ascendancy, decline may be a more complex phenomenon.

Third, causes of change on the power cycle may be either *process*- or *decision-oriented*. Process-oriented causes of change possess high inertia and are not susceptible to much manipulation by government, such as population growth. Decision-oriented causes lend themselves to governmental intervention. Most budgetary allocations fall into this

217

category despite the difficulty in altering entitlements (Baily 1981; Darby 1984).

A fourth set of distinctions concerns origin. In general, cause of change on the power cycle may originate (1) internal to the state itself; (2) internal to competitors; (3) within the external environment in the interaction linking the state and its competitors, including existing economic and political regimes; and (4) as a result of occurrences that are time-bound or restricted to a historical epoch. Identifying where a cause of change originates and whether it is process- or decision-oriented may determine much about the capacity of a government to alter the trajectory of the power cycle and attitudes toward it.

For example, Lynn Williams, International President of the U.S. Steel Workers, notes that labor is not concerned about a relative decline for the United States in which "everyone becomes better off" in the system (personal communication, March 1990), but only relative decline as occurred in Britain involving decline of living standards. Herein lies the crucial importance of both the systemic average against which relative change must be measured, and the origin of causes for decline. In the first case, relative change may be negative (decline) and still satisfactory; in the second case, it is unsatisfactory even if it is positive. This keen insight taps human reaction to relative change more directly. Internal power generation is the key to both absolute and relative power change and its societal impact.

Each of the factors listed in Table 9.1 has to some degree impacted on the US power cycle in recent decades. There is a danger in fixing too much attention on any single cause, or seeking a simple policy solution.

Policy analysts warned of this danger regarding "imperial over-stretch" explanations for U.S. decline (Huntington 1988; Rostow 1988; Nye 1988b, 1990). This is not to deny that military over-extension contributes greatly to relative decline, nor that the escalating costs of its defense commitments have adversely affected the U.S. relative power trajectory (Oye 1983; Gilpin 1981; Kennedy 1988a, b). The point here is that the United States is not suffering from over-extension of the *type or extent* of Imperial Spain or Great Britain, as asserted (Kennedy 1987, 1988a). Rather, the deeper historical analogy with Imperial Spain is the way in which *finance* impinged upon U.S. *productivity* and hence upon its *capacity to generate power* (Hamilton 1934).

The problem for the United States in the 1980s was that very high interest rates had to be maintained to finance the large and growing federal debt for enormous social as well as defense burdens. These interest rates in turn attracted huge amounts of capital from abroad which found the security, size, and potential growth of the U.S. economy attractive. But this capital did what the borrowing of Charles V, combined with the silver bullion from the New World, had done for the Spanish economy. In each case, the exchange rate was inflated, affecting negatively the productivity and output and capacity to export of each economy. In addition, the inflated currency encouraged its citizens to import goods to sustain their high standard of living while compelling the home industries to cease production or to relocate abroad. But a steadfastness of monetary policy, a discipline of fiscal policy, and a new commitment to reform can prevent the U.S. economy from the bankruptcy suffered by Imperial Spain.

Clearly, the causes of decline in general, and *vis-à-vis* the United States in particular, are multiple and interactive.

Historical example and cyclical reversibility: implications for U.S. policy

The founders of modern states commonly attempt to assert that they are the heirs of ancient empire. Hence the argument that the Ommayads (644–750) and the Abbasids (744–1258) have been reborn in the midst of the oil power of modern Saudi Arabia and Iraq; that present-day Iran is built on the foundations of the Sufis (1273–1400); that contemporary China is a triumph of neo-Confucianism that has its origins at least as far back as the eleventh and twelfth centuries. The problem with such assertions of revival and renaissance is that the cycle of power has been broken by long periods of collapse, internally induced or externally imposed. While in cultural and even in territorial terms, the claims of continuity may be legitimate, the continuity of political authority is often disrupted or subject to question.

Within the modern state system, the claim of full recovery to place and status is often obscured by changes of territorial consolidation. Could one argue that the Italian city states of Florence and Venice have enjoyed a modern vindication in the Risorgimento of the nineteenth century? Or that the status of eighteenth-century Prussia found its reincarnation in Bismarckian Germany? Even the lines of dynastic power are difficult to trace in the midst of fragmentation and conquest, reorganization and consolidation. Still, the outlines of statehood and centralized rule often are interpreted as reflections of earlier peaks of brilliance.

Russia in the nineteenth century suffered a decline in relative power caused partly by the industrialization that was going on around it in

219

France, Britain and later Germany, but in which it did not share until the end of the century. Prior to the Russian Revolution of 1917, that dip in the Russian power cycle was reversed. Similarly, the trajectory of Italian power after unification was downward, not upwards, as we have come to expect from the normal pattern.

This historical evidence, sketchy and disputed though it may be, suggests nonetheless that the implacable denial of reversibility is probably on shaky ground. While no full-scale upturn of a major cycle has yet occurred in the period covered by this study, fluctuations that amount to more than temporary perturbations of the cycle are surely evident.

Moreover, while the power cycle may contain persuasive inertia and unrelenting downward pressure on a state once in substantial decline, that inertia is far less for a trend-line containing much variance in the data points, as has been the case for the United States.

POSITION AND TRAJECTORY ON THE U.S. POWER CYCLE

When did the United States reach the apex of its relative power? According to Henry Kissinger in 1968, "The age of the superpowers is now drawing to a close" (Kissinger 1974, p. 56; Art 1990). Perhaps a handful of analysts at the time understood what this outstanding diplomatist and other American policy makers saw immediately. Emerging from this awareness of the American power situation was the Nixon Doctrine which admonished allies to do more to help themselves since henceforth they could not expect as much from the United States. Our own aggregate power index for 1950–85 corroborates these observations: the apex of American relative power, on this index for state capability to carry out and sustain a variety of systemic leadership functions, occurred in the 1960–65 interval. Incremental decline followed during the next two decades.

The economics of America at "high noon" shows *how position on the power cycle (relative share) can drive absolute growth behavior*, and how that behavior in turn can erode relative share and alter the state's trajectory. When a country is so dominant in terms of systemic share, the managers of many of its principal firms find that their industries, like the economy as a whole, are bumping against an upper asymptote to further growth in share. As the second principle of the power cycle demonstrates, the dominant state so heavily weights the growth rate of the system that it is "competing against itself" much more than against other states. Greater increments in absolute output provide very little gain in market share simply because of its huge share. Facing an abrupt change in expectations, the former strategy of maximizing competitive edge is abandoned. Not able to expand market share, the industries shift to a mentality of merely trying to protect that share, or of extracting monopoly rents from that share. The industries become oligopolists not so much by choice as by circumstance.

In contrast, the objective of countries and their industrial managers lower on the power cycle is maximum growth, increase in market share, penetration of foreign markets, and protection of their own economic sphere. Theirs is an offensive strategy built on aggressive exportation and selective and constrained importation. Neomercantilism, augmented by a producer-oriented rather than consumer-oriented set of policies by their home governments, is the strategy of the ascendant economies and their leading industries in the late twentieth century. These self-interested policies further turned the dominant actor's strategy against itself, and turned the open world economy to their great benefit.

Level of U.S. power is slowly beginning to dissipate. Obscuring this trajectory are exchange rate variations, over- or under-valuation of assets, discrepancies in calculating GNP and GDP, and ambiguity about terms and amounts borrowed. Moreover, perception is deceptive. Twentieth-century data, limited to the top of the curve, appear flat. Comparisons with the entire system smoothe the amplitude, making change almost imperceptible.

A different problem in assessing the position and trajectory of U.S. relative power involves misplacing the apex of the U.S. cycle – in terms of both its level and its timing – and hence in either exaggerating or underestimating the extent of U.S. decline. That problem results from disaggregating the concept of power into many separate economic and military strands, and focusing on one to the exclusion of the others. Economic peaking precedes the military apex for the United States. The economic zenith comes during the immediate aftermath of the war, and hence invites either (1) being explained away by the artificial collapse of Japan and Europe to support the "no decline" thesis, or (2) being used to demonstrate both the inevitability and the great extent of decline. By combining the indexes of economic and military power, as is done conceptually by the foreign policy decision maker and as we do in our yardstick for power, the apex is moved forward to the 1960s. Although the rationale for the construction of the aggregate index was not the avoidance of misleading perturbations, the effect of the index is to yield an apex for U.S. power

221

that is not obfuscated by European and Japanese reconstruction.

Notwithstanding the very artificial period of reconstruction after the war when American power was inflated (collapse of Europe and Japan yielded a disproportionately small denominator in the relative power ratio), and the interval of the Reagan defense build-up which once again boosted the military dimension of U.S. power, though at considerable economic cost, the salient observation is that U.S. relative power – economic and military – when considered across the entire span of U.S. history, apparently peaked in the mid-1960s. It is true that in the period 1950–85 some economic indicators showed even absolute decline, such as the share of spending and employment devoted to manufacturing, the savings balance, competitiveness, and the percent of gross fixed capital formation (Lawrence 1984). The point is not that such absolute decline took place on selected indicators, but that decline from the peak occurred in the export share of world markets and in the share of investment in GNP relative to Japan, the NICs, and even Mexico and Brazil (Lodge and Vogel 1987, p. 307.) On average, especially in a phase of rapid world growth (1960–73), but also in slower growth periods (1973–80), gross domestic product grew more slowly for the United States than for many of its major trading partners and for the OECD average.

While relative decline to date has been quite incremental, a continuation of past absolute growth rates will result in much more rapid relative decline in the future. The United States' great initial advantage in level meant that its growth rate contributed so heavily to the "systemic norm" that its rate was not much less than that norm. But the present differential is not sufficient to offset higher growth rates for Japan, Europe, and/or China in the future.

As explained in chapter 3, relative decline can be reversed only through an acceleration in the state's absolute growth or a lowering of the absolute growth rate of its competitors: the state's absolute growth rate must be at least as great as the growth rate of the system for its relative decline to be halted. Conversely, the rate of its relative decline depends upon how much lower its growth rate is than that norm.

These facts must be borne in mind for the United States to accurately assess the degree of inevitability and the likelihood of reversibility of its current pattern of relative decline. *The future U.S. trajectory depends increasingly on having a strong absolute growth rate.* Despite the highly sensitive nature of the U.S. economy, so highly integrated with the world economy, and so vulnerable to endogenous and exogenous shock, the U.S. economy is far more dynamic than many other capitalist economies, to say nothing of the socialist ones, and better able to adjust to crisis (Lodge and Vogel 1987; Scott 1985). On the other hand, the greatest economic challenge to U.S. economic growth has been and will likely continue to be among the Newly Industrializing Countries, the "Little Dragons" and Japan, although neo-mercantilist policies are not in their own best interest considering China's rapid growth rate (see below, p. 235). The United States must achieve a new industrial renaissance, because *economic rebirth to increase its own rate of internal power generation is the only way it can slow its downward trajectory*, and *the only way it can confront the security dilemmas forthcoming during systems transformation*. Three explanations of U.S. decline in relative power suggest alternative paths to recovery.

EXPLANATIONS FOR U.S. DECLINE

Limits to growth preferences. According to this perspective, advanced industrial society is likely to find appealing a trade-off between the alleged costs of growth and the alleged benefits of no-growth or a reduced growth-rate that promises an improvement in the quality of life and in welfare (Meadows, Meadows, Randers, and Behrens 1974). Depending upon how "welfare" is defined, growth may be the antithesis of welfare (work versus leisure or electricity versus acid rain), or at least units of growth cannot be easily converted into increased units of welfare (Wonnacott 1984).

Post-industrial leads and lags hypothesis. According to this hypothesis, the United States is the first post-industrial nation but not the last (Bell 1973). As the other rich countries mature economically, they will follow the patterns of industrial transformation pioneered by the United States. This externally induced source of growth disparity will narrow as other countries catch up with the United States, thus reducing the apparent decline in the U.S. position on its power cycle. A prominent aspect of this hypothesis about industrial maturity is that there is an ineluctable trend away from manufacturing toward the service economy which is much less growth-oriented (Petit 1986).

Power cycle analysis. The cycle interpretation is less subject to automatic adjustment than the post-industrial leads and lags hypothesis, and less subject to immediate societal choice than a shedding of the limits-to-growth outlook or a mere redistribution of military commitments (Scott 1985; Phillips 1986). In the cycle interpretation, reversal requires a reversal of historical precedent via proper management of economic and financial as well as security commitments. It

223

requires an innovation of new governmental responses to a very old pattern of structural change – economic and strategic. It requires an alteration of the inertia involved in the process of incremental decline. Hence it must reverse the economic policies of high noon that devastated its world competitiveness.

ROUTES TO RECOVERY AS PER POWER CYCLE ANALYSIS

If one assumes symmetry for the pattern of U.S. rise and decline on the curve of relative capability, the complete cycle would not soon be completed. But even assuming symmetry, we do not know how long the United States will remain at a plateau near its high point, which would occur if it could maintain growth rates close to the norm for the great power system. Likewise, there is no theoretical, empirical, or historical reason to assume symmetry regarding the level of relative power at which the second inflection would occur.

Actualization of latent capability. Where substantial latent capability has been under-utilized as is almost certainly true in the American case, fuller use will have a positive impact on the pattern of the cycle. Any of the classical factors of production, land, labor, or capital, may be underutilized. An economy far below full employment, a territory underexplored and rich in resources, an intellectual and scientific base poorly integrated with business and commerce, or an untapped tax base that could be readily incorporated into more productive use, all represent a latent capability base that can be actualized.

This awareness of "spare capacity" is not a recipe for Keynesianism, which would focus on demand. Needed instead is a well thought out, consistent strategy of development at the national level that permits firms to make their own long-term choices regarding expansion and development at the micro level. Excessive uncertainty and high costs of capital hinder this latter initiative.

Innovative substitution. A government may seek to change the trajectory of the power cycle by discovering a revolutionary innovation that enables the polity to leap-frog competitors' efforts without changing the actualized-to-latent capability ratio. Examples are the hoped-for discovery of a way to use fusion to produce a virtually infinite, low-cost supply of energy which in turn could be sold to other states, or the Reagan Administration's effort to hurdle

224

the pronounced Soviet lead in state-of-the-art nuclear weaponry and delivery capacity by developing the Strategic Defense Initiative (Kahn 1976, pp. 58–83). Innovative substitution relies upon a stock of resourcefulness that, if applied immediately, can be used to overcome material disadvantage. But, of course, the cost of developing these innovations must not be so prohibitive as to further inflate the federal deficit.

Innovative substitution has the effect of *translating* the power curve upwards by the amount of additional capability that innovation provided solely to the state. As a technique to reverse decline on the power cycle, however, innovation creates a one-time effect that does not alter the shape of the curve, and diffusion of ideas sooner or later will eliminate the monopoly of increased capability it provided.

Accelerated performance. This technique relies neither on an increase of output using latent resources more fully, nor on the impact of a revolutionary innovation giving the state an enormous competitive advantage. Accelerated performance attempts to use reform to improve the quality of the production underlying national capability. Reform can involve either procedures or institutions. Examples are reform of the banking system that enables a government to concentrate savings more effectively and to increase the level of investment or employment without jeopardizing price stability, or reform of the armed forces tripartite division into a unified command that saves money and enhances command effectiveness. Consider the organizational reforms necessitated by aerospace deployment evident within NORAD (Codevilla 1986).

Accelerated performance does not necessarily have an immediate positive effect on national capability but may actually hinder the development of capability in the short-run. A dip in the power cycle may follow reform. But the improvement in efficiency and therefore in output will substantially improve power position in the medium term. Accelerated performance thus has decided intertemporal importance for the power cycle.

IS DECLINE ON THE U.S. POWER CYCLE INEVITABLE? POLICY CHOICES OF HIGH POLITICS

The question of the inevitability of relative decline has, in the U.S. case, been obscured by a fatalistic preoccupation with the seeming imminence of some advanced form of decline. Although the answer may have seemed to many an unambiguous "yes" in the 1970s

225

through mid-1980s, more recent indicators at the very least add ambiguity to that answer. They suggest that the answers to the questions of inevitability and imminence of decline are to be determined by U.S. decision and action (Nye 1990; Rosecrance 1990). What decisions or actions according to power cycle analysis might disprove the imminence and/or inevitability assumptions? Conversely, what decisions or actions might encourage decline?

The need for a new industrial renaissance

Realignment of the U.S. dollar did assist the come-back of American manufacturing. Between 1980 and 1990, federal debt as a percentage of GNP was slightly reduced, though still far too high, and focused on the wrong purposes. Despite the comparatively good news, the debilitating economic reality was that U.S. growth was the slowest and net investment the lowest among the seven largest OECD economies (*Economist*, 27 May 1989, p. 12). The U.S. economy forgot how to manufacture, *even in a host of high tech areas*. Until this situation is reversed, growth will not return. And, as argued in the previous section, *without a strong rate of economic growth, slippage on the U.S. power cycle will continue at an accelerating pace* because the United States no longer has the "safety valve" which its previous high level provided. Conversely, if strong economic growth returns, slippage on the U.S. power cycle can be slowed quite significantly.

American thinking about international political economy is so taken by the notion of fixed factors of production and comparative advantage that firms are often all too ready to concede market share to foreign competition that has a labor cost advantage or even a persistent exchange rate advantage. Of course, some industries are obsolete. Yet what is more insightful is how many industries through technological innovation remain competitive and an important part of the economy. The Japanese did not concede the steel industry to low-labor cost competitors; they innovated new lower cost methods of production and retained their price advantage. The Germans did not move out of the machine tool industry in the face of cheaper output from Taiwan; they found better ways of making high-quality instruments, better adapted to consumer needs, at less cost. Comparative advantage can be created (Scott 1985), and with improved product design and technological innovation can be retained. The metals industries, energy production, and manufacturing will be at the heart of the world economy well into the so-called information age, necessitating measures of power that stress continuity as well as novelty.

226

Policy recommendations for reform of the U.S. economy are straightforward. (1) The United States must reinvigorate the economic base through the use of technological innovation in heavy industry and durables production (as well as in services) and by consciously seeking to maintain a competitive position in the manufacture of the latest technologies. (2) In an era of rapid scientific and technological change, U.S. research and development as a percentage of GNP in non-military areas must remain at the top of the OECD rankings. (3) The United States must improve the quality of the American work force (wages cannot remain comparatively high while quality lags) especially at the elementary and high school levels so that competitiveness exists throughout the labor force, not just at the very top. (4) In order to generate more investment capital, while cutting the federal deficit and dependency on foreign borrowing, the United States must shift preferences from conspicuous consumption to a renewal of private and public saving, resolutely and without abrupt shocks to the economy. (5) Foreseeable problems such as a return of high energy prices, and greater foreign energy dependence, ought to receive attention now when the United States has the leisure to develop solutions through further deregulation, innovation, and substitution. (6) Clean growth, based on decision making that becomes long-term at both the macro and micro levels, must be established as a priority equivalent to the priorities of international exchange rate and monetary coordination, control of inflation, and responses to the business cycle.

Wrestling with the U.S. capability–commitment gap

A paramount policy concern for the United States in coming decades will be reduction not just of the trade and balance of payments deficits, which to some extent through depreciation of the exchange rate are self-correcting, but reduction of the federal budgetary deficit and of the national debt. Rigidity exists because of entitlements and expenditure of funds for future purchases that cannot easily be deferred. Part of the origin of the federal budgetary deficit is external and is cumulative, stemming from decades of large per unit of GNP expenditures for defense. Part of this is the result of excessive consumption versus saving and productive investment. In either case, as the burden of financing these deficits becomes larger, the pressure to reduce governmental expenditures will build.

For the United States and the Soviet Union, something of a capability–commitment gap has developed. A rough index of this gap, overladen by domestic as well as foreign obligations, is the U.S. federal deficit equivalent to some 4 to 5% of GNP and the much larger Soviet deficit in excess of 11% of GNP. Deficits in themselves are not necessarily damaging to an economy, or even very burdensome. Canada, for example, with its strong economy and excellent natural resource base has long had a deficit much larger in per capita terms than that of the United States. But large governmental deficits do "crowd out" borrowing in the private sector. In turn, domestic firms are at an international investment disadvantage.

Suspected over-extension can be dealt with in a number of ways. One way is to exercise greater internal discipline by encouraging greater savings, greater investment, lower governmental spending, and somewhat higher taxes. But this must be carried out in such a fashion as not to send the economy into a recession.

Another way to cope with the deficit is to reduce expenditures on defense. A technique attempting to deal with over-extension might be to reduce the level of assurance, while retaining the same scope of commitments. But lowered assurance is precisely the approach most dangerous to security relations. It attempts to use bluff in place of substance. It invites challenge and security thrusts instead of discouraging them.

In reality, a strong temptation exists for neither the allies nor the United States to bell the "security cat." The tendency is great to paper over the capability–commitment gap until some crisis makes it irremissible. Better forethought and smooth adjustment than non-planned and precipitous change in commitment during a critical interval for one or more of the leading states.

Wrestling with the U.S. fear of interdependence

A paradox confronts the state in relative decline. Interdependence becomes more important, not less important, to the state and to the system as the reduced prestige of a leading state is less effective in itself inducing cooperation. But the temptation is to rely on unilateral rather than concerted action to gain the same ends heretofore obtainable by prestige alone. Moreover, unilateral action comes at a time when it is likely to earn the greatest resistance from other members of the system who feel that it is less than ever justified. The declining state is tempted to dump interdependence at precisely the moment when it is most needed and when unilateral action is most counterproductive.

Consider the handling of the international debt crisis (Malkin 1987;

Buchanan and Wagner 1987; Selowsky 1987). This crisis, following on the heels of the two so-called oil price revolutions of 1973 and 1979, illustrates both the U.S. hesitation (or inability) to rely on interdependence in this period and the propensity to take unilateral action.

International implications of a prolonged U.S. debt crisis

Austerity option. In order to meet current security demands as well as to maintain its living standards into the future, the United States may have to dig more deeply into its current standard of living and social well-being. In this austerity option, by reducing its level of personal consumption and governmental expenditure on such items as welfare, unemployment insurance, educational expenditures, research and development, and retirement benefits, the United States can afford a large military budget even set against a GNP that is not rising as rapidly as in the past, but at least by 2-1/2 to 3%. It could also eliminate its federal budgetary deficit and begin to reduce the carrying cost on the national debt. At least it can curb the rise in the national debt attributable to borrowing from abroad, perhaps the most problematic component of an increasing national debt. But this austerity option will not accomplish very much for future generations, and will be a very painful way of "keeping up appearances" internationally for a limited period, unless the resulting savings are used more productively.

Burden-sharing option. This is a very old option dressed up in the new clothing of post-Gorbachev NATO rhetoric. The objective is to get previously reluctant allies to do more to defend themselves so as to take some of the financial responsibilities off the alliance leader. Several considerations make this option very problematic.

First, given a new more relaxed climate of detente, allies are even less likely to want to divert expenditures away from social goals to strengthen defense. Germany, for example, will be preoccupied with the internal expenses of reviving the former East Germany economy and rebuilding infrastructure.

Second, as ties begin to loosen not just among the former members of the Warsaw Pact, but among some of the members of NATO as well, the meaning of burden-*sharing* will be increasingly questioned as the sense of a common purpose becomes obscured. This can scarcely relieve the financial burdens of defense for the alliance leader since the degree of cooperation and coordination in planning and acquisition will decline. A measure of this tendency is the trouble experienced by

229

the consortium of Britain, Italy, Spain, and West Germany which had planned to build at least 800 Eurofighter planes for the European forces.

Third, some of the members of NATO will begin to harbor poorly suppressed suspicion of the motives and capability of Germany and Japan, the two governments most able to relieve the United States of some of its military burdens. While these governments will do for defense what they believe is in their own self-interest, whatever they do will increasingly be criticized by neighbors, thus discouraging them from certain actions that could be very helpful from the U.S. point of view.

"The Soviets will save us" option. According to this option, what happens on the Soviet and American power cycles in terms of the defense component is extremely interactive. Depending upon how the Soviet Union responds to movement on its power cycle, the United States will adjust its own strategy. Soviet military spending may be reduced, taking pressure off American budgets, either because (1) *perestroika* works, giving the Soviets confidence that their policy of relaxed tensions with the West is on the right track, or because (2) Soviet decline occurs, but the Soviet leadership is able to adjust smoothly and to accept the implications of a smaller Soviet world role and a diminished military presence. Alternatively, Soviet military spending could remain at high levels either because (1) *perestroika* works too well, generating a very large economic base from which to draw military expenditures, or because (2) decline occurs and the Soviet leadership attempts to deny the implications for a constricted Soviet world role.

Under the former circumstances, the Soviets save Western policy by cutting military expenditures, by reducing their military presence first in Eastern Europe, next in the Third World, and finally at home. Western economic choices become easier as overall defense budgets are adjusted downwards. With renewed threat, the Soviets could do what they did with the interventions in Hungary (1956) and Czechoslovakia (1968): they scare the West badly enough to enable it to reorganize its defenses, perhaps in a fashion that is less disproportionately burdensome to the United States. In either case, initiatives for policy change stem from how the Soviet Union adjusts to movement on its power cycle. This option is very passive. Lags in perception and response will scarcely suit planners and may undermine implementation of this option altogether.

Growth option. By reorienting its ratio of saving to consumption, increasing its domestic investment into productive enterprise, retaining a leadership role in the manufacture of essential technologies, enhancing its long-term productivity through a variety of educational and management techniques, and expanding its rate of economic growth, the United States could, through a resulting larger tax base, cover an adequate level of defense expenditures, however the Soviets respond to changes on the Soviet power cycle. But to achieve this option, the United States must reorient its economic priorities, create a business climate that is more propitious, and train and integrate a work force that is more competent and committed when measured by international standards. It must also manage exchange rates in the face of massive continued borrowing so that a repeat of the 1983–86 situation does not return whereby the inflated dollar contributed to a massive trade deficit, thus inhibiting the capacity to earn revenue from exports. This combined strategy, oriented toward environmentally safe growth, is not an option for the short term. Indeed it may become a chimera which policy makers pretend to be pursuing while in fact taking an easier route that leads to the opposite results. It is, however, in many senses a "best" option.

Conclusion

Unlike some past systemic contexts, the leading state in the current system faces challenges that are bifurcated. Military challenge comes from the Soviet Union, since it is the only country that can mortally wound the United States and the only one that seeks to project its power globally. Economic challenge comes primarily from Japan and a group of Newly Industrializing Countries, most of whom are very efficient producers and in addition practice neo-mercantilism, seeking to displace the United States (and Western Europe) from many sectors of the world market while keeping their own economies as closed as possible. Thus, for the United States, challenge comes from two directions. Although no one is on the American "doorstep" to replace it imminently, since no power cycle equals that of the United States in terms of level, the complacency this awareness induces is America's worst enemy. That complacency could erode the long-term economic base underlying American power within a decade or so, such that movement down its power cycle will become virtually impossible to reverse, even though at present reversibility is within the American grasp.

Decline for the United States must be interpreted with respect to these diverse challenges. The only meaningful policy concern regarding decline on the power cycle involves the *internal rate of power*

231

generation. Nor is there much value in lamenting the external aspects of decline attributable to the success of competitors. It is a diversion from the real problems confronting the U.S. economy and, as for Ibsen's "Master Builder," only evokes fears about the "younger generation . . . knocking at my door." Instead, the United States must concentrate on putting its own house in order, and, together with its partners, determine the next stage of construction which will benefit the entire trading system.

It is wrong to equate the slow internal U.S. accession to dominance, much of it reluctant and unsought, with the military hegemonies of the past that attempted to deny place and role for other states, usually through armed force. It is also wrong to suggest that severe decline is imminent and foreordained and, therefore, that radical role adjustments are needed immediately. What is needed is careful planning by the United States and its allies so that changes of capability in the economic dimension (and decisions based on economic concerns) do not undermine the ability to provide security in either the short term or the long term, if not both.

The United States is a strong country still near the peak of its power and role in world politics. It will likely retain a position of leadership for decades to come, regardless of conscious policy choice or societal costs, given the inertia of change in power and role. But it faces tough problems which will determine whether that retention will be at greater or lesser cost to itself, and whether the interval of primary responsibility will be shorter or longer. That nascent relative decline has occurred is a reality. How the United States chooses to deal with this reality is of relevance not only to its own citizens but to the political equilibrium of the international system.

THE ESSENTIAL QUESTION

"Are governments really so myopic? Why haven't they learned from history? They know the power cycle exists, so why have they not adjusted their policies accordingly?" Underlying the challenge for policy is the essential question. What is it that governments do *not* know about the power cycle? What is the lesson which governments must learn from history?

First, strategists instinctively think in relative power terms. But viewed from the outside, the relative power dynamic is misunderstood because it is often counterintuitive. When the difference between absolute and relative power change becomes more fully understood, and when the implications of that difference are spelled out with some precision, even the economic historian enters a different world of interpretation. Suddenly, a new vista of statecraft (international economic as well as international political) is opened for assessment that previously seemed incomprehensible or characterized by misperception.

Second, the foreign policy maker is not myopic. The problem historically has been that governments are taken by surprise when a critical point occurs: their expectations regarding the future trend of relative power, expectations induced by trends in absolute growth, are suddenly shown to be wrong. Governments are conscious of the cycle of relative power and role, but they do not fully understand the conflicting messages in absolute and relative power change, nor the real locus of competition for share, and hence are not prepared for the occurrence of a critical point. *After* the critical point has occurred, governments are all too aware of the *sudden shift in perception* and foreign policy expectations. They belatedly rush to augment or to adjust their position in a way that itself becomes unsettling.

A government does not have to "calculate" shifts on its power cycle for circumstances to force it to make painful foreign policy decisions. All strategic calculation is mediated by perceptions, as Samuel Huntington (1988) has emphasized. It is because the critical point involves a sudden shift in perception that its occurrence is so easily perceived and so troubling. Most alert governments will know about their altered fortunes and will worry about the implications for their foreign policy conduct. Statesmen who are most alert, best informed, and most analytic regarding foreign policy conduct will pick up the signals first. Eventually others will become aware of the same shift in power trend. Those looking to the future and planning strategy will be most perceptive, but they also are subject to the greatest shock and incredulity when they uncover the new perceptions. But worried or not by the new perceptions, the government will eventually have to confront structural change, and respond in some fashion to it. Politically that will not be easy.

Seriously misunderstood today is the future trajectory of Japan's relative power in the great power system. Consider two opposite views regarding Japan's future relative power trajectory. Paul Kennedy (1988) asserts that, *based on a continuation of existing trends*, "for the foreseeable future ... Japan's trajectory continues to rise upward" (p. 467). But, *based on power cycle theory's understanding of the relative power dynamic*, even if one assumes the continuation of existing trends, Japan's relative share of GNP in the great power system is likely to reach its peak in the foreseeable future. Japan's share of GNP

233

in the great power system is already beginning to plateau, but not because of competition from "above." Whether the United States has a 1% or 3% rate of growth will neither postpone nor accelerate the timing of the peak for Japan's share of GNP, although that difference in growth rate greatly affects the rapidity of U.S. decline. Even should Japan's GNP surpass that of the United States, its own era as "systemic leader" is likely to be very short-lived. Why? The competition causing the Japanese cycle to peak comes from "below," from China's rapid growth. In fact, a rapid rate of growth for China would greatly influence the relative power trajectory of each state in the system, and it thus must be a major key in formulating "grand strategy." A strong U.S. economy is in the best strategic interest of Japan as well as of the United States.

Once the nature of the power cycle dynamic is understood, this judgment is so obvious as to appear trivial. No calculations are necessary. But data on "existing trends" in GNP can be used to test whether Japan's GNP will soon peak or will continue to rise in the foreseeable future. Richard Rosecrance (1990) provides "reasonable estimates" of GNP in 1986 and of growth rates for the United States (4 trillion 1986 U.S. dollars, 2.5%), Japan ($2.27 trillion, 4%), the Soviet Union ($2 trillion, 1.5%), and China (0.6 trillion, 7%). As in Kennedy's future projections, he assumes the growth rates remain unchanged and demonstrates that Japan would obtain a GNP nearly equal to that of the United States by 2020. What are the associated *relative* scores for percent share of GNP in that four-actor system? Figure 9.1 (middle row) clearly shows that, in the more than forty years from 1986 to 2032, Japan's increase in percentage share of GNP in that system is *only 5%*. It plateaus at that level in about 2015, and begins to enter decline about a decade later. This is in stark contrast to the *20%* increase in percentage share of GNP in that system which it acquired during the previous forty-year period (1950 to 1990).

These conclusions are robust across growth rates for the United States that vary from 2.0% (Figure 9.1, upper row) to 3.0% (bottom row). Higher U.S. growth rates postpone the point at which Japanese and American curves cross, but they do not appreciably alter the reality that Japan will reach a peak in about the same period, nor that the periodicity of its relative ascendancy will be quite short. Its competition comes from below, as predicted by power cycle theory.

We again see here that trends in relative power are not tied directly to trends in absolute power for any given state (or to internal product cycles). One of the most important aspects of the relative power dynamic is that someday the present trend will undergo an inversion

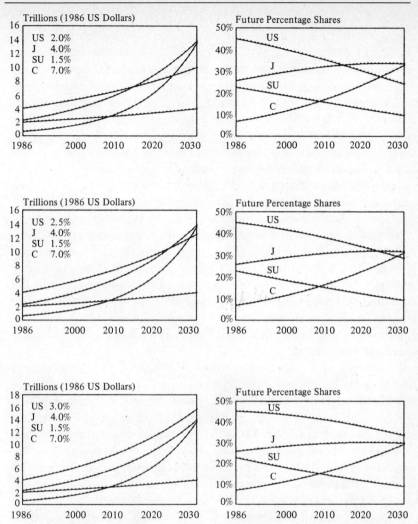

Figure 9.1 Continuation of "present trends" in absolute growth of GNP: the Japanese rise does *not* continue

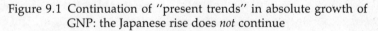

Source: Rosecrance (1990, p. 39) provided the starting values and growth rates (2.5% for U.S.)

even if "everything remains the same" in absolute terms. The bounds of the given system directly affect the dynamic.

But another important aspect of change in the system is that everything does not remain the same. The Soviet Union could once again increase its growth rate above an annual 1.5% of GNP, thus

235

forcing down Japanese relative growth in a fashion reminiscent of the impact that Russia had on Germany in 1910. A united Europe would affect Japanese power even more precipitously. If the effect of the Newly Industrializing Countries is taken into account, Japan may be impacted more sharply than other governments less dependent upon foreign trade, thus reducing the Japanese growth rate below 4% annually. But the quintessential conclusion is that Japanese relative growth in GNP will peak, quite possibly very soon before or after Japan approximates the power level of other leading actors in the system. The tides of history are already shifting against it.

To know that such an inversion of the power trend will occur is in no sense equivalent to knowing how to prevent or manage such an occurrence. Realistic expectations are only the first step.

An analogous decision predicament is that of the monetary economist at the Federal Reserve. Recently the so-called P^* measure has been adopted in a effort to predict inflation and to control future price changes (Kilborn 1989). The challenge is quite similar to that of the statesman attempting to devise a grand strategy to cope with decline and the onset of a critical point. In each case, the effort is to prevent a sudden inversion in the trend. The P^* measure is a good idea, but is it a sufficient policy tool?

The problem for both the statesman and the monetary economist is that there is too much variation unconstrained by available simple policy instruments. For the monetary economist, the temptation is to ignore other more Keynesian factors such as the effect of fiscal policy on how much income is taxed, saved, invested, or consumed. If all the burdens of control are placed on a single instrument, eventually the vacillations in inflation will become too wide for that instrument to contain. Attempts to control will themselves become the source of instability, or will begin to contribute to that instability.

If the architects of grand strategy (1) are unable to postpone decline or contain the rate of decline, and (2) are unable by definition and by past experience to predict the onset of critical points on the power cycle, the alternative is to seek out and to devise additional policy instruments for attempting to manage systems transformation when it occurs. That is the challenge to which we turn in the final chapter.

10 SYSTEMS TRANSFORMATION AND THE NEW IMPERATIVES OF HIGH POLITICS

Returning from a European conference in the fall of 1989, Paul Nitze commented on the impact of the Soviet economic reforms, the debt situation, the attitudes of the European allies, and the future course of U.S. foreign policy in the aftermath of containment: "All is uncertainty." In the midst of the greatest relaxation of East–West tensions since the origin of the Cold War, the first stages of systems transformation are unfolding. Following the euphoria of improved relations, the uncertainties of what all of these changes mean for alliance relationships, the Soviet role, and U.S. leadership are now beginning to bear on contemporary statemen.

Strategic discussion in this chapter emanates from four sets of theoretical argument which form the cornerstone of this book: (1) the theory of the power cycle (of changing systems structure); (2) the theory of war causation; (3) theoretical assessment of the crisis of systems transformation; and (4) the new concept of international political equilibrium.

FUTURE SYSTEMS TRANSFORMATION: THE POWER CYCLE ASSESSMENT

A full transformation of the current system, whatever the period of duration, is likely to have the following characteristics.

(1) The United States is likely to be well past its peak of relative national capability, how far is dependent upon how effectively it is able to put into place the kind of policies assessed in the prior chapter. With a strong economic growth rate, the upper part of the U.S. power cycle will be quite flat, postponing significant relative decline substantially into the twenty-first century. Slowed economic growth will accelerate decline. How the United States administers its economy in the decade of the 1990s will in large part determine the rate of its decline in relative capability.

(2) Somewhat behind the United States in terms of power cycle

237

position, in a fully transformed system the Soviet Union too will have crossed its upper turning point. At that time, the system will have to absorb the shock of the Soviet discovery that it confronts rapid decline. Since the heart of Soviet power is military might, a peak in overall Soviet power is of great consequence for world politics, no matter what the nature of the events that transpire.

(3) Japan, at present well beyond its first inflection point, may or may not have crossed its upper turning point in such a fully trans-formed system. If Japanese power too has peaked, the tensions of adjustment among the three leading states will indeed be substantial. Moreover, whether Japan reaches its peak before the Soviets do, at the same time, or later, will affect very much the kind of foreign policy the United States and other leading governments adopt. In general, if Japan peaks first, perceived pressure on Japan from Moscow is bound to have an effect on the Japanese decision to bolster its defenses. If the Soviet Union enters advanced and permanent decline first, and does so in a fashion that is benign, Japan will have more time to adjust, in concert with the United States or in combination with other govern-ments perhaps inside the region.

(4) China, given its accelerated growth at present, may reach its first inflection point within the overall period of systems transformation under contemplation here, whether from a lowering of its own absolute growth rate or increased growth rates elsewhere in the system. No estimate is possible of its level of relative national capa-bility at that time. Whatever happens to China in power terms affects the Soviet Union first, and *vice versa*, because of the long common border and because each state corresponds to a rival quintessential "land power" as opposed to "maritime state." If the Soviet Union peaks before China reaches its own first inflection point, China is likely to make demands upon the Soviet Union for accommodation of various sorts in South East Asia and perhaps along the common border itself in areas that are considered by China to be in dispute.

(5) Western Europe after 1992 may move incrementally beyond a common monetary policy, a single central bank, and a single currency, toward something resembling a common defense and foreign policy. The odds are against such political spill-over because of the lack of precedent, and because of the monumental task of getting France, Germany, and Britain, the pillars of the community, to yield sufficient sovereignty to Brussels. In the absence of capacity to generate a common foreign policy, Western Europe could become the "Greek city states" of the system in the twenty-first century.

Increasingly the European Community will face strain between the dual strategies of expanding its size and of deepening the cohesion of its economic and political integration. So far the Community, not surprisingly, has taken the easier path of expanding market size. The leading members could always form a new more political union among themselves if the Community as constituted becomes too unwieldy for political progress. But it is not clear that the peripheral members are more of an obstacle to greater political unity than are the three leading members *vis-à-vis* each other. Perceived decline of the United States, removing some of the pressure of dollar hegemony, and of the Soviet Union, leading to a perceived reduction in the threat of military hegemony, could leave the West Europeans with a lower external stimulus, and hence less actual progress, toward integration.

But if progress is made in the decades ahead toward a more coherent sense of West European political identity, whatever problems may arise in the aftermath of German reunification, a new powerful actor would emerge on the world stage capable of shifting power back toward the European continent instead of increasingly toward Asia. The emergence of this new European entity would complete the agenda of full systems-wide, structural transformation. In power cycle terms, the effect of an ascendant Europe would be to demand concessions from the older members of the system in terms of a transfer of status and responsibility for world order.

A unified Europe would be a robust mediator between Washington and Moscow, whatever the nature and degree of their differences at that time, and a factor that both Japan and China would have to weigh in any calculations for extending influence beyond the Asian sphere. Less uncertainty than maturity would be added to the global system by European ascendancy, regarding what at that point will have become a full-fledged balance-of-power system with five actors. At least four of them would have the capability to project military and economic influence world-wide.

(6) In addition, important changes will have occurred in the Third World where Brazil, now the ninth ranked economy, is poised to exercise more than regional leadership, and India, despite its poverty, is capable of expanding its scientific and technological base into civilian and military production that many of its neighbors will be hard put to match. Thus, structural changes on the horizon in the Third World will alternatively reinforce or constrain the horizontal reach of some of the leading states.

Timing and sequencing. How brief will the period of transformation be? When will it accelerate and when will it end? What will

239

the sequence of passages through critical points look like? These are the questions every practicing diplomat will ask, yet also the kind of predictions that no one can with much confidence supply.

This much, however, can be said regarding sequence. Movement on the power cycle of the United States occurred first but may not be the most pronounced. Transformation must start with some relative decline by the United States and the Soviet Union; otherwise movement up and down the hierarchy by smaller polities would create the appearance of "musical chairs" without much profound structural meaning. But the direction of these power shifts is quite important: to Japan, capable of immediately assuming a larger leadership role; to China, preoccupied with internal growth and development; to Europe not yet unified enough to assert focused influence; or outside the central system altogether *vis-à-vis* the NICs and other groupings of states such as ASEAN and OPEC. It is not reasonable to anticipate that in the long term all will benefit equally from redistributions of power in the system.

From the denouement of the European balance of power until the emergence of bipolarity, systems transformation took some sixty years for completion – from the last years of the Bismarckian stewardship to the end of the Second World War. Had management been more successful and the wars averted, the interval might have been foreshortened; conceivably, however, in the absence of the wars the process of transformation might also have been more dilatory.

There is no reason to believe that transformation from bipolarity to multipolarity, or to a new balance-of-power system, can be more expeditiously achieved. Full systems transformation is a process and a condition that governments will have to await for many decades to come.

COPING WITH THE DILEMMAS OF SOVIET FOREIGN POLICY

The United States played a high-stakes game of poker with the Soviet Union in the 1980s. The Soviets eventually chose to fold rather than to raise the stakes. Facing eventual deficits of 11% and more of GNP-equivalent, the Soviet Union decided it could not out-match the Reagan military budget. Given the computer revolution and other high-tech breakthroughs, the Soviets realized they would fall further behind militarily and exhaust their domestic economy in the process. Gorbachev's economic reforms were the logical alternative to an arms race they could not win.

But the high-stakes nature of the American game was that the Soviet Union might have adopted the German strategy of 1914 when confronted with a European arms race which Germany recognized it could not dominate. In my assessment, the tensions were so great that the Soviet Union may have wavered in the direction of possible force use. Arms races are *never* a preferred strategy for peaceful change.

The reason the arms race of the 1980s did not end in armed confrontation was three-pronged. Containment was never drawn too tightly, while overt force use was always made to look far too dangerous for any serious decision maker in the Kremlin to contemplate. Arms control negotiations competed with the arms race in increasing intensity, providing a readily available outlet for policy decision. And, whereas Germany in 1914 was past its peak, the Soviet Union in the 1980s was not, and felt that it had a second chance. Loose containment for an ascendant actor straining to achieve a larger world role was the correct strategy. It made possible the type of self-appraisal and inward reflection necessary to undertake the enormous task of reform eventually adopted by the Soviet Union.

During ascendancy, the Soviet Union like other great states of the past has made and will make claims for a larger role in the system. Some of these claims have been excessive and problematic, others quite legitimate. Soviet dissonance over its foreign policy and relative power position will likely continue as long as the Soviet Union is able to climb higher on its power cycle.

The United States must (1) enhance its own declining relative capability by some combination of the measures discussed in chapter 9, thus sustaining its position in world affairs, and/or (2) adapt and adjust to legitimate demands (emanating from elsewhere in the system, from Japan, China, and eventually perhaps a united Europe or a reinvigorated Soviet Union) for a more visible role in world politics. To opt for neither of these choices and then to demand the same preeminence that the United States has enjoyed since 1945, and to retain the same level of costs it has had to assume in that role, is to deepen the contradictions in the foreign policy outlook of other governments and to worsen the prospects for coping with the crisis of systems transformation. Yet as the state with the greatest level of power, it must continue to lead in world politics.

Once it is clearly evident that Soviet power has peaked and has entered long-term decline on the power cycle – that is, long-term relative decline regarding latent potential and military components as well as productivity – some analysts in the West are likely to recommend caution and appeasement of Soviet claims to increased interests

241

lest the Soviet Union misinterpret the signals from the West concerning its interest in peace. Such a strategy, however, would be the exact opposite of that which is necessary and most workable. Appeasement *vis-à-vis* increased claims at the point of nascent Soviet decline would whet the Soviet appetite for foreign policy adventure, much as the attempt to appease Nazi Germany only elicited suspicions of allied weakness. Once the Soviet Union has crossed the upper turning point on its power cycle, and no longer is in a position to make any further legitimate claims (in that it is not in interest deficit) upon the other members of the system for a larger systemic role, the only correct strategy is opposition and balance to these claims while helping it adjust to its new systemic role. Opposition and balance is the only response that will convince the declining state that foreign policy adventurism is foolish and futile.

These then are the policies which power cycle analysis suggests to manage "peaceful change" *vis-à-vis* the Soviet Union. The United States and the West must accommodate the Soviet Union in its continued rise on its power cycle (without yielding territorial security) in a fashion that seeks to more fully integrate the country into the world trading system and the network of order-maintenance. But once the Soviet Union clearly is in decline in level of relative capability (latent and actualized, economic plus military), the only valid response from the system is to employ balance and opposition regarding greater claims to avoid the potential for expansionism that may at that point find reckless appeal in the Kremlin. Clearly, the choice of correct policy rests on the answer to the three-fold question: Where is the Soviet Union on its power cycle? What is its future projection of power and role? Are its demands on the system legitimate?

Has the Soviet Union passed the apex of its power cycle?

Many commentators are beginning to assert that the Soviet Union – because of its years of economic stagnation, its admission of huge financial deficits, its struggles to reorient its economy away from central planning, its foreign policy pull-backs from Afghanistan, Angola, and elsewhere, its proposals for reductions in the size of the Soviet military, and its top-level effort to change the mission of the Soviet defense forces, *ipso facto*, by these measures and their consequences for future Soviet role – is facing decline in the *level* of Soviet power. Beyond this assertion about declining Soviet power, some observers contend that the Soviet Union has made a *successful* adjustment to aggravated decline and that Gorbachev's trimming of the size and cost of the Soviet military, reduction in the number and duration of Soviet naval deployments, and shift from an "offensive" to a "defensive" military posture all apparently indicate that the Soviet Union has learned to cope with its new downward trajectory of foreign policy role. According to this contention that the Soviet Union has entered serious decline, and has accepted the implications of this decline for a permanently smaller foreign policy role, systems transformation is not likely to be difficult, or dangerous, for the major actors experiencing it.

Indeed, the argument can be carried so far as to claim that power cycle theory itself is fundamentally flawed. Passage through an upper turning point on the power cycle is not traumatic, in that view, because the Soviet Union under Gorbachev has just demonstrated that negotiating a decline in foreign policy role on the heels of a diminished power base is easy, and is acceptable to policy elites, to allies, and to opponents who will not attempt to "exploit" the interval of adjustment to the ultimate disadvantage of the declining state and the system. In short, according to these arguments the recent Soviet experience with adjustment is evidence enough that the perils of systems transformation are mythology and that the international system is entering a period of tranquility and security unparalleled since the onset of the Cold War.

While these arguments based on recent economic and political experience at the margin (though scarcely averaged over a decade or more) contain a certain surface appeal based on the seeming "fit" with recent Soviet policy behavior, the danger here is that the analyst may be reading too much too soon into Soviet intentions, and be dismissing too readily both the empirical evidence of long-term Soviet power growth and, indeed, the long historical foundation of experience underlying power cycle theory.

First, it is very likely that the Soviet Union has *not* passed its peak on the power cycle, which indexes its capability to exert leadership in the international system. At least, insufficient evidence has accumulated to write off *perestroika* as unmitigated failure. Ignored is the enormous underlying latent power base of the Soviet Union indexed by territorial and population size, natural resources, scientific creativity, size and effectiveness of the Soviet armed forces, and the capacity of the Soviet people to accept austerity in the name of national defense. The long-term latent capability of a state must not be confused with shorter-term problems of economic productivity.

Second, at least as important, the Soviet leadership is not responding as though it were in severe relative decline and as though it is making the necessary adjustments for a permanent constriction of foreign policy role and function. On the contrary, current alterations in Soviet policy are thought of in tactical terms as prudent and necessary so as to ensure continued growth in Soviet power and continued projection of an increasing leadership role later. The current alterations in Soviet policy are not indicative of imminent collapse of government or of its polar position in the system. *Rapprochement* with the United States and the West is providential, but scarcely irreversible. Competition stems from power polarization as much as ideological rivalry. A recrudescence of this awareness could, *vis-à-vis* a number of Soviet foreign policy interests, once again emerge, when the time is ripe. The Soviet response (chapter 8) reveals an awareness of the power cycle and an attempt to manage movement along it, not a belief that the Soviet Union has passed its apex and hence must prepare for a permanently diminished foreign policy role in the future.

Third, if Soviet reforms do fail, however, and if the Soviet Union does actually enter genuine long-term decline and is forced to project a decreased future foreign policy role for itself, then power cycle theory will have a test of the causal relation from "critical point" to "increased likelihood for major war" or foreign policy aggressiveness.

What are the possibilities? If the Soviet Union responds to the failure of *perestroika* by aggressive foreign policy adventures, forcing its populace to endure the hardships of expansionist impulse, this would, alas, "affirm" the theory. On the other hand, a "negative" test case would not disprove the theory, since the relationship between a critical point and major war is not deterministic. But more important than the theoretical implications is the foreign policy reality. Other governments have been able to adjust to the new projection of power and role at a critical point without major warfare. A "no instability" result would credit the wise guidance of the then leaders of the Soviet Union, and the equally prescient leaders of the other nations of the world who would successfully have contended with a possibly interventionist Soviet foreign policy.

Finally, the very flatness of the Soviet cycle near the apex, the very fact that it is at or near the apex at growth that is virtually zero, means that it may enjoy perhaps a decade or two in which to adjust to the possibility of an inversion of trend in future power and role. In other words, the very protracted nature of the Soviet turning point, because of the long slow ascendancy of the Soviet Union, may perhaps make adjustment less painful.

If the United States is able through prescient judgment and skillful administration to postpone further significant decline on its own power cycle, it will be much more able to deal with a Soviet Union traumatized by the crossing of a critical point. Rapid structural change elsewhere will mean that attentive application of the appropriate strategic response to Soviet decline will be all the more important.

POTENTIAL SNAGS IN THE TRANSFORMATION PROCESS

Despite the best effort to disengage the process of systems transformation from major war through an understanding of the dynamics of change on the power cycle, the process will probably remain tension-ridden.

(1) At the top of the list of problems to be managed during systems transformation will be *the possible inability of the Soviet Union to cope with its own sudden discovery of decline* – at the top because of both the enormity of military capability which the Soviet Union now enjoys and the severe economic and political crisis currently confronting it. The size and earnestness of this problem for the system must not be underestimated. Both France and Germany found the upper turning point on their power cycles to be a tumultuous event. Other states, including the United States, have struggled with acceptance of imminent relative decline. In the Soviet case, the southern rim of the Soviet Union is porous, not protected by "buffer states" and thus easily rationalized in expansionist terms, and difficult for non-regional actors to police.

(2) *The perils of too-rapid Japanese ascendancy* cannot be disparaged. In some ways, the problems Wilhelmine Germany created for itself and the system are the problems Japan is creating today. Germany industrialized at such a rapid pace that it generated expectations in Berlin of perpetual rise. When Germany reached the zenith of its power cycle, the shock was all the more traumatic because of the rapidity of the prior crescendo of activity. A state which reaches the top of its power cycle while still at a very high rate of growth in relative power will feel the effect of that upper asymptote very abruptly (chapter 3). The government must confront all at once the idea that its relative power position will reach a limit, an idea that would have come more easily if its rate of growth had begun to slow down somewhat earlier, allowing a more gradual approach to the limit.

Similarly, Japan today is so rapidly increasing its share of the world's total manufacturing and its share of the total export market in manufactures, services, and finance that other governments – notably

245

the United States – are not as easily able to adjust as in the past. Protectionism in Europe and the United States is a direct function of the need, but the political inability, to establish a new trade equilibrium fast enough through exchange rate depreciation so as to correct imbalances.

At the same time, the rocket-like growth of Japan has left its own society and government unable to adapt to new circumstances. On the one hand, the growth has elevated internal elite expectations, especially on the right, that Japan will become a future superpower capable of "taking over" responsibilities of hegemonic leadership which Japan has been led to imagine the United States now possesses. On the other hand, the meteoric economic growth has not given Japanese society enough time to match internal policies with new external obligations. Lingering restrictions on foreign investment in Japan, non-tariff restrictions on high-tech imports, an inefficient internal distribution mechanism that serves to exclude foreign products, and anachronistic power groupings with narrow-minded positions on foreign assistance and trade, all beset the country that is now the world's leading financial actor and the hub of the world manufacturing economy. Too-rapid growth has created gaps internal and external for Japan between role and capability that will make passage through an upper turning point on the Japanese power curve especially stressful.

Contrasts between late-nineteenth-century Germany and late-twentieth-century Japan are of course also instructive. Japan is not militarized in the way that Germany was, and the increased military participation we advise would not make it so. The international system today is far more interdependent than a century earlier, meaning that all of the leading actors are in contact with the central system in a way that the United States and Japan of 1914 were not. Japan presently is locked in a trading competition that generates its own vulnerabilities on foreign markets and therefore its own set of constraints in a way that did not operate on Imperial Germany.

Japan is needed as a leader, not a reluctant follower, regarding trade reform and reform of international financial assistance. More progress has been made in the latter area than in the former. But Japan must lean against the temptation of some governments like France to use foreign assistance as a vehicle for export promotion, although since Japanese goods are of such high quality and priced so competitively, the costs of diversion to them is probably not so great. Becoming a major international lender to the Third World, albeit on Japanese terms, is essential if liquidity is to grow in the international financial system and a bottleneck is to be avoided in which a single actor experiences huge foreign surpluses while other large economies suffer seemingly perpetual deficits. From the Japanese point of view, the money was earned through legitimate enterprise and ought to be spent for purposes that are not solely altruistic. This is understandable and there is certainly room for a higher Japanese standard of living (apart from further support for inflated Tokyo land prices). But part of the burden of being on top is to shoulder the financial costs internationally, and to address the interests of all states.

Second, Japan is more dependent upon an open trading system than any other major trading partner. Therefore, Japan must take the lead with the United States in defending openness, or see the world trading system fragment and begin to close. The last vestiges of neomercantilism look anachronistic for a country so dependent upon the liberal trade order. A hierarchical view of trade relationships that ties states lower on the development ladder to acceptance of a narrowly prescribed role, in return for a place in that trade order, will generate political grievance. If Japan takes the lead voluntarily on multilateral trade reform, it will raise its stature immensely within the central system and become a model for the NIC's in yet another way.

(3) *Can Germany – and the system – adjust to Germany's new ascendancy?* At the bottom of its power cycle, and starting over, is Germany. Unification of the Germanies did not precede the crossing of the lower turning point. This fact has important implications both for German politics and for the theory of the power cycle. The Federal Republic reached its low point (8%) and stabilized at that level around 1965–68, not beginning to turn up until a decade or so later. Unification came only in the last decade of the twentieth century, and only because it was allowed to occur. Thus, the impulse to unify formally followed and did not precede the occurrence of the lower turning point for the Federal Republic.

This fact of sequencing explains much. It explains the dynamism felt in the Federal Republic in terms of its economy and the confident diplomacy of Chancellor Kohl. It explains the unease within the international system over the prospect not just of a unified Germany, but of a once-again vibrant and even assertive German state. Not only near neighbors with fearful memories – France, Poland, and Czechoslovakia – but the Soviet Union itself had some misgivings about the prospect of an ascendant Germany in the heart of central Europe. Despite the reality that Poland, too, was reluctant to face elites over the relinquishment of claims to territory in Lithuania, the electoral hesitancy of the Kohl government to quickly accede to a formal treaty

247

relinquishing territory east of the Oder–Neisse did not of course dissipate anxiety among the Poles themselves. All of these sudden, unanticipated changes in the status and projected future foreign policy and territorial role of Germany are in keeping with the normal dynamic of the power cycle at a critical point. The question in the German case is whether the international system can absorb the strains and whether Germany is a saturated state, or whether once again history will show a break-down of order.

Any propensity for a renewal of German expansionism seems fully offset by other factors. Without question, Germany will experience buoyant economic growth, combining abundant capital with the skilled and relatively cheap labor of the East, a fresh new industrial base and infrastructure in the East, and the renowned capacity for discipline and hard work that is a German trademark. But democracy has deep roots in West Germany. A unified Germany will have a population around 80 million in the early 1990s but an economy less than half the size of the Japanese economy. The United States, the Soviet Union, China and Japan all will continue to tower over Germany in terms of latent national capability. The resulting inter-national political equilibrium will reflect these factors and reinforce a stable and saturated German state.

In addition, the German crossing of its turning point is not likely to be troublesome to the international system for other reasons. First, for more than a decade West Germany will be preoccupied with consoli-dation and internal development. Germany will have a difficult time lifting its gaze from these concerns. Second, *Ostpolitik* for Germany is not dead in the aftermath of the Russian withdrawal from Eastern Europe but is likely only to take a different more commercial form. German banks will probably provide credit for much of Eastern Europe's economic recovery. This overall economic renaissance is likely to demand much of Germany in terms of leadership, time, and financial energy. Third, Germany will remain fully committed to the European Community, whatever the direction of its emphasis, greater compass or greater depth of integration. Though Germany's other involvements may slow down the pace of European integration somewhat, the opposite could happen if German political leadership is adequately meshed with that of Paris and London and not treated as a looming intra-European threat. Finally, the removal of Russian troops from Eastern Europe thus reducing the danger of surprise conventional attack, and the continued extension of the U.S. nuclear commitment, minimizes the need for Germany to reorganize its defenses in a precipitate fashion. In particular, these considerations

248

mitigate having to face an immediate decision on German military nuclearity, thus giving German decision makers and the central system time to adjust to all of this structural change without having to comtemplate a fracture of the Nuclear Non-Proliferation Agreement to which Germany is a signatory.

In short, because of the considerations examined here, Germany has so far responded to this sudden change in its power and future foreign policy outlook in a sensible and constrained fashion.

(4) *Is Asia large enough for both an ascendant China and an increasingly predominant Japan?* It is easy to see the complementarity of the foreign policies of the two states in the later twentieth century, but also the competitiveness. Japan needs the huge Chinese market, but wants to transfer only the less sophisticated technology. Japan has the capacity to develop a military arm with a global reach, but China has nuclear weapons and a huge land army. Both countries share Confucian values, and a commitment not to allow the events of the first half of the twentieth century to repeat themselves.

However, well into the interval of systems transformation, each polity will cross a critical point. The event will be as destabilizing for these countries as for others. What happens when each government possesses far more military capability and correspondingly expects a far broader range of foreign policy interests? Every interest inside the region can be regarded by either Japan or China as vital, from the discovery of oil and gas in the South China Sea, to the fate and future of Taiwan and of South Korea.

In an interval where the United States does not siphon off tension in the way that it has since 1945, and does not act as a mediator in most disputes in the region, the surfaces of Japanese and Chinese foreign policy will rub against each other directly. Will this friction generate heat that can in various ways be vented, or will it become pent up and focused within a territorial space that is after all very tight? These are unanswerable questions from the vantage point of the twentieth century. But these are not questions that should remain unasked, or that may remain without answers throughout the interval of systems transformation (Inoguchi 1983).

(5) *Russia at the apex, China at an inflection.* This is the combination that is perhaps most worrisome to grand strategists of international relations. It is reminiscent of the geostrategic concern of the confrontation between one great land power (the Soviet Union) and the great maritime power (the United States) which in turn allows a second great land power (China) to rise on the outskirts of the system, creating an inescapable challenge to the former, predominant land

power, therefore precipitating another world war (Liska 1980). But, from the perspective of the power cycle notion, the dilemma is only perplexing when there is a confluence of critical points, that is, a situation in contemporary structural terms where the Soviet Union is defensive because it has passed the zenith of its curve, and where China is frustrated because it has discovered that its hopes for the future have been dashed by a new lower growth rate in future power and role. China has long thought in terms of ascending and deteriorating power, dividing the central system analytically into these two categories of states. All the more frightening is the reality then when such a government discovers that it is among the declining set even though it had always imagined itself to be among the rising powers.

Problematic for world order is the possibility that these two great land powers, with their long common border, might together discover that their future role aspirations face abrupt, massive alteration. Lack of concern about a Sino-Soviet war is due to awareness that today neither state seeks war with the other, not that there is no objective prospect for such war in their foreign policy conduct. What is more, the simultaneous passage through critical points, involving all of the accompanying trauma over role and power, could very sharply increase the probability of such war. Whether such a confluence of disturbing structural change will take place is impossible to predict. That such a confluence of passage through critical points would be difficult for the respective states and the system to absorb is indubitable.

(6) *Suppose Western Europe does not coalesce?* The larger probability is that Western Europe will not get beyond the stage of a more sophisticated economic common market. How will the absence of a single, large European political entity affect global international political equilibrium, if at all?

With Europe as a major player, the central system would have a three-continent base: North America, Asia, and Europe. No geopolitical orientation in the eventual, mature, multipolar system would possess an advantage. Emergence of a united Europe somewhere late in the period of systems transformation would restore a focus that will by then have drifted in the direction of Asia. Despite the reality that the United States will still probably remain the largest single actor in the system, in the absence of a united Europe, an Asian focus in power terms will begin to predominate.

Without a united Europe, the Soviet Union in nascent decline will feel much less inhibited in its actions globally. The United States, itself in relative decline, will have a much harder time balancing Soviet initiative and will always have to rely upon either Japan or China to offset potential Soviet expansionism. If aggressive actions stem from an Asian base, the United States would have to rely much more directly on the Soviet Union to halt the challenge. Thus, the absence of a united Europe would leave something of a vacuum in a mature, multipolar system of the twenty-first century.

On the other hand, the emergence of Europe would place some stress on the central system as the number of actors increased and as the united Europe made claims for a larger role and set of global responsibilities. Thus while there would be many theoretical advantages to the membership of a unified Europe in the leadership of a mature multipolar system, getting there might be difficult. The paradox of systems transformation is that the conditions which ease its management may not be the same as those that conduce to a smooth operation of the mature international system which eventually replaces bipolarity.

(7) Although the task of this analysis has been to explain major war involving members of the central system, in the period of future systems transformation *major war can become very serious for systems stability without the participation of one of the principal governments*. At the regional levels, governments also follow cycles of power and critical points. Instability may in the next decades become more common and dangerous in the Third World as the principal actors avoid (for fear of escalation) vetoing, or intervening against, wars that may drag on as long as the Iraq–Iran war did. Nuclear proliferation, combined with broad availability of weaponry capable of pinpointing accuracy on targets hundreds or even thousands of miles away (*Discriminate Deterrence*) is changing the nature of warfare such that a big war can happen anywhere and much more suddenly than in the past.

(8) Whatever the limits of leadership within each configuration, both nineteenth-century balance of power and recent bipolarity contained very well-defined central systems. Systems transformation may lead to a condition where the *central system deteriorates*. Power diffuses throughout the system as a whole. The hierarchy of national capability collapses to a considerable extent, increasing the degree of anarchy felt everywhere in the system.

Yet insofar as this resulting multipolar system is able to operate without the shocks of critical change for the major powers, the members will learn to evolve their own norms of economic and political interaction. The snag here is that the norms and rules of behavior in *one* type of international system cannot automatically be transferred to another. Coping with nuclear weapons after 1945 was

251

far different than constraining chemical weapons after 1919. Dealing with non-tariff barriers is quite different from arranging tariff reductions. The new system must have time to evolve its own patterns of state interaction. Systems transformation wipes the international political slate clean.

U.S. POLICY AND WORLD ORDER DURING SYSTEMS TRANSFORMATION

Caution is the hallmark of U.S. policy in a period of nascent systems transformation, inducing the United States neither to abandon traditional allies, nor to forge new political associations. U.S. policy will not be merely passive, however, responding to events rather than attempting to shape them. A new concept of world order will gradually evolve. For the near future at least, the Soviet Union is the only country that could mortally wound the United States and, therefore, U.S. strategy for dealing with structural change will continue to be very much influenced by Soviet behavior and attitudes.

Insofar as Soviet passage through a critical point on its power cycle is still unresolved, leading to the kind of policies of contraction and consolidation pursued by Gorbachev in 1990, the United States ought to contemplate the incremental development of a new relationship with the Soviet Union (Brzezinski 1989).

A mutual no-undercut pact

In the period of impending systems transformation, world order is dependent upon new understandings between the superpowers, new care during crisis not to misread signals, new comprehension regarding mutual interest in stability. The United States and the Soviet Union face a choice. They can continue to undercut each other in the Third World, waste each other's resources, and damage world order. Or, they can reinforce each other's attempts to sustain world order, avoid unnecessary and debilitating competition, pursue parallel and positive steps towards the maintenance of fragile regional and local stability regimes, and accommodate structural change while eliminating explosive power–interest gaps. If the superpowers continue to undercut each other, each will accelerate the other's decline, and therefore its own decline. Third powers will rise prematurely on the outskirts of the system, without fully being ready to shoulder the responsibilities of world order, possibly triggering war with one or other of the superpowers, while foregoing integration into a more comprehensive and structurally stable system of world order.

Lessons of Vietnam and Afghanistan ought to be clear. Support for "wars of liberation" change the international balance. They upset local stability. They unsettle neighboring regimes. Thus, for a new stable equilibrium to emerge, such a strategy of political destabilization must have been foregone. Moreover, expansion of influence is far easier than the maintenance of that influence. Attrition from the countryside is far cheaper and simpler than a defense of the cities. Yet it is in the cities that the stability of local governments increasingly will establish itself. The Soviet Union and the United States have unending capacity to leave each other far worse off after confrontation than before, and therefore, to leave world order in tatters, just at a time when overall systems transformation demands constructive interaction.

Thus, choice confronts Washington and the Kremlin. A no-undercut pact implicitly adhered to, or publicly signed, is in the respective interest of each government. Parallel action, not condominium which third governments would resent and fear, is the desired course. Mutual agreement to minimize difference and maximize communality may yield results for world order during the crisis of systems transformation beyond anything either government can do in isolation or in common with third governments. This is a positive world order program that need not wait.

Shifting coalition strategy

Suppose, however, that relative decline for the Soviet Union is either precipitous, thus greatly reducing its substantial capacity for mischief, or that the Gorbachevian efforts at reform are deep and lasting, thus leading to a more defensive-oriented military posture and a more open democratic government from which its neighbors perceive they have little to fear. Ideology in the latter case has been replaced by the market: the Soviet Union becomes one polity like others, not the center of world communism. In either case, the United States may find that before the period of systems transformation ends, its farflung alliance relations are in disarray despite its best effort to seek coordination.

Under these circumstances, the United States may be forced to adopt a shifting coalitional focus composed of overlapping and more temporary arrangements that seek to stabilize equilibrium much as Bismarck sought to do in the aftermath of the Franco-Prussian War, albeit without the offensive military provisions of some of his alignments. Insofar as the source of aggressive behavior emerges elsewhere in the system, such coalitional flexibility will become more essential. Indeed, although not likely in the short term, seen from the present perspective, the two declining superpowers might find themselves on the same side of an effort to contain the military expansion of one or more of the ascending polities should the effort to accommodate such rising power fail.

A strategy of shifting coalitions also has much in common with the role played by Britain *vis-à-vis* the Continent in the nineteenth century. Britain regarded herself as "holder of the balance" on the Continent and retained her "splendid isolation." The United States would become an equivalent of the island, maritime power in the twenty-first century. Surrounded by three oceans, preeminent in aero-space activity, the United States could attempt to maintain equilibrium through a tripping of the balance against whatever "continental" power threatened bellicosity.

One of the reasons this analogy must not be stretched too far, however, is that such a system would contain not one but two such "island" states, the other being an island in the strict sense, Japan. Culturally beholden to Europe, the United States nonetheless in economic and geostrategic terms continues to have much in common with Japan. A central system composed of two "island" states is likely to be looser and more prone to temporary coalitional behavior, because of the sensitivity of such polities to shifts of equilibrium, than a central system of the nineteenth-century European variety.

Meg-alliance

Suppose, however, that one of the negative scenarios regarding Soviet politics emerges and that a belligerent Soviet Union for whatever reason again is featured. Suppose also that the capability to meet such a centralized threat has declined both because of dwindling U.S. force capability and a set of alliance relationships that are in disarray. Under these circumstances, quite a different kind of coalitional strategy may be called for in Washington.

One prospect is to attempt to bind together the two wings of the alliance, NATO and Japan. While the Soviet Union might claim that such a firming up of alliance structures amounts to "encirclement," or a reconstitution of containment, a bellicose Soviet Union in decline has no claim on the international system for increased rights and responsibilities, and can only anticipate defensive actions of those threatened. Accommodation is not the appropriate response; balance is.

254

Instead of tinkering around the edges of NATO and of the bilateral alliance with Japan and South Korea, attempting to extract a bit more of a commitment on the margin from each member, the United States might consolidate its principal alliances into a single, revitalized organization. The new alliance would have a global focus. It would bring together the wings of security responsibility. It would retain as a pivotal concern the necessity of halting aggression and expansion on the part of the Soviet Union. But it would accomplish this objective more efficiently and by a better mix of commitments from Western Europe, from Asia, and from North America. Instead of resting upon two pillars, the meg-alliance would rest upon three. Three legs are stronger and more capable of withstanding turbulence than two. An alliance based on two pillars constantly risks collapse because of the danger of breaking in half. Meg-alliance meets stress criteria far better.

Each of the legs of the alliance could determine its level of defense contribution according to a revised formula of authority-sharing within the organization. Greater equality of responsibility, and of contribution, would characterize operation of such a meg-alliance. Each of the legs ought to acknowledge opportunity costs. Increasing fragmentation can only weaken Western security. And increasing fragmentation can only magnify the actual financial and administrative costs of defense far beyond those required by collective defense under a revised organization format. Some form of rationalization of function and contribution will be necessary as systems transformation proceeds because the United States will become less and less capable of absorbing disproportionate defense expenditures.

Most importantly, the meg-alliance would acknowledge global defense responsibilities. A secondary purpose of the alliance, subject to the full support of its members, would be to provide security in regions outside those of immediate adjacency to the members. The Persian Gulf actions would fall into this category since the interests of Europe and Japan are at least as paramount as those of North America in terms of the free flow of world oil.

OPPORTUNITIES IN THE TRANSFORMATION PROCESS

Systems transformation creates not only problems but new opportunities. At the end of the Second World War, two legacies of unfinished business from the attempt to assimilate the defeated hegemonic powers, Germany and Japan, were the divided states. West and East Germany and South and North Korea formed two of the

255

worst trouble spots in the post-1945 landscape (the third was Vietnam). Systems transformation offers an opportunity in the soft light of detente to reduce the animosity between the two halves of divided societies and bifurcated political structures that, untended, become flashpoints of global belligerence.

From the current perspective, that attempt at Yalta to design a post-war structural solution for the problem of world peace was a considerable success. Not only have the prior hegemonic powers been assimilated, but the specter of other assimilative efforts, the rise of a third hegemonic threat (in this case the Soviet Union) has been mollified. Containment worked; communism is reforming itself. Systems transformation now offers to Eastern Europe a fresh start. Pluralism is taking root as the memory of democratic institutions has returned. Germany and Japan now face new challenges and opportunities: Germany that it can accept a leadership role inside Europe without harboring illegitimate political goals (and Europe that it can allow this place to Germany, or to whomever becomes the dominant rising power in Europe); Japan that it can adjust to its systemic responsibilities now and when it finally does bump against the upper limits of its relative growth.

Hence, according to power cycle interpretation, out of "competitiveness" and "complementarity" emerges international political novelty. Something new is created. Systems transformation is the interval in which this novelty is generated. The realism of power and role merge with the idealism of a new order with new possibilities for statecraft. The future should not so much be one that is hedged by anxiety as one that is filled with promise for statecraft. Ideological change is an example of that promise.

Communism is not dead, as the reversals in China show, no matter how bankrupt the ideology might be on grounds of human rights or of economic output. Nor should the West trumpet its victories in such a fashion that they undermine the very process that is now inchoate, but that holds out such promise. Ideology pales before power in structural terms. But in terms of the individual and in terms of society, ideology may mean virtually everything. Systems transformation brings forth the opportunity to the individual and to society that ideology may lose its malignancy, among the advanced industrial states in particular, as well as much of its past malevolence. But communal ethnocentrism may destroy the prospect for democracy that the dissipation of ideology has so recently made attractive. Power and role will still drive the essential flow of structural change, whatever the ideological focus, within the international system.

256

Hence, although the primary imperative during systems transformation is to maintain an equilibrium between power and interests on the respective power cycles of the leading states, transformation also facilitates the creation of new interests, or changes in the priorities of old interests. Those interests favoring the creation of a more just world order have an opportunity to rise to the top of state agendas.

Sustainable development, for example, is not a code word but a necessity. While many unfounded claims have been proffered by environmentalists over the years such as the exhaustion of physical resources, no one has disproved the multiplicative effects of trends such as very rapid population growth and worsening pollution. A more just world order will require some transfer of financial capability from rich, advanced industrial countries high on their power cycles to poor polluters lower on theirs so that equilibrium between power and interest for all concerned can be maintained. Sustainable development, as the theorists of interdependence have long argued, cannot be achieved in national isolation, a fact reflected in the power cycle dynamic.

Similarly, human rights are now seen among Marxist states, former and present, as possibly essential to, rather than incompatible with, governance. Systems transformation must not be regarded as entirely a negative process, nor a process limited to structural considerations.

CONTRASTING PARADIGMS OF WORLD POLITICS

In the contemporary international system, change occurs far more quickly than in previous centuries, systems possess less durability, and the decentralized character of each type of international system remains a precondition of its acceptability to the constituent units, the nation–state. Yet the systems of past history reveal to us the function of systems transformation in contemporary terms. (1) The central system must expand to encompass new members. (2) As the relative power of individual states changes, so does the scope of state interest and role. (3) A new equilibrium of power and role among the principal governing units must emerge for stability to be preserved.

On the one hand, these statements are comfortably familiar; on the other, they challenge the sufficiency of existing paradigms for preserving world order during such massive structural change. International systems analysis, of which the power cycle notion is one part, calls into question the static idea of an international system based on the conventional notion of balance. Alone, the static, flat chessboard of strategy cannot account for the realities of international political

257

behavior. As with the Ptolemaic view of the physical universe, it collapses from the weight of complexities required to "save" the theory. But does the "systemic" view of foreign policy behavior provide a valid and significant "Copernican" alternative?

By a "paradigm shift" to a dynamic "vertical" perspective, the unique international relations (systemic structural) orientation emerges. At the heart of this new orientation is the concept of relative power, or systemic share of power attributable to each state. But outside the context of the full dynamic of change in relative power, of the state power cycle, relative power itself is likely to be, and has been, misunderstood.

Once rendered clear, that dynamic reconciles seeming puzzles of history: the perspective and concerns of contemporaneous statesmen do not "make sense" from the traditional paradigm. The puzzles dissolve when one grasps the fundamental difference between absolute and relative power – the nature of their trajectories – and hence the full significance of systemic bounds. The reality is traumatic when a meteoric rise in relative power suddenly peaks even as absolute power makes its greatest gains. Surprises of history are the essence of all critical changes on the power cycle. With a paradigm shift, reinterpretations of history, new perspectives on the causes of war, and alternative paths to world order become plausible. When the concerns of statesmen are seen clearly, the paradox of peaceful change begs reconsideration.

For over thirty years, a variety of debates have surrounded the emerging systemic view and its implications for war and peaceful change, highlighting conceptual problems and paths to their resolution. Debates over "neorealism," "hegemonic stability," and "rise and decline" are only the most recent variants. Criticism and debate are essential. But any theory of world politics must not be digested in pieces (the reductionist fallacy). It must be examined in the whole, with assumptions intact, and with empirical tests that actually determine whether "the sun rises or the earth rotates" in terms of the international political equivalents.

Historical relevance and logical rigor are only part of the challenge confronting international relations theory. When all is said and done, a theory which is essentially structural, and therefore behavioral, becomes in its essence more profoundly *ethical*. Norms protect the ideals of the state as well as the integrity of the system (group). They are minimum guidelines necessary for the establishment of a world order that seeks to be just as well as secure. A further question for debate is whether these minimum guidelines are acceptable, and whether they thus might be accepted.

258

On the one hand, the theory does not accede to the fallacy of inevitability. Improvement in rate of absolute growth is possible for all states at all times in their historical development. The rate of internal power generation ultimately determines whether a state experiences improvement or worsening of its current relative power and position in the international system. Moreover, cooperation is always a predominant characteristic of international relations, especially in an international system where technology expands the universe of opportunity equally for all states.

On the other hand, states "in decline" must be prepared to yield some political role, and states "in ascendancy" must be satisfied with a limited albeit larger stake in the world system and prudently assume the responsibilities that are conveyed therein. Reliance upon force as the ultimate defense of vital interests has not been abolished. Yet that force, in the power cycle perspective, is contained within new limits and observes new norms more fitting to the circumstances of a post-nuclear world and an international system in transformation.

APPENDIX
MATHEMATICAL
RELATIONS IN THE POWER
CYCLE

For a function of one variable, a *critical point* is a point at which the derivative is zero (at which the tangent is horizontal).

The concept of *critical points in the dynamic*, as used in power cycle theory, refers to (1) critical points on the relative power curve itself, and (2) critical points on the curve of the dynamic of change in relative power, that is, on the curve of the rate of change in relative power. Hence, the critical points in the dynamic are (1) the maximum and minimum of the relative power curve itself, and (2) the points of inflection on the relative power curve, since these are the maximum and minimum of the curve of the first derivative.

Likewise, *inflection point* is as defined in both calculus and differential geometry. The calculus definition stems from calculus of variations and differential manifolds theory: the second derivative is zero (note that the first derivative is *not* required to be zero, which is a special case of inflection point of importance in catastrophe theory) (Bronshtein and Semendyayev 1985, pp. 242–8). The differential geometry definition (pp. 554–55) is based on curvature conditions, namely, that the curvature changes sign at the point of inflection. A few algebraic steps show that the curvature condition required at the inflection point occurs for the general asymmetric logistic precisely when the second derivative is zero.

DEFINITIONS:

* Actors: a, b, . . . , k compose the system, tot : = [a, b, . . ., k]
* Time: $t_1, t_2, \ldots, t_{n+1}$ are times corresponding to data points
* Absolute power score for actor b at time t_i : $Abs_b(t_i)$ is observable
* Relative power score for actor b at time t_i : $Rel_b(t_i)$ is defined in terms of $Abs_b(t_i)$ as : $Rel_b(t_i) := \dfrac{Abs_b(t_i)}{Abs_{tot}(t_i)}$ where $Abs_{tot}(t_i)$ is the sum of $Abs_a(t_i)$ as a ranges the system

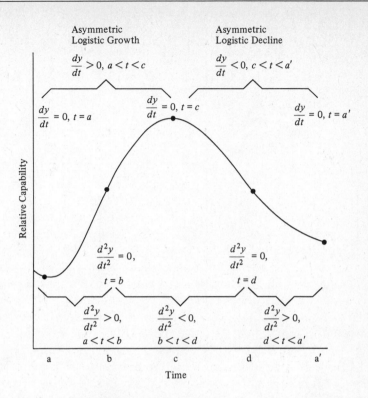

Figure A.1   Generalized curve of relative capability: mathematical
relations

Legend: $a, b, c, d, a' =$ critical points in the dynamic
$t =$ time
$y =$ relative capability of the state
$(dy/dt) =$ rate of change (velocity) in relative capability over time
$(d^2y/dt^2) =$ rate of change of change (acceleration) in relative
capability over time

Source: Conceptualized by Charles F. Doran (1971, pp. 46–51,
191–94).

* Rate of growth of absolute capability of actor b from time t_i to
$t_{i+1} : AGR_b([t_{i'} \ t_{i+1}]) : = \dfrac{Abs_b(t_{i+1}) - Abs_b(t_i)}{Abs_b(t_i)}$

$AGR_{tot}([t_i, t_{i+1}])$ is the "systemic norm" (absolute growth rate
of the system) in that interval

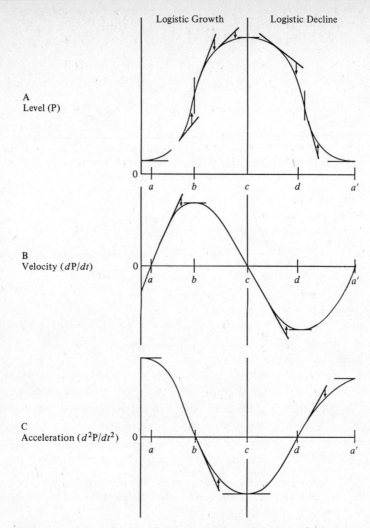

Figure A.2 Level, rate of change, and acceleration of relative capability

Legend: a, b, c, d, a' = critical points in the dynamic
      a, c, a' = turning points (maximum or mimimum value) of level
      b, d = inflection points (points where tangent reverses direction) and hence turning points with respect to the derivative
      ↑ = actual value greater than linear projection
      ↓ = actual value less than linear projection

Source: Conceptualized by Charles F. Doran (1971, pp. 191–94, 210). Also published in Doran and Parsons (1980, p. 950).

NECESSARY AND SUFFICIENT CONDITIONS FOR RELATIVE POWER CHANGE:

"That at least one state in the system has a different absolute growth rate is necessary and sufficient for the relative power of some states in the system to change."

$\sim [AGR_a ([t_i, t_{i+1}]) = AGR_b ([t_i, t_{i+1}]) = \ldots = AGR_k ([t_i, t_{i+1}])]$ i.f.f.
$\sim [Rel_a (t_i) = Rel_a (t_{i+1})$ & $Rel_b (t_i) = Rel_b (t_{i+1})$ & $\ldots$ & $Rel_k (t_i)$
$= Rel_k (t_{i+1})]$ or, equivalently, the contrapositive.

Proof:

$[AGR_a ([t_i, t_{i+1}]) = AGR_b ([t_i, t_{i+1}]) = \ldots = AGR_k ([t_i, t_{i+1}])$
$= AGR_{tot} ([t_i, t_{i+1}])]$
i.f.f.
$[AGR_a ([t_i, t_{i+1}]) = AGR_{tot} ([t_i, t_{i+1}])$ & $AGR_b ([t_i, t_{i+1}])$
$= AGR_{tot} ([t_i, t_{i+1}])$ & $\ldots$ & $AGR_k ([t_i, t_{i+1}]) = AGR_{tot} ([t_i, t_{i+1}])]$
i.f.f.
$[Rel_a (t_i) = Rel_a (t_{i+1})$ & $Rel_b (t_i) = Rel_b(t_{i+1})$ & $\ldots$ & $Rel_k (t_i)$
$= Rel_k (t_{i+1})]$,
because, for any state b in the system,
$AGR_b ([t_i, t_{i+1}]) = AGR_{tot} ([t_i, t_{i+1}])$ i.f.f. $Rel_b (t_i) = Rel_b (t_{i+1})$
(proof identical to that of the first fundamental principle below).

In other words, that a state's absolute growth rate does not equal the systemic norm is necessary and sufficient for its relative power to change.

THE FIRST FUNDAMENTAL PRINCIPLE OF THE POWER CYCLE

"The rate of growth of absolute capability of actor b is greater than (equal to, less than) the systemic norm if, and only if, actor b's relative power is increasing (constant, decreasing)."

$AGR_b([t_i, t_{i+1}]) \gtreqless AGR_{tot}([t_i, t_{i+1}])$ i.f.f. $Rel_b (t_{i+1}) \gtreqless Rel_b (t_i)$

Proof:

$AGR_b([t_i, t_{i+1}]) \gtreqless AGR_{tot}([t_{i+1}])$

263

$$\frac{Abs_b(t_{i+1}) - Abs_b(t_i)}{Abs_b(t_i)} \gtreqless \frac{Abs_{tot}(t_{i+1}) - Abs_{tot}(t_i)}{Abs_{tot}(t_i)}$$

$$\frac{Abs_b(t_{i+1})}{Abs_b(t_i)} \gtreqless \frac{Abs_{tot}(t_{i+1})}{Abs_{tot}(t_i)}$$

$$\frac{Abs_b(t_{i+1})}{Abs_{tot}(t_{i+1})} \gtreqless \frac{Abs_b(t_i)}{Abs_{tot}(t_i)}$$

$$Rel_b(t_{i+1}) \gtreqless Rel_b(t_i)$$

THE SECOND FUNDAMENTAL PRINCIPLE OF THE POWER CYCLE:

"Relative power growth (decline) within the major power system is homologous to asymmetric logistic growth (decline)." Generalized Asymmetric Logistic Equation (Integrated Form):

$$P(t) = k / [1 + \exp(Z(t))] + d$$

Generalized Asymmetric Logistic Differential Equation:

$$P'(t) = [-Z'(t) \cdot (P(t) - d)] \cdot [1 - (P(t) - d)/k]$$
$$\text{[Growth factor] [Retarding factor]}$$
where $Z(t) = 1n(m) + at + bt^2 + ct^3$

Applied to relative capability, $P(t)$ is a state's relative power score at time t; the constants $(k+d)$ and d are the upper and lower asymptotes, respectively, established by the state's scores; $Z(t)$ is a polynomial function of time whose parameters are determined by least squares fit.

Proof:

As in the first non-trivial case (thought experiment on p. 4), and in the simulations (chapter 3), key to a proof are:

(1) starting ratio of absolute levels (state ÷ system)
(2) each state's absolute growth rate (allowed to vary over time)
(3) changing systemic norm (even when growth rates do not vary)
(4) fixed number of percentage shares (bounds of the system)

"RATIO TESTS" FOR RELATIVE POWER CHANGE: POWER CYCLES AND POWER BALANCE

Comparison of appropriate ratios is necessary and sufficient to test for relative power convergence or divergence, and a number of equivalent ratio tests are used intuitively by statesmen in assessing change on the power cycle and changing balance of power (Doran 1971, pp. 46–51; 1974a). Note that most of these ratios obscure the effect of the bounds of the system.

Definitions and conventions

n-actor system: states A, B, C, ..., N
"A-complement" is all the states in the system except A
$A(t)$ = absolute score for state A at a given time (t)
$S(t) - A(t)$ = absolute score for A-complement at a given time (t)
$\triangle A = A(t+1) - A(t)$ = change in absolute score for state A in interval
$\triangle S = S(t+1) - S(t)$ = change in absolute score for system in interval
$\triangle(S-A)$ = change in absolute score for state-complement in interval
$A(t) - B(t)$ = difference in absolute scores for states A and B at time (t)

I. Power cycle: Equivalent "ratio tests" to determine whether a state is rising or declining in relative power in a system – whether it is diverging from ($>$) or converging to ($<$) the rest of the system. Proof by algebra.

Rel. score for state A at time $(t+1) \gtreqless$ Rel. score for state A at time (t)

iff:

1(a)

$$\frac{\text{Abs.score for state A at time } (t+1)}{\text{Abs.score for system at time } (t+1)} \gtreqless \frac{\text{Abs.score for state A at time } (t)}{\text{Abs.score for system at time } (t)}$$

$$\frac{A(t+1)}{S(t+1)} \gtreqless \frac{A(t)}{S(t)}$$

This ratio bounded below by 0, above by 1.

1(b) The denominator of the ratio may be A-complement rather than the system, but that ratio is unbounded.

2(a)

$$\frac{\text{Abs.score for state A at time } (t+1)}{\text{Abs.score for state A at time } (t)} \gtreqless \frac{\text{Abs.score for system at time } (t+1)}{\text{Abs.score for system at time } (t)}$$

$$\frac{A(t+1)}{A(t)} \gtreqless \frac{S(t+1)}{S(t)}$$

2(b) The right-hand ratio may involve A-complement rather than the system.

3(a)

$$\frac{\text{Increase in abs.score for state A}}{\text{Increase in abs.score for system}} \gtreqless \frac{\text{Prior abs.score for state A}}{\text{Prior abs.score for system}}$$

$$\frac{\triangle A}{\triangle S} \gtreqless \frac{A(t)}{S(t)}$$

This ratio bounded below and above as in case 1(a).

3(b) The denominator of the ratio may be A-complement rather than the system, but that ratio is unbounded.

$$\frac{\triangle A}{\triangle(S-A)} \gtreqless \frac{A(t)}{S(t)-A(t)}$$

4(a)

$$\frac{\text{Increase in abs. score for state A}}{\text{Prior abs. score for state A}} \gtreqless \frac{\text{Increase in abs. score for system}}{\text{Prior abs. score for system}}$$

$$\text{(Rate of abs. growth for state A)} \qquad \text{(Rate of abs. growth for system)}$$

$$\frac{\triangle A}{A(t)} \gtreqless \frac{\triangle S}{S(t)}$$

4(b) The right-hand ratio may be the rate of absolute growth for A-complement.

$$\frac{\triangle A}{A(t)} \gtreqless \frac{\triangle(S-A)}{S(t)-A(t)}$$

II. Balance of power: Equivalent "ratio tests" for determining whether the relative power trajectories of a pair of states in the n-actor system are diverging (>) or converging (<). Proof by algebra. Assume A > B in interval.

A's rel. $(t+1)$ – B's rel. $(t+1) \gtreqless$ A's rel. (t) – B's rel. (t)

iff:

(1)

$$\frac{\text{Diff. in abs. scores at time } (t+1)}{\text{Abs. score system at time } (t+1)} \gtreqless \frac{\text{Diff. in abs. scores at time } (t)}{\text{Abs. score system at time } (t)}$$

$$\frac{A(t+1) - B(t+1)}{S(t+1)} \gtreqless \frac{A(t) - B(t)}{S(t)}$$

(2)

$$\frac{\text{Diff. in abs. scores at time } (t+1)}{\text{Diff. in abs. scores at time } (t)} \gtreqless \frac{\text{Abs. score system at time } (t+1)}{\text{Abs. score system at time } (t)}$$

$$\frac{A(t+1) - B(t+1)}{A(t) - B(t)} \gtreqless \frac{S(t+1)}{S(t)}$$

Additional ratio tests involving the "increase (decrease) in the difference in absolute scores" can also be constructed.

Observations:

–Note that the system is the "norm" which determines both the nature of a state's relative power trajectory and, a separate issue, whether the trajectories of two states in the system are converging or diverging.

– The maximum difference in relative power for two states need not occur when one of the states is at a maximum or minimum on its power cycle.

– A "transition" occurs at some time t at which $[A(t) - B(t)] = 0$. The time of transition is thus the same in both absolute and relative power.

REFERENCES

Ajami, Fouad. 1981. *The Arab Predicament: Arab Political Thought and Practice Since 1967*. Cambridge: Cambridge University Press.

Albertini, Luigi. 1952–57. *The Origins of the War of 1914*. London: Oxford University Press.

Allen, G. C. 1981. *The Japanese Economy*. London: Weidenfeld & Nicholson.

Allison, Graham, Albert Carnesale, and Joseph Nye, eds. 1985. *Hawks, Doves and Owls: An Agenda for Avoiding Nuclear War*. New York: Norton.

Anderson, Paul. 1983. "Decision-making by objection and the Cuban Missile Crisis." *Administrative Science Quarterly* 28 (June), 201–22.

Anderson, Paul, and Timothy McKeown. 1987. "Changing aspirations, limited attention, and war." *World Politics* 40, 1–29.

Aristotle. 1961. *The Politics*. In *The Great Political Theories* edited by Michael Curtis. Vol. 1, New York: Avon.

Art, Robert J. In press. *Containment, Grand Strategy, and America's Foreign Policy*.

Ascher, William. 1978. *Forecasting: An Appraisal for Policy-Makers and Planners*. Baltimore: The Johns Hopkins University Press.

Aspaturian, Vernon V. 1980. "Soviet global power and the correlation of forces." *Problems of Communism* 29, no. 3 (May–June).

Axelrod, Robert. 1968. *Bureaucratic Decision-Making in the Military Assistance Program*. Santa Monica, CA: The Rand Corporation.

Baily, M. N. 1981. "Productivity and the services of capital and labor." *Brookings Papers on Economic Activity*, no. 1, 1–50.

Bairoch, Paul. 1979. "Europe's gross national product: 1800–1975." *Journal of Economic History* 5, no. 2 (Fall), 273–337.

    1982. "International industrialization levels from 1980," *The Journal of European Economic History* 11, no. 1, 269–334.

Baldwin, David. 1979. "Power analysis and world politics: New trends versus old tendencies." *World Politics* 31, no. 2 (January), 161–94.

Barnett, A. Doak, and Ralph Clough, eds. 1986. *Modernizing China, Post-Mao Reform and Development*. Boulder, CO: Westview Press.

Barnett, Harold J., and Chandler Morse. 1963. *Scarcity and Growth: The Economics of Natural Resource Availability*. Baltimore: The Johns Hopkins University Press.

Baumont, Maurice. 1978. *The Origins of the Second World War*. New Haven, CT: Yale University Press.

Beitz, Charles. 1979. "Bounded morality: justice and the state in world politics." *International Organization* 33, no. 3 (Summer), 405–24.

Bell, Daniel. 1973. *The Coming of Post-industrial Society*. London: Heinemann.

Bergson, Abram. 1978. "The Soviet economy in the eighties." In *NATO, the USSR in the Eighties*. Brussels: NATO.

Bergson, Abram, and Herbert S. Levine, eds. 1983. *The Soviet Economy: Toward the Year 2000*. London: Allen & Unwin.

Berman, Larry. 1982. *Planning a Tragedy*. New York: Norton.

Bernardi, Aurelio. 1970. "The economic problems of the Roman empire at the time of its decline." In *The Economic Decline of Empires*, edited by Carlo C. Cipolla. London: Methuen.

Bestuzhev, I. V. 1966. "Russian foreign policy February–June 1914." In *1914: The Coming of the First World War*, edited by Walter Laqueur and George L. Mosse. New York: Harper & Row.

Betts, Richard K. 1983. "Analysis, war, and decision: why intelligence failures are inevitable." In *Power, Strategy and Security*, edited by Klaus Knorr. Princeton, NJ: Princeton University Press.

Blainey, Geoffrey. 1973. *The Causes of War*. New York: The Free Press.

Bleicher, S. 1971. "Intergovernmental organization and the preservation of peace: A comment on the abuse of methodology." *International Organization*, 25, no. 2 (Spring), 298–305.

Bobrow, Davis. 1972. *International Relations: New Approaches*. New York: The Free Press.

1989. "Japan in the world: opinion from defeat to success." *Journal of Conflict Resolution*, 33, 571–604.

Bobrow, Davis, and Neal E. Cutter. 1967. "Time-oriented explanations of national security beliefs: cohort, life stage, and situation." *Peace Research Society (International) Papers* vol. 8, 30–52.

Boulding, Kenneth E. 1962. *Conflict and Defense*. New York: Harper & Row.

Boxer, C. R. 1965. *The Dutch Seaborne Empire, 1600–1800*. London: Hutchinson.

1970. "The Dutch economic decline." In *The Economic Decline of Empires*, edited by Carlo C. Cipolla. London: Methuen.

Bracken, Paul. 1983. *The Command and Control of Nuclear Forces*. New Haven, CT: Yale University Press.

Braudel, Fernand. 1979. *The Perspective of the World*, vol. 3. New York: Harper & Row.

Brenner, Reuven. 1985. *Betting on Ideas: Wars, Invention, Inflation*. Chicago: University of Chicago Press.

Bronshtein, I. N., and K. A. Semendyayev. 1985. *Handbook of Mathematics*, New York: Van Nostrand Reinhold.

Brown, Harrison, ed. 1982. *China Among the Nations of the Pacific*. Boulder, CO: Westview Press.

Brzezinski, Zbigniew. 1986. *Game Plan*. Boston: The Atlantic Monthly Press.

1989. *The Grand Failure: The Birth and Death of Communism in the Twentieth Century*. New York: Charles Scribner's Sons.

Buchanan, James M., and Richard E. Wagner. 1987. *Democracy in Deficit*. Orlando, FL: Academic Press.

Bueno de Mesquita, Bruce. 1978. "Systemic polarization and the occurrence and duration of war." *Journal of Conflict Resolution* 22, no. 2 (June), 241–67.

1981. "Risk, power distribution, and the likelihood of war." *International Studies Quarterly* 25, no. 4 (December), 541–68.

1983. "The costs of war: A rational expectations approach." *American Political Science Review* 77, no. 2 (June), 347–57.

Burckhardt, Carl J. 1935–67. *Richelieu*, 4 vols.

Calleo, David P. 1978. *The German Problem Reconsidered*. Cambridge: Cambridge University Press.

1982. *The Imperious Economy*. Cambridge, MA: Harvard University Press.

Carr, E. H. 1949. *The Twenty Years' Crisis, 1919–1939: An Introduction to the Study of International Relations*. London: Macmillan.

1951. *German–Soviet Relations Between the Two World Wars, 1919–1939*. Baltimore: The Johns Hopkins University Press.

Central Intelligence Agency. 1979. *A Dollar Cost Comparison of Soviet and U.S. Defense Activities, 1968–1978*, SR–79–1004. Washington, D.C.: Government Printing Office, January.

Chan, Steve. 1984. "Mirror, mirror on the wall . . . are the freer countries more pacific?" *Journal of Conflict Resolution* 28 (December), 617–48.

Choucri, Nazli, and Robert North. 1968. "The determinants of international violence." *Peace Research Society (International) Papers* 12:33–63.

1974. *Nations in Conflict*. San Francisco: W. H. Freeman.

Churchill, Winston. 1948. *The Gathering Storm*. New York: Bantam Books, 1961 edn (originally published by Houghton Mifflin).

Cipolla, Carlo C., ed. 1970. *The Economic Decline of Empires*. London: Methuen.

Claude, Inis. 1962. *Power and International Relations*. New York: Random House.

Cline, William R. 1979. "A quantitative assessment of the policy alternatives in the NIEO negotiations." In *Policy Alternatives for a New International Economic Order*. New York: Praeger. 3–62.

Codevilla, Angelo. 1986. "Strategic defenses now." *Global Affairs* 1, no. 3, 17–33.

Coffey, John W. 1987. "The path of Soviet imperialism: A review essay." *Comparative Strategy* 6, no. 1, 91–98.

Cohen, Benjamin. 1979. "Europe's money, America's problem." *Foreign Policy* no. 35 (Summer), 31–48.

Cohen, Stephen F. 1985. *Sovieticus: American Perceptions and Soviet Realities*. New York: W. W. Norton & Co.

Collingwood, R. G. 1956. *The Idea of History*. New York: Oxford University Press, Galaxy edition.

Commission on Integrated Long-Term Strategy. 1988. *Discriminate Deterrence*. Washington, D.C.: U.S. Government Printing Office.

Conant, Melvin A. 1982. *The Oil Factor in U.S. Foreign Policy*. Lexington, MA: D.C. Heath.

Copeland, Dale. 1988. "Towards a new vertical theory of international relations." Class paper, The Johns Hopkins University – SAIS.

Cracraft, James, ed. 1983. *The Soviet Union Today: An Interpretive Guide*. Chicago: University of Chicago Press.

Dahl, Robert A. 1957. "The concept of power." *Behavioral Science* 2:201–15.

Darby, M. R. 1984. "The U.S. productivity slowdown: A case of statistical myopia." *American Economic Review* 74, no. 3 (June), 301–22.

Davies, J. C. 1969. "Political stability and instability: some manifestations and causes." *Journal of Conflict Resolution* 13 (March), 1–17.

Dehio, Ludwig. 1962. *The Precarious Balance: Four Centuries of the European Power Struggle*, trans. Charles Fullman. New York: Knopf.

Deibel, Terry L. 1988. "Changing patterns of collective defense: U.S. security commitments in the third world." In *Alliances in U.S. Foreign Policy: Issues in the Quest for Collective Defense*, edited by A. N. Sabrosky. Boulder, CO: Westview Press.

Denton, Frank H., and Warren Phillips. 1968. "Some patterns in the history of violence." *Journal of Conflict Resolution* 12 (June), 182–95.

Dessler, David. 1987. "Structural origins of major war." Ph.D. Diss., The Johns Hopkins University – SAIS.

1989. "What's at stake in the agent–structure debate?" *International Organization* 43, 3 (Summer 1989), 441–73.

Deutsch, Karl W. 1968. *The Analysis of International Relations*. Englewood Cliffs, NJ: Prentice-Hall.

Diehl, Charles. 1970. "The economic decline of Byzantium." In *The Economic Decline of Empires*, edited by Carlo C. Cipolla. London: Methuen.

Doran, C. F. 1971. *The Politics of Assimilation: Hegemony and Its Aftermath.* Baltimore: The Johns Hopkins University Press.

1972. "'Equilibrium' and rank disequilibrium." Unpublished working paper.

1974a. "A conceptual and operational comparison of frustration–aggression, rank disequilibrium, and achievement discrepancy models: Towards synthesis via a general theory of conflict dynamics." Paper presented at the International Studies Association Annual Meeting, St. Louis.

1974b. "A simulation of war and national power." Paper presented at the Southern Political Science Association Meeting, New Orleans, November.

1975. "Hierarchic regionalism from the core state perspective: The U.S. case." In *The Analysis of Foreign Policy Outputs*, edited by William O. Chittick. Columbus, OH: Charles E. Merrill.

1980a. "Modes, mechanisms, and turning points: Perspectives on the analysis of the transformation of the international system." *International Political Science Review* 1, no. 1, 35–61.

1980b. "Change, uncertainty, and balance: A dynamic view of United States foreign policy." *International Journal*, 35, no. 1, 563–79.

1985. "Power cycle theory and system stability." In *Rhythms in Politics and Economics*, edited by Paul M. Johnson and William R. Thompson, 292–312. New York: Praeger.

1986. "Theoretical perspectives on superpower conflict: Systems transformation, the power cycle, and U.S.–Soviet relations." Paper presented at the American Political Science Association Annual Meeting, Washington, D.C.

1989a. "Political change, power cycles, and systems transformation." Paper presented at the International Studies Association Annual Meeting, London, 31 March.

1989b. "Power cycle theory of systems structure and stability: commonalities and complementarities." In *Handbook of War Studies*, edited by Manus I. Midlarsky. Boston: Unwin Hyman.

1989c. "Systemic disequilibrium, foreign policy role, and the power cycle: challenges for research design." *Journal of Conflict Resolution* 33, no. 3 (September), 371–401.

1989d. "Trade policy for the new administration." *SAIS Review* (Winter/Spring). 141–56.

1990a. "Conflict resolution, assimilation, and the state power cycle." Paper presented at the Rutgers–USIP Seminar on Domestic and Global Conflict Resolution, February 27.

1990b. "Yardsticks and metersticks: implications for the analysis of systems structure and major war." Paper presented at the annual meeting of the International Studies Association, Washington, D.C.

Doran, C. F., Kim Q. Hill, and Kenneth R. Mladenka. 1979. "Threat, status disequilibrium, and national power." *British Journal of International Studies* 5:37–58.

Doran, C. F., Kim Q. Hill, Kenneth R. Mladenka, and K. W. Wakata. 1974. "Perceptions of national power and threat: Japan, Finland, and the United States." *International Journal of Group Tensions* 4, no. 4 (December), 431–54.

Doran, C. F., and Eduardo Marcucci. 1990. "Broken trends, and viscosity of power, and major wars." Prepared for publication in *Studi Urbinati: Economica Sociologia*.

Doran, C. F., and Wes Parsons. 1980. "War and the cycle of relative power." *American Political Science Review* 74, no. 4 (December), 947–65.

Doran, C. F., with Terrence Ward. 1977. "A general theory of power and conflict." Working paper.

Dupuy, T. N. 1979. *Numbers, Predictions, and War*. Indianapolis, IN: Bobbs-Merrill.

Elder, Robert E., Jr., and Jack E. Holmes. 1985. "International economic long cycles and American foreign policy moods." In *Rhythms in Politics and Economics*, edited by Paul H. Johnson and William R. Thompson. New York: Praeger. 239–63.

Fairbank, John King. 1986. *The Great Chinese Revolution, 1880–1985*. New York: Harper & Row.

Falkowski, Laurence S., ed. 1979. *Psychological Models in International Politics*. Boulder, CO: Westview Press.

Farrar, L. L., Jr. 1977. "Cycles of war: Historical speculations on the future of international violence." *International Interactions* 3, no. 1:161–79.

Feieraband, Ivo K., Rosaline L. Feieraband, and Betty A. Nesvold. 1972. "Social change and political violence: cross-national patterns." In *Anger, Violence, and Politics: Theories and Research*, edited by I. K. Feieraband, R. L. Feierabend, and T. R. Gurr. Englewood Cliffs, NJ: Prentice-Hall.

Ferris, Wayne H. 1973. *The Power Capabilities of Nation States*. Lexington, MA: D.C. Heath.

Finley, M. I. 1970. "Manpower and the fall of Rome." In *The Economic Decline of Empires,* edited by Carlo C. Cipolla. London: Methuen.

Fischer, Fritz. 1967. *Germany's Aims in the First World War.* New York: Norton.
 1975. *War of Illusions: German Policies from 1911 to 1914.* London: Chatto and Windus.

Fisher, Charles A. 1966. "The changing dimensions of Europe." In *1914: The Coming of the First World War,* edited by Walter Laqueur and George L. Mosse. New York: Harper and Row.

Fisher, H. A. L. 1984. *A History of Europe,* vol. 2. Glasgow: Fontana-Collins, originally published 1935.

Forrester, Jay W. 1968. *Principles of Systems.* Cambridge, MA: Wright–Allen Press.
 1971. *World Dynamics.* Cambridge, MA: Wright–Allen Press.

Fournari, Franco. 1974. *The Psychoanalysis of War.* New York: Doubleday.

Fournier, August. 1911. *Napoleon I,* vol .2. New York: Henry Holt.

Freedman, Robert O., ed. 1984. *The Middle East Since Camp David.* Boulder, CO: Westview Press.

Friedberg, Aaron L. 1988. *The Weary Titan: Britain and the Experience of Relative Decline, 1895–1905.* Princeton, NJ: Princeton University Press.

Galambos, Lewis, 1982. *America at Middle Age.* New York: New Press.

Galtung, Johann. 1966. "A structural theory of aggression." *Journal of Peace Research* 2:146–77.

Garthoff, Raymond L. 1985. *Detente and Confrontation: American–Soviet Relations from Nixon to Reagan.* Washington, D.C.: Brookings Institute.

Garvy, George. 1943. "Kondratieff's theory of long cycles." *The Review of Economic Statistics,* 25, no. 4, 203–20.

Geiss, Imanuel. 1966. "The outbreak of the first World War and German war aims." In *1914: The Coming of the First World War,* edited by Walter Laqueur and George L. Mosse. New York: Harper and Row.

Gelb, Leslie and Richard Betts. 1979. *The Irony of Vietnam.* Washington, D.C.: Brookings Institute.

Gelman, Harry, 1986. "Gorbachev's dilemmas and his conflicting foreign policy goals." *Orbis* 30, no. 2 (Summer), 231–47.

George, Alexander. 1984. "Crisis management: the interaction of political and military considerations." *Survival* 26, no. 5, 223–34.

George, Alexander, and Richard Smoke. 1974. *Deterrence in American Foreign Policy: Theory and Practice.* New York: Columbia University Press.

Gilpin, Robert. 1975. *U.S. Power and the Multinational Corporation.* New York: Basic Books.
 1981. *War and Change in World Politics.* New York: Cambridge University Press.
 1987. *The Political Economy of International Relations.* Princeton, NJ: Princeton University Press.

Gleditsch, Nils Peter. 1970. "Rank theory, field theory, and attribute theory: three approaches to interaction in the international system." Research Report No. 47, Dimensionality of Nations Project, University of Hawaii.

Goldman, Marshall L. 1983. *USSR in Crisis: The Failure of an Economic System.* New York: Norton.

Goldstein, Joshua. 1988. *Long Cycles: Prosperity and War in the Modern Age*. New Haven, CT: Yale University Press.

Goodpaster, Andrew J., and Walter J. Stoessel, Jr., co-chairmen, and Robert Kennedy, Rapporteur. 1986. *U.S. Policy Towards the Soviet Union: A Long-Term Western Perspective, 1987–2000*. Washington, D.C.: The Atlantic Council of the United States.

Graham, Daniel O. 1979. *Shall America Be Defended?* New York: Arlington House.

Gramsci, Antonio. 1977. *Selections from Political Writings*, 2 vols. New York: International Publishing Co.

Great Britain Foreign Office. 1915. *Collected Diplomatic Documents Relating to the Outbreak of the European War*.

Greenwood, David. 1984. "Strengthening conventional deterrence." *NATO Review* 32, no. 4 (August), 8–12.

Griffiths, William E. 1964. *The Sino-Soviet Rift*. Cambridge, MA: MIT Press.

Gulick, Edward V. 1955. *Europe's Classical Balance of Power*. Ithaca, NY: Cornell University Press.

Gurr, Ted R. 1970. *Why Men Rebel*. Princeton, NJ: Princeton University Press.

Haas, Ernst. 1953. "The balance of power: prescription, concept or propaganda?" *World Politics* 5, no. 4, 446–77.

Hamilton, Earl. 1934. *America's Treasures and the Price Revolution in Spain: 1501–1650*. Cambridge, MA: Harvard University Press.

Hansen, Roger D. 1979. *The North–South Stalemate*. New York: McGraw Hill.

Hawtrey, R. G. 1930. *Economic Aspects of Sovereignty*. London: Longmans, Green.

Hermann, Charles. 1979. "Why new foreign policy challenges might not be met: constraints on detecting problems and setting agendas." In *Challenges to America: United States Foreign Policy in the 1980s*, edited by Charles W. Kegley, Jr. and Patrick J. McGowan. Beverly Hills, CA: Sage Publications.

Hirschman, Albert O. 1958. *The Strategy of Economic Development*. New Haven, CT: Yale University Press.

Hitler, Adolf. 1961. *Hitler's Secret Book*, trans. S. Attanasio. New York: Grove Press.

Hobsbawm, Eric. 1969. *Industry and Empire: From 1750 to the Present*. London: Pelican.

1989. *The Age of Empire: 1875–1914*. New York: Vintage Books.

Hoffmann, Stanley. 1960. "International relations as a discipline." In *Contemporary Theory in International Relations*, edited by Stanley Hoffmann. Englewood Cliffs, NJ: Prentice-Hall.

1968a. *Gulliver's Troubles: Or the Setting of American Foreign Policy*. New York: McGraw Hill.

1968b. "Balance of power." *International Encyclopedia of the Social Sciences*. Vol. 1. New York: Macmillan, 506–10.

1978. *Primacy of World Order: American Foreign Policy Since the Cold War*. New York: McGraw-Hill.

1984. *Duties beyond Borders: On the Limits and Possibilities of Ethical International Politics*. Syracuse, NY: Syracuse University Press.

Holsti, Kal J. 1970. "National role conception in the study of foreign policy." *International Studies Quarterly* 14, no. 3 (September), 233–309.

Holsti, Ole R. 1972. *Crisis, Escalation, War*. Montreal: McGill-Queen's University Press.

Holsti, Ole R., and Alexander George. 1975. "The effects of stress on the performance of foreign policy makers." *Political Science Annual* 6.

Houweling, Henk and Jan G. Siccama. 1988. *Studies of War*. London: Martinus Nijhoff Publishers.

Howard, Michael. 1984. *The Causes of War*, 2d edn, enlarged. Cambridge, MA: Harvard University Press.

Hower, Gretchen, and Dina A. Zinnes. 1990. "International political conflict: A literature review." In *Annual Review of Conflict Knowledge and Conflict Resolution*, edited by Joseph P. Gittler. New York: Garland.

Huntington, Samuel. 1983. "Conventional deterrence and conventional retaliation in Europe." *International Security* 8, no. 3 (Winter), 31–39.

1988. "Coping with the Lippmann gap." *Foreign Affairs* 66, no. 3, 453–77.

Hussein, S. M., Bruce Bueno de Mesquita, and David Lalman. 1987. "Modelling war and peace." *American Political Science Review* 81, no. 1 (March) 221–32.

Huth, Paul. 1988. "Extended deterrence and the outbreak of war." *American Political Science Review* 82, no. 2 (June), 423–43.

Inoguchi, Takashi. 1988. "Four Japanese scenarios for the future." *International Affairs* 65, no. 1 (Winter), 15–28.

Janis, Irving L., and Leon Mann. 1977. *Decision Making: A Psychological Analysis of Conflict, Choice, and Commitment*. New York: The Free Press.

Jelavich, Barbara. 1964. *A Century of Russian Foreign Policy, 1814–1914*. Philadelphia: J. B. Lippincott.

Jervis, Robert. 1976. *Perception and Misperception in International Politics*. Princeton, NJ: Princeton University Press.

1979. "Deterrence theory revisited." *World Politics* 31, no. 2 (January), 289–324.

Job, Brian. 1976. "Membership in international alliances, 1815–1965: Exploration using mathematical modelling." In *Mathematical Models in International Relations*, edited by Dina Zinnes and John V. Gillespie. New York: Praeger.

Jockel, Joseph T., and Joel J. Sokolsky. 1986. *Canada and Collective Security: Odd Man Out*. New York: Praeger.

Jones, A. J. 1980. *Game Theory: Mathematical Models of Conflict*. New York: John Wiley.

Kagan, Donald. 1987. "World War I, World War II, World War III." *Commentary* 83, no. 3 (March), 21–40.

Kahn, Herman. 1976. *The Next 200 Years: A Scenario for America and the World*. New York: William Morrow.

Kahn, Robert L., Doland M. Wolfe, Robert P. Quinn, and J. Diedrick Snoek. 1964. *Organizational Stress Studies in Role Conflict and Ambiguity*. New York: John Wiley and Sons.

Kahneman, D., and P. Slovic, eds. 1982. *Judgment Under Uncertainty: Heuristics and Biases*. Cambridge: Cambridge University Press.

Kamel, Mohamed Ibrahim. 1986. *The Camp David Accords: A Testimony*. New York: Routledge & Kegan Paul.

Kann, Robert A. 1974. *A History of the Hapsburg Empire, 1526–1918*. Berkeley: University of California Press.

Kaplan, Morton. 1961. "Problems of theory building and theory confirmation in international politics." In *The International System: Theoretical Essays*, edited by Klaus Knorr and Sidney Verba. Princeton, NJ: Princeton University Press.

Katz, Mark. 1985. *Russia and Arabia: Soviet Foreign Policy Toward the Arabian Peninsula*. Baltimore: The Johns Hopkins University Press.

Kegley, Charles W., Jr., and Eugene Wittkopf. 1976 "Structural characteristics of international influence relationships." *International Studies Quarterly* 20:261–300.

Kelley, H. H. 1965. "Threats in interpersonal negotiations." *Journal of Conflict Resolution* 9 (March), 79–105.

Kennan, George F. 1979. *The Decline of Bismarck's European Order*. Princeton, NJ: Princeton University Press.

Kennedy, Paul. 1980. *The Rise of the Anglo-German Antagonism, 1860–1914*. London: George Allen & Unwin.

   1984. "The First World War and the international power system." *International Security* 9, no. 1 (Summer).

   1985. "The First World War and the international power system." In *Military Strategy and the Origins of the First World War*, edited by Steven E. Miller. Princeton, NJ: Princeton University Press.

   1988a. *The Rise and Fall of the Great Powers: Economic Change and Military Conflict from 1500 to 2000*. New York: Random House.

   1988b. "The end of empire: Can we decline as gracefully as Great Britain?" *Washington Post*, Outlook section, 24 January.

Keohane, Robert. 1984. *After Hegemony: Cooperation and Discord in the World Political Economy*. Princeton, NJ: Princeton University Press.

   1989. "Theory of world politics: structural realism and beyond." In *International Institutions and State Power: Essays in International Relations Theory*. Boulder, CO: Westview Press, 35–73.

Keohane, Robert, and Joseph Nye, Jr. 1977. *Power and Interdependence: World Politics in Transition*. Boston: Little, Brown.

Kilborn, Peter T. 1989. "Federal reserve sees a way to gauge long-run inflation." *New York Times*, 13 June.

Kindleberger, Charles. 1981. "Dominance and leadership in the international economy." *International Studies Quarterly* 25, no. 3 (June), 242–54.

Kinross, Lord. 1977. *The Ottoman Centuries: The Rise and Fall of the Turkish Empire*. New York: Morrow Quill.

Kirton, John J. 1972. "The consequences of integration? The case of the defense production sharing agreements." Paper presented at the Inter-University Seminar in International Relations, Ottawa, 8 April.

Kissinger, Henry. 1974. *American Foreign Policy*. New York: W. W. Norton.

   1984. "A plan to reshape NATO." *Time*. 5 April.

Klingberg, Frank I. 1952. "The historical alternation of moods in American foreign policy." *World Politics* 4, no. 2 (January), 239–73.

1979. "Cyclical trends in American foreign policy moods and their policy implications." In *Challenges to America: United States Foreign Policy in the 1980s*, edited by Charles W. Kegley, Jr. and Patrick J. McGowan. Beverly Hills, CA: Sage Publications.

Knorr, Klaus. 1956. *The War Potentials of Nations*. Princeton NJ: Princeton University Press.

1970. *Military Power and Potential*. Lexington, MA: D.C. Heath and Company.

ed. 1983. *Power, Strategy and Security*. Princeton NJ: Princeton University Press.

Koch, H. W., ed. 1972. *The Origins of the First World War*. London: Macmillan.

Krasner, Stephen D. 1985. *Structural Conflict: The Third World Against Global Liberalism*. Berkeley, CA: University of California Press.

Krauss, Melvyn. 1986. *How NATO Weakens the West*. New York: Simon & Schuster.

Kuznets, Simon. 1930. *Secular Movements in Production and Prices: Their Nature and Their Bearing Upon Cyclical Fluctuations*. Boston: Houghton Mifflin.

1961. *Capital in the American Economy: Its Formation and Financing*. Princeton NJ: Princeton University Press.

1966. *Modern Economic Growth: Rate, Structure, and Spread*. New Haven, CT: Yale University Press.

Lakatos, Imre, and Alan Musgrave, eds. 1970. *Criticism and the Growth of Knowledge*. Cambridge: Cambridge University Press.

Lamborn, Alan C. 1985. "Risk and foreign policy choice." *International Studies Quarterly* 29, no. 4 (December).

Landes, David S. 1969. *The Unbound Prometheus: Technological Change and Industrial Development in Western Europe from 1750 to the Present*. Cambridge: Cambridge University Press.

Lawrence, Robert W. 1984. *Can America Compete?* Washington, D.C.: Brookings Institution.

Lebow, R. N. 1981. *Between War and Peace*. Baltimore: The Johns Hopkins University Press.

Lefebure, G. 1953. *Napoleon*. Paris: Presses Universitaires.

Leibenstein, Harvey. 1978. *General X-efficiency Theory and Organisational Analysis*. New York: Harper and Row.

Levi, Isaac. 1986. *Hard Choices: Decision-Making Under Unresolved Conflict*. Cambridge: Cambridge University Press.

Levy, Jack S. 1983a. "Misperceptions and the causes of war." *World Politics* 35, no. 1 (October), 76–99.

1983b. "World systems analysis: A great power framework." In *Contending Approaches to World Systems Analysis*, edited by William R. Thompson. Beverly Hills, CA: Sage Publications.

1987. "Declining power and the preventive motivation for war." *World Politics* 40, no. 1 (October), 82–107.

Levy, Jack S., and Rick Collis. 1985. "Power cycle theory and the preventitive war motivation: A preliminary empirical investigation." Paper presented at the American Political Science Association Annual Meeting, New Orleans.

277

Lewis, W. Arthur. 1978. *Growth and Fluctuations, 1870–1913*. London: George Allen & Unwin.

Lieberman, Seymour. 1965. "The effects of changes in roles on the attitudes of role occupants." In *Human Behavior and International Politics*, edited by J. David Singer, 155–68. Chicago: Rand McNally.

Limbert, John W. 1986. *Iran: At War with History*. Boulder, CO: Westview Press.

Lindblom, Charles. 1959. "The science of muddling through." *Public Administration Review* 19:79–88.

Liska, George. 1957. *International Equilibrium*. Cambridge, MA: Harvard University Press.

1967. *Imperial America: The International Politics of Primacy*. Baltimore: The Johns Hopkins University Press.

1982. *Russia and the Road to Appeasement: Cycles of East–West Conflict in War and Peace*. Baltimore: The Johns Hopkins University Press.

1990. *The Ways of Power: Pattern and Meaning in World Politics*. London: Blackwell.

Lodge, George C., and Ezra F. Vogel, eds. 1987. *Ideology and National Competitiveness: An Analysis of Nine Countries*. Boston: Harvard Business School Press.

Luttwak, Edward N. 1983. *The Grand Strategy of the Soviet Union*. New York: St Martin's Press.

1987. *Strategy: The Logic of War and Peace*. Cambridge, MA: Harvard University Press.

Maier, Charles. 1988. "Wargames: 1914–1919." *Journal of Interdisciplinary History* 18, no. 4, 581–90.

Malkin, Lawrence. 1987. *The National Debt*. New York: Henry Holt.

Mansbach, Richard W., and John A. Vasquez. 1981. *In Search of Theory: A New Paradigm for Global Politics*. New York: Columbia University Press.

Marantz, Paul, and Blema Steinberg, eds. 1985. *Superpower Involvement in the Middle East*. Boulder, CO: Westview Press.

March, James G. 1955. "An introduction to the theory and measurement of influence." *American Political Science Review* 49, no. 2 (June), 431–51.

Marchildon, Gregory and Charles F. Doran. "Relative national capability: a new index of power 1800–1990." Forthcoming.

Markham, James M. 1989. "Gorbachev's vision." *New York Times*. 8 July.

Masserman, J., ed. 1963. *Violence and War with Clinical Studies*, vol. 6 of *Science and Psychoanalysis*. New York: Grune & Stratton.

May, Ernest R. 1973. *Lessons of the Past: The Use and Misuse of History in American Foreign Policy*. New York: Oxford University Press.

May, Robert M. 1975. "Biological populations obeying difference equations: stable points, stable cycles, and chaos." *Journal of Theoretical Biology* 51:511–24.

Mayer, Kenneth R. 1983. "War and the power cycle." Class paper, Yale University.

McGowan, Patrick J. 1974. "Adaptive foreign policy behavior." In *Comparing Foreign Policies*, edited by James Rosenau. Beverly Hills, CA: Sage Publications.

1989. "State-agents, international structures, and foreign policy behaviour: thinking seriously about foreign policy analysis." Forthcoming in *International Affairs Bulletin* (Johannesburg).

McKeown, Timothy J. 1983. "Hegemonic stability theory and 19th century tariff levels in Europe." *International Organization* 37, no. 1 (Winter), 73–91.

Meadows, Donella H., Dennis L. Meadows, Jorgen Randers, and William W. Behrens III. 1974. *The Limits to Growth*. New York: New American Library.

Meyer, Cord. 1989. "Uneasy stirrings at the wayside." *Washington Times*, 3 March.

Meyer, Stephen M. 1984. "Soviet national security decision-making: what do we know and what do we understand?" In *Soviet Decision-Making for National Security*, edited by Jiri Valenta and William Potter, 255–97. London: George Allen & Unwin.

Midlarsky, Manus I. 1969. "Status inconsistency and the onset of international warfare." Ph.D. Diss., Northwestern University.

1988. *The Onset of World War*. Boston: Unwin Hyman.

ed. 1989. *Handbook of War Studies*. Boston: Unwin Hyman.

Miller, Steven E., ed. 1984. *Strategy and Nuclear Deterrence*. Princeton, NJ: Princeton University Press.

ed. 1985. *Military and Strategy and the Origins of the First World War*. Princeton, NJ: Princeton University Press.

Mitchell, B. R. 1980. *European Historical Statistics, 1750–1970*. New York: Columbia University Press.

Miyoshi, Osamu. 1987. "Soviet strategy in Asia: A Japanese view." *Comparative Strategy* 6, no. 1, 1–27.

Modelski, George. 1978. "The long cycle of global politics and the nation–state." *Comparative Studies in Society and History* 20, no. 2 (April), 214–35.

Montague, M. F. A. 1968. *Man and Aggression*. New York: Oxford University Press.

Moore, Geoffrey H. 1986. *Business Cycles, Inflation, and Forecasting*, 2nd edn. National Bureau of Economic Research Studies in Business Cycles, No. 24. Cambridge, MA: Ballinger.

Morgenthau, Hans J. 1967. *Politics Among Nations*, 4th edn. New York: Knopf.

Most, Benjamin A., and Harvey Starr. 1976. "The spread of war." Bloomington, IN: Center for International Policy Studies.

Mowat, Charles L., ed. 1968. *The New Cambridge Modern History*. Vol. 12, *Shifting Balance of World Forces 1898–1945*. Cambridge: Cambridge University Press.

Muller, Edward N. 1972. "A test of a partial theory of potential for political violence." *American Political Science Review* 66, no. 3 (September), 928–59.

Myers, Kenneth A., ed. 1980. *NATO: The Next Thirty Years*. Boulder, CO: Westview Press.

Neilson, Francis. 1916. *How Diplomats Make War*. New York: B. W. Huebsch.

Niou, Emerson M. S., Peter C. Ordeshook, and Gregory F. Rose. 1989. *The Balance of Power: Stability in the International Systems*. Cambridge: Cambridge University Press.

Nitze, Paul. 1976. "Assuring strategic stability in an era of detente." *Foreign Affairs* 54 (January), 207–32.

Nomikos, E., and R. C. North. 1976. *International Crisis: The Outbreak of World War I*. Montreal: McGill-Queen's University Press.

Nye, Joseph S., Jr. ed. 1984. *The Making of America's Soviet Policy*. New Haven, CT: Yale University Press.

1988a. "Old wars and future wars: causation and prevention." *Journal of Interdisciplinary History* 18, no. 4 (Spring).

1988b. "Understanding U.S. strength." *Foreign Policy* no. 72 (Fall), 105–29.

1990. *Bound to Lead: The Changing Nature of American Power*. New York: Basic Books.

Oliver, F. R. 1982. "Notes on the logistic curve for human populations." *Journal of the Royal Statistical Society* vol. A, 359–63.

Olson, Mancur. 1982. *The Rise and Decline of Nations: Economic Growth, Stagflation and Social Rigidities*. New Haven, CT: Yale University Press.

Olson, Mancur and Richard Zeckhauser. 1966. "An economic theory of alliances." *Review of Economics and Statistics* 4, no. 3 (August), 266–79.

Organski, A. J. K. and Jacek Kugler. 1980. *The War Ledger*. Chicago: University of Chicago Press.

Osgood, Robert E. and Robert W. Tucker. 1967. *Force, Order, and Justice*. Baltimore: The Johns Hopkins University Press.

Oye, Kenneth. 1983. "International systems structure and American foreign policy." In *Eagle Defiant: United States Foreign Policy in the 1980s*, edited by Kenneth Oye, Robert Lieber, and Donald Rothchild. Boston: Little, Brown, 3–32.

Parrott, Bruce. 1987. *The Soviet Union and Ballistic Missile Defense*, no. 14. Washington, D.C.: The Johns Hopkins Foreign Policy Institute/Westview Press.

Pearl, Raymond. 1924. *Studies in Human Biology*. Baltimore: Williams and Wilkins Co.

Peterson, Walter J. 1986. "Deterrence and compellence: A critical assessment of conventional wisdom." *International Studies Quarterly* 30, no. 3 (September).

Petit, Pascal. 1986. *Slow Growth and the Service Economy*. New York: St. Martin's Press.

Phillips, Kevin. 1986. *Staying on Top: Winning the Trade War*. New York: Vintage Books.

Plato. 1961. *The Republic*. In *The Great Political Theories*, edited by Michael Curtis, 2 vols. New York: Avon Discuss Books.

Pokrovski, M. N. 1970. *Russia in World History*. Ann Arbor, MI: University of Michigan Press.

Pollack, Jonathan. 1978. "The opening to America." In *Revolutions Within the Chinese Revolution, 1966–79*, edited by R. MacFarquhar and J. K. Fairbank. Vol. 15 of *The Cambridge History of China*. Cambridge: Cambridge University Press.

Porter, B. 1975. *The Lion's Share: A Short History of British Imperialism 1850–1970*. London: Longman.

Putnam, Robert D., and Nicholas Bayne. 1984. *Hanging Together: The Seven Power Summits*. Cambridge, MA: Harvard University Press.

Quandt, William B. 1986. *Camp David: Peacemaking and Politics*. Washington, D.C.: Brookings Institute.

Ravenal, Earl C. 1982. "Counterforce and alliance: The ultimate connection." *International Security* 6, no. 4 (Spring), 26–43.

Reischauer, Edwin O. 1977. *The Japanese*. Cambridge, MA: Harvard University Press.

Renouvin, Pierre. 1969. *World War II and Its Origins*. New York: Harper & Row.

Riker, William H. 1964. "Some ambiguities in the notion of power." *American Political Science Review* 58, no. 2 (June), 341–49.

Roberts, J. M. 1983. *The Pelican History of the World*. New York: Penguin Books.

Rosecrance, Richard. 1963. *Action and Reaction in World Politics: International Systems in Perspective*. Boston: Little, Brown.

1986. *The Rise of the Trading State: Commerce and Conquest in the Modern World*. New York: Basic Books.

1990. *America's Economic Resurgence: A Bold New Strategy*. New York: Harper & Row.

Rosecrance, Richard, Alan Alexandroff, Brian Healy, and Arthur Stein. 1974. *Power, Balance of Power, and Status in Nineteenth Century International Relations*. Beverly Hills, CA: Sage Publications.

Rosenau, James N. 1969. *Linkage Politics: Essays on the Convergence of National and International Systems*. New York: The Free Press.

Rostow, Walt W. 1971. *Politics and the Stages of Growth*. New York: Cambridge University Press.

1975. "Kondratieff, Schumpeter, and Kuznets: trend periods revisited." *Journal of Economic History* 35, no. 4 (December), 79–53.

1978. *The World Economy: History and Prospect*. Austin, TX: University of Texas Press.

1988. "Beware of historians bearing false analogies." Book Review Essay, *Foreign Affairs* 66, no. 4 (Spring), 863–68.

Ruggie, John G. 1983a. *The Antinomies of Interdependence and National Welfare and the Division of Labor*. New York: Columbia University Press.

1983b. "Continuity and transformation in the world polity: toward a neorealist synthesis." *World Politics* 35, no. 2 (January), 261–85.

Russell, Sir William Howard. 1856 (1966). *Russell's Despatches from the Crimea 1854–1856*, edited by Nicholas Bentley. London: Andre Deutsch.

Russett, Bruce. 1983a. *The Prisoners of Insecurity*. New York: W. H. Freeman.

1983b. "Prosperity and peace." *International Studies Quarterly* 27, no. 4 (December), 381–88.

1985. "The mysterious case of vanishing hegemony." *International Organization* 39:207–31.

Russett, Bruce, and P. Huth. 1984. "What makes deterrence work?" *World Politics* 36, no. 4 (July), 496–526.

Sabrosky, Alan Ned. 1975. "From Bosnia to Sarajevo: a comparative discussion of interstate crises." *Journal of Conflict Resolution* 19 (March), 3–24.

Schlesinger, Arthur M. 1949. *Paths to the Present*. New York: AMS Press.

Schlesigner, Arthur M., Jr. 1986. *The Cycles of American History*. Boston: Houghton Mifflin.

Schmidt, Gustav. 1985. *Der europäische Imperialismus*. Munich: R. Oldenbourg Verlag

Scott, Bruce R. 1985. "National strategies: Key to international competition." In *U.S. Competitiveness in the World Economy*, edited by B. R. Scott and George C. Lodge. Boston: Harvard Business School.

Selowsky, Marcelo. 1987. "Adjustment in the 1980s: an overview of issues." *Finance and Development* 24, no. 2 (June), 11–14.

Shapley, L., and M. Shubik. 1954. "A model for evaluating the distribution of power in a committee system." *American Political Science Review* 48: 787–92.

Shaw, Stanford J. 1976. *History of the Ottoman Empire and Modern Turkey*. Cambridge: Cambridge University Press.

Shwadran, Benjamin. 1985. *Middle East Oil Crises Since 1973*. Boulder, CO: Westview Press.

Simes, Dimitri. 1983. "The new Soviet challenge." *Foreign Policy* no. 55:113–31.

Simon, Herbert A. 1953. "Notes on the observation and measurement of power." *Journal of Politics* 15, no. 3 (August), 500–16.

1957. *Models of Man*. New York: John Wiley & Sons.

Singer, J. David. 1961. "The level of analysis problem in international relations." In *The International System: Theoretical Essays*, edited by Klaus Knorr and Sidney Verba. Princeton, NJ: Princeton University Press.

ed. 1979. *The Correlates of War*. Vol. 1, *Research Origins and Rationale*. New York: The Free Press.

ed. 1980. *The Correlates of War*. Vol. 2, *Testing Some Realpolitik Models*. New York: The Free Press.

Singer, J. David, and Associates. 1979. *Explaining War: Selected Papers from The Correlates of War Project*. Beverly Hills, CA: Sage Publications.

Singer, J. David, and Melvin Small. 1972a. *The Strength of Nations*. New York: Macmillan.

1972b. *The Wages of War, 1816–1956: A Statistical Handbook*. New York: John Wiley & Sons.

Singer, J. David, Stuart Bremer, and John Stuckey. 1972. "Capability distribution, uncertainty, and major power war, 1820–1965." In *Peace, War, and Numbers*, edited by Bruce M. Russett, 19–48. Beverly Hills, CA: Sage Publications.

Siverson, Randolph M., and G. T. Duncan. 1976. "Stochastic models of international alliance initiation." In *Mathematical Models in International Relations*, edited by Dina Zinnes and John Gillespie. New York: Praeger.

Small, Melvin, and J. David Singer. 1979. "Conflict in the international system, 1816–1977: historical trends and policy futures." In *Challenges to America*, edited by Charles W. Kegley, Jr. and Patrick J. McGowan. Beverly Hills, CA: Sage Publications.

Smith, Denis Mack. 1954. *Cavour and Garibaldi, 1860: A Study in Political Conflict*. Cambridge: Cambridge University Press.

1959. *Italy: A Modern History*. Ann Arbor, MI: University of Michigan Press.

Smith, Steve. 1987. "The development of international relations as a social science." *Millennium* 16: 189–206.

Smoke, Richard. 1977. *War: Controlling Escalation*. Cambridge, MA: Harvard University Press.

Snyder, G. H., and P. Diesing. 1977. *Conflict Among Nations*. Princeton NJ: Princeton University Press.

Snyder, Jack. 1985. "Perceptions of the security dilemma in 1914." In *Psychology and Deterrence*, edited by R. Jervis, R. Lebow, and J. Stein. Baltimore: The Johns Hopkins University Press, 153–79.

Solomon, George I. 1970. "Psychodynamic aspects of aggression, hostility and violence." In *Violence and the Struggle for Existence*, edited by David N. Daniels, et al. Boston: Little, Brown.

Stadelmann, Rudolf. 1948. "Die Epoche der deutsch-englischen Flottenrivalitat." In *Deutschland und Westeuropa* (Wurttemberg: Laupheim).

Stein, Arthur. 1984. "The hegemon's dilemma: Great Britain, the United States, and the international economic order." *International Organization* 38, no. 2 (Spring), 355–86.

Steinberg, Jonathan. 1966. "The Copenhagen complex." In *1914: The Coming of the First World War*, edited by Walter Laqueur and George L. Mosse. New York: Harper & Row.

Steinbruner, John D. 1974. *The Cybernetic Theory of Decision: New Dimensions of Political Analysis*. Princeton, NJ: Princeton University Press.

1981. "Nuclear decapitation." *Foreign Policy* 45 (Winter 1981–82), 16–28.

Stoll, Richard and Michael Ward, eds. 1989. *Power in the International System*. Boulder, CO: Lynne Rienner.

Storry, Richard. 1983. *A History of Modern Japan*. New York: Penguin.

Sylvan, Donald A., and Steve Chan, eds. 1984. *Foreign Policy Decision-Making*. New York: Praeger.

Taylor, A. J. P. 1954. *The Struggle for Mastery in Europe, 1848–1918*. Oxford: Clarendon Press.

1963. *The Origins of the Second World War*. New York: Penguin Books.

1967. *Europe: Grandeur and Decline*. New York: Pelican.

1979. *How Wars Begin*. New York: Atheneum.

Thomas, R. H. 1952. *Liberalism, Nationalism and the German Intellectuals, 1822–1847*. Cambridge: Cambridge University Press.

Thompson, William R. 1983. "Cycles, capabilities and war: An ecumenical view." In *Contending Approaches to World System Analysis*, edited by William R. Thompson. Beverly Hills, CA: Sage Publications, 141–63.

Thompson, William R., and Gary Zuk. 1982. "War, inflation and the Kondratieff long wave." *Journal of Conflict Resolution* 26 (December), 621–44.

1986. "World power and the strategic trap of territorial commitments." *International Studies Quarterly* 30, no. 3 (September), 249–68.

Trevelyan, George Macaulay. 1922. *British History in the Nineteenth Century and After: 1782–1919*. New York: Penguin Books, 1965 printing.

Trevor Davies, R. 1965. *Spain in Decline: 1621–1700*. London: Macmillan.

Tucker, Robert W. and David C. Hendrickson. 1990. *Empire of Liberty: The Statecraft of Thomas Jefferson*. Oxford: Oxford University Press.

Tuchman, Barbara. 1962. *The Guns of August*. New York: Dell Publishing.

Ulam, Adam. 1974. *Expansion and Coexistence: Soviet Foreign Policy, 1917–73*, 2nd edn New York: Praeger.

van Evera, Stephen. 1985. "Why cooperation failed in 1914." *World Politics* 38, no. 4 (October), 80–117.

Vasquez, John A. 1983. *The Power of Power Politics: A Critique*. New Brunswick, NJ: Rutgers University Press.

1986. "Capability, types of war, peace." *Western Political Quarterly*, 38: 313–27.

Vernon, Raymond. 1966. "International investment and international trade in the product cycle." *Quarterly Journal of Economics* 80: 190–207.

Vives, Jaime Vincens. 1970. "The decline of Spain in the 17th century." In *The Economic Decline of Empires*, edited by Carlo C. Cipolla. London: Methuen.

Vlek, Charles, and Pieter-Jan Stallen. 1980. "Rational and personal aspects of risk." *Acta Psychologica* 45.

Vogel, Ezra F. 1963. *Japan's New Middle Class*. Berkeley, CA: University of California Press.

von Mach, Edmund. 1916. *Official Diplomatic Documents Relating to the Outbreak of the European War*. New York: Macmillan.

Waldmann, Raymond J. 1986. *Managed Trade: The New Competition Between Nations*. Cambridge, MA: Ballinger.

Wallace, Michael D. 1973. *War and Rank Among Nations*. Lexington, MA: D. C. Heath.

Wallerstein, Immanuel. 1974. *The Modern World System*. 2 vols. New York: Academic Press.

Walt, Stephen M. 1987. *The Origins of Alliances*. Ithaca, NY: Cornell University Press.

Waltz, Kenneth. 1967. "International structure, national force, and the balance of world power." *Journal of International Affairs* 21, no. 2, 215–31.

1979. *Theory of International Politics*. Reading, MA: Addison-Wesley.

Wedgwood, Charles V. 1962. *Richelieu and the French Monarchy*. New York: Collier.

Weede, Erich. 1976. "Overwhelming preponderance as a pacifying condition among contiguous Asian dyads, 1950–1969." *Journal of Conflict Resolution* 20 (September), 395–412.

Weinstein, F. 1969. "The concept of commitment in international relations." *Journal of Conflict Resolution* 13 (March), 39–56.

Weitzman, Martin. 1983. "Industrial production." In *The Soviet Economy: Towards the Year 2000*, edited by Abram Bergson and Herbert S. Levine. London: George Allen and Unwin.

Wight, Martin. 1946. *Power Politics*. London: Royal Institute of International Affairs.

Wildavsky, Aaron. 1964. *The Politics of Budgetary Process*. Boston: Little, Brown.

Wohlforth, William C. 1987. "The perception of power: Russia in the pre-1914 balance." *World Politics* 39: 353–81.

Wohlstetter, R. 1962. *Pearl Harbor: Warning and Decision*. Stanford, CA: Stanford University Press.

Wolf, John B. 1970. *Toward a European Balance of Power, 1620–1715*. Chicago: Rand McNally.

Wonnacott, Paul. 1984. *Macroeconomics*. Homewood, IL: Richard D. Irwin.

Wright, George. 1985. *Behavior Decision-Making*. New York: Plenum Press.

Wright, Quincy. 1942. *A Study of War*. Chicago: University of Chicago Press.

Yoon, Young-Kwan. 1987. "Political economy of foreign investment and productivity." Ph.D. Diss., The Johns Hopkins University – SAIS.

Young, Oran. 1968. "Political discontinuities in the international system." *World Politics* 20, no. 3 (April), 367–70.

Zartman, I. William, and Maureen R. Berman. 1982. *The Practical Negotiator*. New Haven, CT: Yale University Press.

Zinnes, Dina. 1967. "An analytical study of the balance of power theories." *Journal of Peace Research* 4, no. 3, 270–88.

Zinnes, Dina, John V. Gillespie, and G. S. Tahim. 1978. "A formal analysis of some issues in balance of power theories." *International Studies Quarterly* 22, no. 3 (September), 323–56.

Index

* alternative descriptors for power cycle dynamic (changing systems structure)

Vlek, Charles, 26
Vogel, Ezra F., 77, 222–3
von Mach, Edmund, 129–30

Wagner, Richard E., 229
Wakata, K. W., 39
Waldmann, Raymond J., 194
Wallace, Michael D., 34
Wallerstein, Immanuel, 118
Walt, Stephen M., 139
Waltz, Kenneth: central system, 57;
"Copernican" systems structure
perspective, xiii, 2; structural change,
149
war, major: defined 21, 95, 251; empirical
tests, 132–40; power cycle explanation
summarized, 20–2; *see also* First World
War; Second World War
Ward, Michael, 50
Ward, Terrence, 35, 134
Wedgwood, Charles V., 70
Weede, Erich, 147
Weinstein, F., 180

Weitzman, Martin, 204
Westphalia, Peace of, 4, 69
Wight, Martin, 30
Wildavsky, Aaron, 96
Williams, Lynn, 218
Wohlforth, William C., 79–80, 87, 93, 113
Wohlsetter, R., 116
Wolf, John B., 143
Wolfe, Oland M., 29
Wonnacott, Paul, 223
world order: structural foundation, xvii,
1, 166–7; just, based on power cycle
dynamic, 186–91; *see also* equilibration
Wright, George, 14, 26
Wright, Quincy, xvi

Yalta, 75, 256
Yoon, Young-Kwan, 77

Zartman, I. William, 179
Zeckhauser, Richard, 185
Zinnes, Dina, 42, 143, 145
Zuk, Gary, 14